Lucy Lapwing

LOVE IS A TOAD

Exploring our relationship with nature

First published in the UK in 2026 by Blink
An imprint of Bonnier Books UK
5th Floor, HYLO, 105 Bunhill Row,
London, EC1Y 8LZ

Copyright © Lucy Hodson, 2026

All rights reserved.

No part of this publication may be reproduced, stored or transmitted in any form or by any means, electronic, mechanical, photocopying or otherwise, without the prior written permission of the publisher.

The right of Lucy Hodson to be identified as the Author of this work has been asserted by her in accordance with the Copyright, Designs and Patents Act, 1988.

A CIP catalogue record for this book is available from the British Library.

Hardback ISBN: 978-1-78512-014-5

Also available as an ebook and an audiobook

1 3 5 7 9 10 8 6 4 2

Design and Typeset by Envy Design
Printed and bound by CPI (UK) Ltd, Croydon CR0 4YY

"We Shake with Joy" by Mary Oliver
Reprinted by the permission of The Charlotte Sheedy Literary Agency as agent for the author. Copyright © 2009, 2017 by Mary Oliver with permission of Bill Reichblum

Every reasonable effort has been made to trace copyright holders of material reproduced in this book, but if any have been inadvertently overlooked the publishers would be glad to hear from them.

The authorised representative in the EEA is
Bonnier Books UK (Ireland) Limited.
Registered office address:
Block B, The Crescent Building
Northwood, Santry
Dublin 9, D09 C6X8, Ireland
compliance@bonnierbooks.ie

www.bonnierbooks.co.uk

To my family.

Sal and Fred for sibling bickering, middle fingers and endless laughs.

Dad, for tree scrambling and bows and arrows.

To mum, for letting us all run wild with Hodson feet.

And, of course, the absolute *puppity wups*.

Contents

Author's Note ix
INTRODUCTION **The Squeaks** 1
CHAPTER 1 **A Nod and a Wink** 17
CHAPTER 2 **A Telltale Peep** 45
CHAPTER 3 **Do Beetles Feel Glee?** 75
CHAPTER 4 **Hoardyceps** 101
CHAPTER 5 **Pincushion of Opportunity** 121
CHAPTER 6 **The Granny Pine** 149
CHAPTER 7 **Slugliness** 177
CHAPTER 8 **Whatever It Was, It Wiggled** 197
CHAPTER 9 **For the Love of Oil Beetles** 223
CHAPTER 10 **The Pink People** 243
CHAPTER 11 **The Antlebump-tumps** 265
CHAPTER 12 **Face Down, Bum Up** 291
CHAPTER 13 **Two for Joy** 321
References 339
Acknowledgements 341

Author's Note

I've believed for a while that you don't need to know the name of every species in order to be a 'good naturalist'. Being able to list off the two-part, scientific names of every bird, plant and fungus is impressive, sure. But it isn't necessary. Being a good naturalist means knowing nature in more ways than just a rigid, orderly catalogue; it's something we come to know in our bodies, in sight and sound and touch.

That said, the names of things are undoubtedly important. Be it a Latin label, a local name derived from folklore, or even a name you made up yourself, the way we humans relate to other life inevitably involves giving them names. Names signify recognition, familiarity and respect.

When I use a species' name, I prefer to capitalise it. We do this with fellow humans all the time; when I write Nadia's name, I always use a capital 'N'. It gives her the respect she so deserves as the fabulous person she is. So it feels odd to me, that for equally fabulous beings, like Oaks or Kestrels, the usual treatment is to not capitalise.

Not capitalising species feeds into the mindset of a hierarchy of species we often encounter in conservation, separating non-human life from ourselves. It also makes for some potential confusion. If I don't use capitals and I tell you about a gorgeous little ring plover I saw, am I telling you about a Little Ringed Plover (*Charadrius dubius*), or a Ringed Plover (*Charadrius hiaticula*) that was quite dinky?

In her book *Braiding Sweetgrass*, Robin Wall Kimmerer discusses the importance of the personhood of all species, and gifts the plants she writes about with capitalised names. And so, in this book, I have treated the species I write about similarly. When I discuss a specific species, I capitalise. And so I meet Bramble and Blackbird and Fox. Where I talk about life less specifically – a category like finches and wasps and mosses – I don't.

Of course, one of the best things about nature is that it doesn't fit neatly into our boxes. And so inevitably there are instances where it's hard to apply these rules; or where I have got it wrong. Oh well!

INTRODUCTION

The Squeaks

A bucketful of toads yields the most wonderful noise. *The squeaks. I did not expect the squeaks.* An adorable, guttural sort of peep, nothing dainty about it and better than any sound effect. I lifted my toad-laden plastic tub and rested my chin upon the brim, ear tilted downwards into the amphibious amphitheatre. Squeak. Squeak. Squeaksqueak. How utterly bloody mint.

On this particular evening my vessel held about 40 warty little souls. Their voices peaked, troughed and harmonised in a sort of grumpy symphony as I trundled along, the bucket swaying gently with each welly-booted step. In my other hand I clutched my toad-finding torch – complete with a zooming beam and the power of a billion candles (or something) – swinging it in front of me and casting a rigid ray of light over tarmac, verge and hedgerow.

Aha. There. I'd heard your rustling in the paper-dry leaf

LOVE IS A TOAD

litter, but your mudpuddle browns and mosslog greens had camouflaged you too well. Now you crouched in the middle of the tarmac river ahead, squat and hunkered, illuminated by my searchlight and followed by a comically skewed shadow.

A light jog and a gentle scoop, and I found myself cupping your wonderful bum in my gloved palm. Your flight response was, quite frankly, terrible. Slow and clumsy, you barely bothered to attempt an escape as I wrapped my fingers tenderly under your warty belly in the face of approaching headlights. Perhaps you, Bufo bufo, were confident enough in your bufotoxin-soaked skin, sure to make any would-be toad-scoffer spit you right back out. Ogling you more closely, I stared into those eyes. I reckon I could use all the words I know to describe the gold within them – spangled, mottled, gilt, doused – but none would do them any justice.

Have you ever seen something that's simultaneously extraordinarily beautiful and fascinatingly disgusting? Something so creepy, gross and ick-inducing that you simply can't stop looking at?

There were more glistening bodies than it was possible to count and every single one of them was on the move. They'd reacted immediately, becoming a frenzied, shimmering and quivering mass of scuttling things as soon as I'd prised the slab of old slate from the spreading mat of grass. Ants' nest. Uh oh. But wait . . . it was safe. They were Black Ants. By the age of five, I'd already learnt Red Ants meant 'ouch' and Black Ants meant a bit of a pinching tickle at most.

THE SQUEAKS

I crouched in my jelly shoes, holding the slate up, only mildly worried about them scuttling over my toes, unable to tear my eyes away. There were so, so many ants. A million ants at least. Or that's what it felt like to five-year-old me. The immediate panic within the disturbed colony had now transformed into a frantic organisation. Clusters of chubby white ant grubs sat in chambers and tunnels, carved out of the stodgy dark soil. Worker ants had begun picking them up; a line of grub-shifters had formed, moving them to the safety of the nest underground. The tiny, pale larvae looked like rice pudding, and I hated rice pudding. Ew. Gross. And yet I couldn't stop watching.

There I was, a kid – a weird kid – drawn to any interaction, observation or encounter with living creatures. I mentally drooled over them in the same way I physically drooled over the promise of a treat from the sweetie tin. What else could you want, if you had Ladybirds? If fascination and entertainment lay under every rock, sat upon every flower and whizzed through the air – what else could you possibly need? When I was little, all of my micro-adventures inevitably led to encounters with life. Glorious, messy and never-endingly diverse life. Plants, bugs, birds and critters, entwined and interacting with each other. From my earliest memories they all transfixed me: if it wriggled, hopped, slithered or fluttered I was in love.

With filthy fingernails I'd probe and explore every nook and cranny in the garden, finding excitement and wonder in unremarkable places, like the underside of old bricks or the dusty corners of a shed. I didn't know it then, but something was brewing, building, blossoming. Like the slow growth

LOVE IS A TOAD

of Ivy up a tree trunk, tendrils of a lifelong fascination were taking root.

Every March, when the wind is low and the moon is dim and the temperature exceeds eight degrees, a magnificent migration begins. Toads start to move, clumsily crawling from their winter refuges in woodlands and scrub, back to the breeding ponds, lakes or canals from which they had emerged as youngsters. Upon arrival, a mass spawning frenzy commences, as broad, fat females couple up with smaller, clingy (and squeaking) males. The result of this amphibious sex fest is laid bare in miles and miles of toadspawn. Quite different to frogspawn, toadspawn resembles stringy tangled ladders of jelly, dotted satisfyingly down its length with developing toadpoles. It's gorgeous stuff.

The Common Toad's breeding strategy worked well until the advent of tarmac. You see, roads and toads do not a good combination make. Toads only begin breeding when they're a few years old and they often move en masse during migration. When migration routes meet busy roads, a population-knocking disaster can occur in just one evening. So, every spring, teams of folks across the UK don wellies and hi-vis vests, pack torches and set out on Toad Patrol. Toad Patrol! It's an annual highlight, better than the first Chiffchaff of spring, better than August blackberries and much, much better than Christmas. In groups, volunteers patrol sections of road known for toad migrations, intercepting animals on the move and picking them up before they get squashed. Toads are given a helping hand to get to whatever body of water

THE SQUEAKS

they're trying to reach, hopefully avoiding becoming a toad pancake.

I grew up and the nature fascination followed me around, like a lazily stalking Horsefly follows my thighs in summer. It was there in the background as I went to high school and learnt to swear and do trigonometry and wear really bad eyeliner. It followed me to college where I met new mates. We wore skinny jeans and studded belts, and posted selfies on MySpace with *oh so moody* profile songs. We filled pop bottles with cheap rosé wine and got the bus into town. We drank vodka in parks and saw indie bands in grungy clubs and kissed strangers and put on even more eyeliner. I still loved finding Frogs in spring and climbing trees in summer.

I learnt there was such a thing as 'conservation' and was sold visions of working in faraway places with Tigers, Orangutans or Polar Bears. Subconsciously, I came to understand that nature was elsewhere and that it needed white kids like me to come along and save it. But I still didn't know the nature under my toes. I didn't know the names of the wildflowers or whose voice that was belting from the Hawthorn hedgerow. I didn't know the wild beings I shared my childhood with – not closely. We don't learn about Blackbird or Oak or Cowslip at school. We aren't taught their names or when they'll appear each spring and what they like. Here, to learn about any of the species we live alongside takes a concoction of opportunity, privilege and luck. I had some of these of course, growing up in a large cabbage-growing village in west Lancashire – privilege gave me a garden and fields to play in and luck gave me parents who let us muck about. But I still didn't learn about nature outside of my own nosiness. That came later. After uni, I worked in retail for two years until my lovely nana died. After helping with her care the year before she passed away, I decided it was time to try to get a foot in the conservation door. That's easier said than done when you can't afford to do an unpaid internship and your current volunteering experience is nil, but somehow I managed to blag a job with the RSPB without knowing what a Jay or a Pied Wagtail was (sorry, RSPB). It was a tough year, attending events and recruiting members for the charity as a sort of glorified chugger. But I learnt a lot about nature, how to identify common birds and flowers and critters. I met proper nerds and found myself noticing things I'd never noticed before. And then I got ill.

And so I found myself bald, bloated and jobless at the age of 24 (more on that later). Months out of work, boredom, skintness and luck combined into the gift of time – time I spent getting to know the nature that was within walking distance of my doorstep. Gradually, I came to know the names of things; gradually, a sense of familiarity and closeness crept in.

Before I knew it, I'd found this thing. A nature thing, a nature joy, rich and thick like syrup. Now I was thirsty for it. I just wanted to slurp it all up – a tasty concoction of knowledge, sensations and experience. I learnt 'nature joy' was real, as tangible as a Wren, or a Garden Snail or a favourite conker. Within a year, I found myself utterly obsessed and enthralled by all things wildlife. I'd whip my phone out in the pub to show mildly interested mates the latest beetle or damselfly, or I'd jump up with excitement

THE SQUEAKS

in the beer garden, knocking over pints as I looked for the Nuthatch I could hear calling in the treetops. I'd found more than just a passion for 'animals'; I'd found an intimacy with the ordinary and wonderful wildlife around me. And with it came wonder and fascination, ecstasy and joy.

I was too late. The distance was too great, the approaching car going too fast. I ran to try to reach you but my slightly-too-big wellies slopped pathetically around my ankles, making me slow and clumsy. The winter-white light from my torch floodlit your little body as I watched you disappear under thick tyres. A sickening, gristly crunch. The fading of an engine. Clumping rubber soles on tarmac and then a horrid silence as I reached your flattened form. Little toad. I wondered if you were an individual I'd picked up before, on previous year's patrols.

As much as Toad Patrol was brilliant, it could also be heartbreaking. Road casualties were an inevitability: no matter how many toads you managed to pick up, some would evade detection and end up being run over. Our patrol covered about a mile of road and, with only four volunteers, it sometimes felt like that old arcade game 'Road Frog', or some sort of amphibious Whack-a-Mole. On some nights, when the weather didn't feel quite right for toad migration, we'd call off the patrol. It was gutting to hear the next day that some toads had ventured out anyway and unsuccessfully attempted a crossing. I felt the guilt and sadness churn in my tummy when we lost 50 in one night.

Toad Patrol could also be unsettling in other ways. Nightfall in March coincides with rush hour, and an endless

LOVE IS A TOAD

stream of teatime traffic flying past on a road with no pavement is quite intimidating. Even with flashing hazard lights and our bespoke triangular road sign bearing a giant toad silhouette, plenty of cars would still zoom past us at over 60mph.

Then there were the road-ragers. Most nights, at least one person would blast their horn as they passed us and we'd regularly get people slowing down to shout abuse at us. Drivers would fling litter out of their windows, casting empty energy drink cans and Maccies wrappers on to the verge. After a while, I added a litter picker to my kit. I'd mutter to myself, feeling the anger bubbling at people's callousness and indifference as I filled my bucket with wrappers and pop bottles on quiet toad nights.

More headlights, as another speeding car flew around the corner. They slowed down just enough to hurl abuse at Bob, the 80-year-old who leads our patrol group, and whose knees mean he struggles to jump up on to the high verge like the rest of us.

Finding nature joy felt like finally opening a filthy, muck-crusted window I'd been trying to look through for so long. Things felt clear, brighter. It was as though I'd been introduced to a bottomless pit of treasures, one I could spend the rest of my life digging through and never, ever reach the bottom of.

But this new sense of intimacy revealed other things too. In learning about the beauty of Turtle Doves, I also discovered they'd declined by 98 per cent since the 1960s. When I knew how to recognise the silhouette of the Ash tree, I started noticing the dead, dieback-stricken trees

THE SQUEAKS

lining skylines everywhere. I read headlines about shit-filled rivers, the possible local extinction of the Hedgehog and an impending 'insect apocalypse'. It started to feel as though I was surrounded by loss.

Now, whenever I took a weekend trip to the Peak District or walked out of town into the countryside, I could see wounds and sickness surrounding me. Stretches of land cut, sprayed, burned and grazed into relative silence. I'd walk for hours, following miles of flailed hedgerows devoid of bird and insect life. I felt my head wobbling, my mind descending into a constant state of anxiety and worry as I learnt about threat after threat, loss after loss.

Inevitably, this much worry began to ferment and congeal. Before long, I felt anger starting to brew; a sort of discombobulated rage simmered inside me without any direction or focus. My nerves were frayed and frazzled, and I struggled to sleep. Headlines about nature's decline, loss and destruction ricocheted around my skull at 2am like a moth rattling round a light bulb.

My sense of self-righteous anger was acute and raw; I walked around with a perpetually clenched jaw and furrowed brow. I was snappy and bad-tempered with the people I loved. And I was stubbornly insistent that I knew the truth: the world was fucked, nature was fucked and people were the problem. Things would change, I thought, if only I screamed loud enough. The destruction of nature could be fixed and reversed if I worked hard enough and if people would just listen to me. I even thought, in my darkest moments, that perhaps Earth would be better off without us. Us – the filthy polluters, takers, destroyers. Eugh.

LOVE IS A TOAD

What I didn't realise at the time – as I sulked and moped my way through work and family barbecues and Friday nights at the pub – was that I was grieving. All of these feelings of rage and resentment, of sorrow and soul-numbing despair were the manifestation of a deep grief, a grief I'd not yet learnt to put a name to. Like an unknown beast I sensed stalking me through shadowed woods. I hadn't turned around to stare them down, to look them in their hungry, burning eye.

Nature grief, I came to realise, was as real and tangible as nature joy; as inseparable as the fleas on the Wren, the slime of the snail and the rot of the conker.

With a screech of rubber on tarmac, the car revved away, exuding impatience and annoyance. Bob hauled himself upright, hobbling away from the verge he'd leant into to avoid the vehicle. After he assured us that he was all right, we continued the evening's patrol and I added another couple to my bucket of two dozen toads. After a few minutes, more headlights rounded the bend ahead, accompanied by loud exhaust and thumping base. This car slowed down as it reached me and I braced myself for another angry arsehole. It rolled to a stop and a tinted window went down to reveal four gawping young lads, probably in their late teens. They were accompanied by the pungently fragrant scent of weed, which wafted across me as the front passenger asked me what I was doing. 'Why's there a massive frog on a sign?' the lad grinned, cocky in a friendly sort of way. I answered the question simply, tilting my bucket forwards so they could see inside it. 'Collecting toads!' I laughed as I watched their

THE SQUEAKS

somewhat addled minds explode with confusion. Shrieks, giddiness and collective 'Whaaaaaaaaaa?!' ensued as I explained to the red-eyed foursome all about Toad Patrol. They thanked me before driving away.

Later that evening, a mum and daughter stopped to see what we were doing. The little girl was enthralled by my bucket of warty wonders, her eyes widening as she heard the chorus of squeaks. Another nosey lady Bob spoke to earlier in the week ended up joining our patrol a fortnight later. I suppose Toad Patrol wasn't all bad.

My shower was full of outside things. Bits of leaf and moss fell from my hair as I lathered shampoo; grit and mud followed the suds down the plughole. I plucked a Bramble thorn from my knee, embedded at a particularly red point of a scratch that stretched halfway down my shin. My ankle was red too, my skin raised and lumpy like angry bubble wrap after I'd traipsed through a patch of Nettles.

Nettle stings are one of the best things. Painful, yes. But reframe them as a sensation, a connection or an interaction – and they become awesome. Herbaceous chemicals tingling nerves, creating a hot and fresh sting that reminds you quite forcefully that you're alive. Especially when you accidentally squat into a patch of them when having a bush wee. Do I like it? I think so. A plant that fights back. How brilliant.

It was summer in that weird old lockdown year and I'd taken to rooting out new nooks and crannies on my doorstep, little patches of wild behind retail parks and under bridges where I could find nature on my daily walks. This often meant a bit of light trespassing, wandering along non-existent routes and scrambling through patches of thorny, brambly and Nettle-filled scrub.

It was also the year I picked up a new book. I'd no idea what it was about, but I'd seen a few folks on Instagram mentioning *Braiding Sweetgrass* and a lady called Robin Wall Kimmerer. I opened the first page and felt myself falling in, gulping down delicious words about plants, nature and our relationship with it, like a glass of iced water after a long, hot walk. By the end of lockdown summer, my copy was battered and filthy, the pages covered in mud and pencil marks, and stuffed with bookmarks devised out of Tawny Owl and Wood Pigeon feathers.

Here was a book that shifted my perspective. Reading it, I felt a sense of unshackling and release, as Kimmerer put names to concepts I'd felt but never consciously thought about. I felt connections form; linking systems and ideologies with nature's fate. The ideas she shared gave me permission to alter my relationship with nature, to let go of the expectations of what makes a 'good naturalist'. Now I felt empowered to informalise that relationship, to make it about fun and silliness over science and labels.

Whenever I found something interesting, beautiful or weird, I felt an urge to let that excitement bubble over. I simply needed to share it. Putting these experiences and observations into words helped me appreciate the natural world from all angles, like twizzling an especially knobbly gall around in your fingers. And so I found a love for writing about wildlife, scrawling notes or tapping furiously into the notes app on my phone to help me process what I'd seen, smelt and heard.

It's easy to gush about what we love. And we're quite good

THE SQUEAKS

at it when it comes to nature, sharing stories with one another and painting pictures of the beauty of it all. A gorgeous owl, a perfect slug, sunlight tinkling through Rowan leaves in a way that's just right. To put that warmth out into the world feels natural. Our bodies buzz and pulse with the joy of it. But what about the other stuff? Those murky feelings hiding in the shadows? Our bodies pulse with those too.

As months ticked by, I found myself also reflecting on the other things I'd been feeling. The flip side of a lichen-encrusted coin, where sadness and grief lie. When it comes to naming and sharing our grief for nature, it feels as though we're not able to be so open. Sure, it might bubble and spill out in moments of intense loss or anger – like the rage I had felt. But lots of us don't know how to sit with grief, tend to it, let it rest in our bones. We deny or suppress our sadness, dousing it in a shower of distracting positivity. To look these feelings in the eye and feel them is uncomfortable and painful, like prodding that Bramble thorn deeper into your skin.

This grief we're experiencing isn't obvious. It doesn't sit at the surface – flashing garish warning colours like a wasp – it's hidden somewhere deeper. A slow burning, more chronic grief, one we've perhaps not fully come to label yet because we're still in the midst of loss. It feels complex and layered, mixed in with nature joy and lots of other feelings into a thick compost.

When I started trying to think about all of the ingredients of this compost, there were too many to count: love, fascination, awe, sadness, fear, despair. I couldn't figure it out. And then I had an idea. I could combine all of these things I love doing – seeing wildlife and sharing love for it with other people, other nerds. If there's one thing I like to do with nature, it's tease it apart and explore inside it. And so I figured I could do this with all of these feelings too.

This book isn't trying to fix nature. I don't hold much power to mend, to heal, to restore, to rewild. At least not in a traditional conservation sense. But what about healing ourselves? I suspect much of our broken relationship with the Earth comes down to how we relate to it. And relationships are about feelings – about emotions, attitudes, perceptions and beliefs. In the following pages, I want to hold up my hand lens to these feelings and take a closer look, to scratch and sniff all the elements that make each side of that encrusted coin. I want to prise open the petals of nature joy and burrow through the mulched layers of nature grief. I want to understand how we carry such conflicting emotions within ourselves, and how we clutch joy tightly in the face of bleakness and sorrow.

So, I'm about to head off on a bumble. Spring is fully spronging, and I'm setting off on a sunshine, wind and mud-splattered quest around the isles I've grown up on. I want to meet fellow wild beings, feathered ones and slimy ones and leafy ones. I also want to meet fellows of my own species. Because I'm starting to see now that it's people who've uncovered this world of treasures for me. Offering a palm full of glinting seashells and pebbles, acorns and feathers, revealed with a slow and enticing unfurling of muddy fingers. The value of these gifts – of shared knowledge, excited chatter, spent time and long walks – is immeasurable, and I owe much of my love and understanding of the natural world to the givers of them.

THE SQUEAKS

Twelve months stretch ahead of me. As they blend and melt into each other, as life ebbs and flows through the calendar, I'll head out on some walks. Twelve people, twelve places, a bin-load of nature. We'll natter and nerd out together. I'll hear their thoughts and watch critters and creatures with them. Together we'll explore fascination and joy, sadness and grief. All with muddy fingernails, midge bites and birdsong ringing in our ears.

CHAPTER 1

A Nod and a Wink
Love | Heartbreak

NADIA SHAIKH
Isle of Bute – 16 May

THE WHALE

'*A*nd IIIIIIIIIIIIIII WHALE always love yooooooooou!' Nadia was laughing as she sang, her hands stuffed into her pockets, shuffling from foot to foot in a fizz of anticipation and excitement. This was just her latest performance from a suite of whale-themed lyrics. We'd been there nearly two hours and we were freezing. The heavy November sun had already sunk below the skyline, way up on the hill behind us. Across the water, the sunshine was still tickling the very top of the opposite slope, a tideline of light illuminating the late-autumn bracken like glowing, orange embers. The shadows below contrasted in cool blueish grey. It was so pretty.

We saw the message about the whale only a few hours ago. Two phones vibrating in different rooms, both receiving the same set of words on WhatsApp. A whale!

LOVE IS A TOAD

A Humpback, seen across the way from us, from the mainland. Somebody had shared a photo, the whale's fluke raised in the air as it dived downwards. In the background was a big shed – unmistakably the shed of the boatyard just up the road. Oh my god. It was nearby! In a scurrying flurry, we legged it outside and down to the seafront, Nadia running alongside me with her scope, me with my binoculars. We set up a makeshift lookout post and strained our eyes, peering up Loch Striven, the sea loch across the water from Bute. The air distorted with the distance – the point we peered at must've been a couple of miles away. And no matter how hard we squinted, we absolutely, definitely could not see a whale.

I glanced at the time and saw an opportunity. There was a ferry leaving from the north end of the island in 20 minutes. I did the maths: the crossing itself is only five minutes and it'd be another quarter of an hour to reach the banks of the loch. Where we'd potentially see a Humpback Whale. Screw it, it was too exciting to resist.

And so there we stood, fingers numb and aching, scanning the water's surface. We were looking for anything: a large ripple, a cetaceous swell, a breaking of surface by a smooth and colossal mammalian spine. Nope, nowt. Close to our shore, a nosey Grey Seal slunk past. It gave us a suspicious side-eye.

'Cause of my hump-back, my hump, my hump, my hump-back, my lovely little hump-back.'

Oh god. Nadia had transitioned to a whaley rendition of the Black Eyed Peas' 'My Humps'. Distracting ourselves from the cold and the wait, we'd been inserting whalean lyrics into any song we could think of. It was definitely very nearly, pretty much dark.

'THERE! THERE! THERE!'

Nadia was flapping and jumping and squealing. She pointed elatedly to the far side of the loch. An inky black form smoothly breached the surface of the water, the arch of its back flowing in an almost unending way. It was huge. We froze and gawped as it slid smoothly under the surface without so much as a splash. I couldn't believe it.

We erupted; Nadia was running in circles and I jumped up and down, utterly buzzing. There wasn't a soul around to hear our joyous mania. Well, not a human soul.

The whale resurfaced again. This time, as its spine arched, it blew an immense jet of whaley breath; we could hear the powerful, rushing hiss of it from across the loch. I imagined what it must smell like, that cloud of hot, wet air, so recently constrained by a whale's lungs. I bet it stunk. I bet it was brilliant.

I fixed my binoculars on the whale as it started to sink again. And then, a tail! A lobed fluke that paused in the air for a second in a perfect silhouette. I could practically see the water dripping from it, the gleam of seawater on blubbery skin. Then it was gone. Disappearing in a smooth flow, melding into the darkness of the loch.

We jumped and danced. We carried on singing. We hugged in a collision of giddiness, fizzing excitement and disbelief. It felt bizarre to see a life form that was so enormous. I spend so much time looking at tiny things – woodlice, Daisies, Wrens. And here my eyeballs were clapped upon an actual swimming, stinky-breathed whale.

LOVE IS A TOAD

The moon took over the sky so that the water became hard to see. Then the cold took a firm grip of our cores. In a haze of satisfaction and elation, we tumbled back into the car and turned the key. A shudder, a sputter. The battery... dead. But it didn't matter. Because that day we saw a Humpback Whale.

The whirring was incessant. Biologically mechanical and never-pausing, it sounded a bit like a fishing rod being reeled in. It was coming from the deep-green density of a Gorse bush ahead of us. It sounded almost like a high-pitched purr and I could feel the tiny vibrations from it in my throat. As we drew closer, we saw the noise creator. A little avian sculpture, brown and mottle-backed, mouth agape. A Grasshopper Warbler. I adore these little brown jobs. This one looked like a little feathered robot, perched stiffly upon a branch, beak wide open with that almost artificial sound pouring out of it – rattling, clicking, whirring. Close your eyes and the noise transforms into something more reminiscent of meadows and verges on a hot day in late summer – the inane chatter and buzz of their namesakes. Come to think of it, their tone reminds me specifically of Roesel's Bush Crickets.

As I lowered my binoculars, my gaze landed on Nadia's bum, clad in shorts despite the drizzle. She was hunched over the verge at the side of the path admiring some Cow Parsley. Its satisfyingly arranged flower heads were splayed like bike spokes and topped with platforms of fluffy, white flowers.

'Oh my god. There's so much going on here. Look at that little snail. Look at this little mosquito's fuzzy antennae! And ooh, what are these again?'

A NOD AND A WINK

She pointed at a jet-black little insect, covered in black fuzz and beholding a bulging pair of eyes. A St Mark's Fly, slow and sluggish. You see loads of them each spring when they seem to land on you out of nowhere, grateful for a rest. This little male (the females have tiny beady eyes) sat motionless on a flower head that was otherwise bustling with insect activity.

It was that sweet spot of spring, the month of May. There's a tangible energy in the air at this time of year – one of fizzling and busyness and flirting that you can almost taste. Plus, it's a month of meeting old friends, familiar faces who turn up every year, responding to nature's innate calendar, RSVP always 'yes'. I asked Nadia what her favourite thing is about May.

'Uh . . . strimmers. Yep. Strimmers,' she answered sarcastically. Earlier we'd walked past a stretch of shaved embankment. It looked raw and sterilised, contrasted with the juicy bushiness that wants to swell out of every nook and cranny at this time of year.

'Oh, a Mayfly! Ooh!' The little insect was perched upon another cloud-like poof of Cow Parsley, its outstretched front legs forming a pose like it was bowing in prayer. The veins on its wings formed an intricate pattern that reminded me of lace. 'Nice, that's my first one of the year. There! That's something I like about May. It's got things named after the month. Like Maybugs.' Nadia smiled, satisfied with her answer.

We bumbled further along the stony, bumpy track sandwiched between fields. There was zipping activity ahead of us, things flitting from one patch of green to another. Swallows swooped in slick, fluid motions, snarfling insects from the moist, thick air. And Linnets, too, perched on phone wires in pairs and threes, tinkling and woohoo-ing as we walked past.

'Ugh. Fences though, what are they even about?!' Nadia's Geordie inflections made me smile, even as she gestured to the shiny, brutal structure ahead of us. The fence in question had recently been installed. It marked the boundary of a sheep field, a barrier of straight lines garnished with sinister barbed-wire prongs. It was raw and severe. Behind it lay the remains of the field's previous border, gnarls of Gorse bushes piled high.

Gorse is a brilliant plant. I love its form, all twists and contortions. I love the deep green of its spiny leaves and the way it stings in a sort-of-nice way when they scratch my thighs. Couple the spines with the yellow of its flowers and it looks almost like an old photograph, the colours tinged with a hint of sepia.

Here it had been cut and wrenched from the earth. Metres and metres, bushes and bushes. The coconutty scent of its sunshine-yellow flowers still wafted through the damp air. This time last year, that very Gorse hedgerow was blooming. Garishly and gorgeously yellow, its flowers buzzed with insect busyness. Its thorny density provided an impenetrable barrier for sheep, and an impenetrable shelter for Long-tailed Tits and Grasshopper Warblers building their nests. It hung over the gravel path, silhouetted against the sky like dramatic saffron clouds. But not any more. In its place, the new fence stood. Big, brutal and bossy. Uniformity replacing unruliness.

'Just, why?! It's mad,' Nadia tutted.

I love Nadia even more than I love Gorse. She's mad, she's

weird, she fizzes with energy in the same way a Wren belts its song out of the undergrowth. She's bold and artistic, and absolutely hilarious. And she's always up for a skinny dip; I've seen her naked almost more times than I've seen myself. Nadia taught me a lot about love – of the intimate, platonic, friendship kind. She also taught me loads about nature.

The first time I met her I was shitting myself, and not because of her bolshiness and sparkle – Nadia was interviewing me for a job. I saw her in the visitor centre at RSPB Sandwell Valley, as she walked past, all confidence and extroversion. Somehow, despite my nerves, I got the job. From there, we grew closer. Nadia took me on birdy adventures, not only teaching me how to identify things, but how to immerse myself unselfconsciously in moments of joy and excitement. After the whirlwind of Covid and the uncertainty that followed, we both found ourselves in weird circumstances, free and untethered to place or work. Nadia upped sticks from her home in the Midlands and moved to the Isle of Bute; I followed her a few months later. Here we live together, huddled in our little home office, running out on our lunch breaks to plunge into the sea or collect Limpet shells on the beach. So many Limpet shells.

Nadia is thoroughly entangled with my own journey of getting to know nature. So I thought she'd be the perfect person to talk to about nature joy in its purest form.

Trundling out of our flat that morning, we'd decided to go out for a wander despite the heavy-bellied grey clouds stretching in every direction. The bumpy track we took climbed gently upwards in a way that reddens the cheeks and warms the hands. We soon reached the hump of a small hill, opening up a wide view across part of the island. Looking down on Rothesay, we could see the nine o'clock ferry pulling into the port of the little town where we regularly poked around in our favourite charity shop and howled 'Big Yellow Taxi' at the little karaoke bar.

In the foreground, a patch of juicy-looking Nettles lay at our feet. We spied some dots of shimmering, metallic colour punctuating their fuzzy leaves: a pair of beetles, unmistakably mid beetley love session. Their wing cases a deep, rusty red and shoulders an iridescent green, they looked like something you'd colour in as a kid. I googled them later and found out they were Knotgrass Leaf Beetles, and indeed they were fond of Nettles. They sat motionless and mid-copulation, different hues ricocheting around their shells as you lowered your eyes to their level.

'Obscene,' muttered Nadia, ogling the pair unashamedly. She's a bit like me in the way she watches wildlife: wide-eyed and full of nosiness. I told her I reckoned we would've been best mates as kids, and she described how when she was younger, she'd watch little red mites on the wall in the garden and poke jellyfish on the beach. When she'd found lots of tiny little Frogs on the lawn, she'd pleaded with her parents not to mow it. Yep, we definitely would've been friends. I thought back to my own solo playing as a kid and remembered my butterfly bin.

My butterfly bin was cream and speckled. The sort of ordinary plastic bin you'd find in the kitchen. A forked fissure snaked down one side; Mum had chucked it out when it'd split and I'd swiftly nabbed it from the rubbish for my 'friends'.

A NOD AND A WINK

Light and easy to carry with a swinging lid, it was perfect. I'd collect handfuls of any plants I could tug up. Juicy grasses, Daisies and Dandelions – they'd all go in there. Stuffed into the bin with green-tinged fingers. It had to be *just right*.

Once my makeshift vivarium was ready for its residents, the fun would begin. Now, it was time to embody the hunter. Prowler, stalker, pouncer. Creeping on muddy tiptoes, I'd sneak ever so slowly up to an unsuspecting 'friend'. It was a complicated business, butterfly catching. Even at the age of five, I'd honed my skills to become a champion sneaker. Where was my shadow falling? Which way was the wind blowing? If I approach from this direction, will you detect me? Arms outstretched, hands braced for gentle-but-firm cupping, I'd get as close as I dared before swooping in for the capture. YES! Success. There were the giveaway tickles, battering my skin like a little lepidopteran massage. A treasure. As light as air. Fluttering, whispering wings against sticky pink palms. A treasure peeked at, illuminated in a tiny crack of light between rigidly clasped thumbs. Beady-eyed treasure. Blobs on wiggling antennae. How exciting.

Honestly, the squirt of adrenalin I felt catching butterflies as a kid is still hard to match. It was pure glee, the most innocent ecstasy. Into the bin the butterfly would go and the prowl would start all over again. I spent hours doing this, following Cabbage Whites, Peacocks and Small Tortoiseshells around the garden in a state of giddiness.

Nadia and I meandered along beside each other, the path we were following becoming gradually engulfed in high-sided hedges of stunted Beeches. Lacking the thick trunks of mature

LOVE IS A TOAD

trees, they still oozed oldness in their lumpy gnarls and cloaks of mosses. The leaves were at a point of mid-emergence, soft and moist and poking out in fresh lime tufts from between bushes of paler green lichens. The hedgerows were busy, with a mix of chattering Chaffinches and tits flocking alongside us, all noisiness and energy.

Stopping to squeeze through a kissing gate, I spied a curled black sausage nestled in the grass at my feet. 'Bloody hell, you chonks!' Nadia bent down for a closer look and I crouched next to her. Plump and chubby and adorned with protruding hairs, it was a sizeable caterpillar – the length and thickness of my pinky. I gently scooped it up, moving it out of the way of any more boots, and it coiled up softly in the palm of my hand. It felt like velvet and sat with a surprising heftiness – chunky and solid. Its dark body was mottled with molten orange speckles and, combined with its whorled posture, it looked somewhat cosmic – a bit like a photograph of a swirling galaxy. I recognised it as the caterpillar of the Drinker (what a name) – a big caterpillar that becomes a big moth, fluffy and ginger and slightly reminiscent of a puppy. We took a moment to indulge in admiration – our noses only inches from the coil of speckles and hairiness. A deep, satisfying sigh, a minute of unfocused bliss. It was all rather relaxing.

I asked Nadia about it – if this sort of moment is when she finds she's in her element of nature joy. 'God, yes – if I'm out on my own, wandering without purpose, without any constraints on time. And obviously if I've got a good packed lunch . . .' Nadia trailed off. We mutually understood the importance of packing some good butties for a long walk.

A NOD AND A WINK

'It's those days you spend slowly exploring. Seeing what happens around you and being surprised by your own ability to get lost in something. Some kind of archetypal British moment: a hot summer's day lying in a meadow, watching insects fly past, or going rock pooling, or one of those crisp, misty mornings in autumn. All of these little private moments.'

I could picture each of the scenes as she spoke, seeing a Nadia in a state of tranquillity and peacefulness. We squelched along, wobbling across the muddiness underfoot and the wetness of spring. A small burn, trickling vigorously, intersected the path in front of us and a rickety footbridge saved us from having to go for a paddle. The water flowed steadily; with all the rain, it had swollen up and over its narrow banks, combing the grass either side like parted hair.

Nestled in the green and submerged under the flow was a sliver of grey. I plucked the sopping feather from the stream and preened it softly with my fingers, arranging the barbs and tidying its edges to reveal its identity. A pale, smoky grey, punctuated by blurred bars the colour of storm clouds, with a band of cream down the left side: I held in my fingers a feather dropped by a Sparrowhawk. How *cool* and how apt. The Beech hedges had opened out into a spacious corridor, flanked each side by Birch scrub and Gorse bushes. I'd already given it a nickname on previous walks – Sparrowhawk Alley. It seemed to be a favoured place for these avian annihilators. I'd regularly seen one zooming silently and determinedly along the open ride, on the tail of the Chaffinches we'd seen earlier. As we continued to walk, I kept an eye out for the telltale shadow, the flap-flap-glide, but there was no sign. The alleyway was quiet today.

LOVE IS A TOAD

I handed the feather to Nadia and she twirled it in her fingers, admiring its stripes and paddle-like form. 'For me, nature joy comes in two types,' she mused. 'There's Type One – those moments which are really acute and explosive. Like seeing that Humpback – it was an uncontained, unadulterated, unfiltered joy!' Ahh. The whale. I think about it often and smile every time I do. 'Type One moments are those when you identify or recognise something, and you're just absolutely buzzing. I'll either scream and be silly, or I'll just cry. It's a rush that's so heavy. It's, like, observer joy.'

Observer joy – those moments of *wow*, when you recognise a species and you know exactly what it is or why it's doing what it's doing. It could be when you see something you've read about in books or heard other people excitedly discuss. I've had plenty of experiences that fit into this type. Like the time I'd got lost in some woods and in trying to take a shortcut back to a path had slipped into a ditch. With sog seeping into my knickers, I realised I'd stumbled across something awesome: a small, vivid-orange matchstick of a mushroom, my first ever Bog Beacon Fungus. I'd seen pictures of it in a mushroom book and fantasised about meeting it for a couple of years, and here it was, glowing against the gloom of the dark water like a little lighthouse. I was ecstatic. Or there was the time I first saw Ivy Bees. I'd climbed up on to the rickety shed roof in my back yard to get a closer look at the stripy bums I could see zooming about and one momentarily landed, looking just like the pictures I'd seen online. *So* exciting.

By now, we'd traversed a little further along the West Island Way, passing from Sparrowhawk Alley to Gorse Avenue.

A NOD AND A WINK

Here the path was squeezed by Brambles and Gorse, which grappled at our jackets as we pushed through. I pinched a couple of flowers from a vibrant Gorse bush and nibbled on them, relishing the pungent combination of planty bitterness and coconut. The weighty, plump clouds above had started to release chunky droplets of rain that quickly soaked us, our socks soggy and a constant trickle running down our foreheads and noses.

Nadia continued her train of thought, licking her lips in between to catch raindrops. 'Then there's Type Two. Exquisite nature joy. It's totally different. Like getting into a warm bath. It's a completely different high, almost transcendental.'

As the avenue opened up into a waterlogged field of Soft Rush, the towering mountains of Arran appeared in the distance, jagged and dramatic and partly obscured by pillowy clouds. Scattered across the field were white pompoms of Cotton Grass, static and bob-less on such a still day. It was tranquil, the gentle pattering of rain continued and the smell it left, also infused with the earth and vegetation, hung heavy around us.

'Type Two is when you feel it in your body. When it seeps in, when it becomes part of you. To be salty-skinned, or when your hands smell like crushed leaves, or you feel the rain pouring down your face.' She laughed, experiencing the latter as she spoke. 'I guess it's the moment when you transition from civilised human into something more creature-like.'

To be creature-like. That was *exactly* it. I'd never thought about it this way before. Type Two definitely feels like something tangible and distinct. To fully sink into the animalistic side of oneself and simply *be* in a habitat,

LOVE IS A TOAD

a dynamic bundle of nerves and senses and processing. Sniffing stuff, watching stuff, licking stuff. It's there in those long, quiet moments when you find a spot – a tree, a pond, a bench – and hunker down, settling into a state of stillness and softness. When you melt into the background and let nature carry on around you. When I find myself in this state, I can feel it physically, a twinkling and sparkling sensation, sitting behind my eyeballs somewhere deep inside my skull, like goosebumps of the brain. I feel it in my chest too – a deep, satisfying ache, like the sweet spot at the top of a stretch. In these moments every sense is heightened, eyes wide, lungs full, skin tingling. It might be autumn sunlight dappling through a fiery canopy of Oak and Beech. It might be the thrum and buzz of a meadow in summer, the perfect pose of a bumblebee upon some Knapweed. It could even be a barefoot beach walk in midwinter, aching toes and bubbling Curlew and the *hisssss* of the waves through pebbles and sand. In these moments there are no rigid, human-language thoughts. In these moments I don't matter. In these moments everything *makes sense*.

I spoke my thoughts aloud and Nadia agreed. 'Yes, totally! When I do have those transcendental moments, I don't feel big in this world at all, I feel tiny.' She hoiked up over a stile, wobbling slightly as her muddy boots struggled to grip the slippery, damp wood. 'And it's not about me any more – it's about wholeness beyond me. I've tapped into the system; it's like finally getting the USB the right way up, joining the network. *Thunk!*' she said, miming the action as she talked. 'There are all of these human systems and problems that we live alongside – the patriarchy, capitalism, colonialism . . .

A NOD AND A WINK

We're plugged into them all of the time. When you're in nature you can disconnect from all of that and reconnect to something way more ancient. And that's why it feels so good. You're plugging into something far greater than just you.'

Nail on the head! She's right. Perhaps if more people – some of the ones hardened by power and wealth and privilege – had the chance to experience Type Two, we might begin to make a little headway with some of those problems.

Our route, traversing across the island from home, had taken us on to a winding, single-track road. As we trundled along it sloped into a dip, the sort of place where wetness naturally collects. The plants in the fields on either side of the track spoke of this dampness, growing in a thick flush of sedges, rushes and Bog Myrtle. In the branches of a young Alder, a Sedge Warbler sat stiffly and sturdily – they love this vein of succulence forking through the fields and I see them here each spring. Another little brown job, they're beautiful in their subtleties. A pale eye stripe accentuates their brow like golden eyeshadow. Their song ricochets around your head when you hear it, an amalgamation of rasps and scratches, whistles and *pew-pew-pews*.

The verges either side of us were engorged with bushy greenery typical of May, dense clumps of Cow Parsley and Hemlock Water Dropwort jostling in the bright light. The road ahead snaked into a mouth-like archway of trees, so that it looked like it was being swallowed by big Beeches and towering Oaks. As we slunk under the trees, the hedgerow plants gave way to shade lovers. The early spring plants of woodlands are some of my favourites – there's just something about them; perhaps it's that association with lovely-jubbly things to come. They're professional canopy racers, hurrying to bloom before the trees awaken, gobbling their sunlight before Oak leaves erupt and block out the sunshine for the summer. All around us, Bluebells glowed indigo hues in the shadows, and sprinkles of Greater Stitchwort – a cartoon-like flower you'd doodle in an exercise book – gave the impression of scattered star constellations.

We paused to admire the woodland galaxy at our feet and I asked Nadia about that second way of experiencing nature. Had it changed over time?

'Yes, oh my god. I feel Type Two so much more now. I feel like the older I get, and the further away I get from conservation and from institutionalised nature work, the more personal and the more private my relationship with nature gets.'

Nadia's a reformed conservationist. She considers herself to be 'post-charitable industrial complex' – the term used to describe the way that a lot of large charities are linked closely with the activities of large corporations and governments, effectively being part of the same churning machine, and so operating with a growth-based mindset. She, like many, feels the conservation sector has lost a bit of its soul. Despite being full of wonderful people and projects, it is in many ways fundamentally flawed. Many of our nature charities are now huge and powerful organisations, and they profit from the very practices that caused harm to nature in the first place. Extraction (think flogging crap in gift shops to raise funds 'for nature'), exploitation (benefiting from the free labour of volunteers, which lots of people can't afford to do) and exclusion (keeping people off land and only the right sorts of people being allowed to be 'in nature'). So many of us are disempowered from nurturing and working with nature ourselves, so instead we donate a fiver a month to someone else, in return for an acrylic-furred cuddly Hedgehog and the promise of 'saving nature'.

The constellations of Stitchwort had given way to another cosmic woodland flower. A smattering of Wood Anemones twinkled from a bank to the right of the road, looking like the forest floor's answer to a starry night sky.

We paused to admire them and Nadia continued her train of thought, telling me how over time her connection with the natural world had become both stronger and simpler. No longer was it about textbooks or science, and nor was it performative. 'It's not anything! It's just being outside, seeing nature with a little nod and a wink. I guess the same way you'd be around a partner – that intimacy you have with really strong love.'

Love. I find it hard to think of a more fitting word for my relationship with the natural world. It's the first one that springs to mind. Something strong and warm, something fundamental. This is taking one of the most human experiences and applying it to the way we feel about other, non-human life, and our place amongst it. It's the thing I say most often when I'm talking about wildlife. 'I bloody LOVE toads!' 'Oh my god, I love the smell of White Clover so much.' I even say it to creatures in passing: 'Mornin', Robin, love you!' But it's more than sentimental gushing. It's the stuff I feel privately too, the way Nadia described. I think of the places I've sat in a state of contentment, with the warmth of the sun caressing my skin and the lumpiness of the earth and the leaf litter digging into my bum through my shorts. Or perhaps a dragonfly landing on my bare, muck-dusted toes, birdsong bubbling in my chest and the air saturated with the smell of living things. This is a feeling of intimacy and closeness, of deep affection, and a sense of being surrounded by the peaceful, mundane busyness of other life. I feel it bursting in my chest like mushrooms erupting from a pine-needled forest floor. I feel it like butterflies in my tummy. Small Coppers, I reckon.

But is it *actually* love? To me, love itself isn't an emotion but an amalgamation of things. A thick mud, made from a compost of components: affinity, intimacy, commitment, care, affection, passion, trust. These are all things I can apply to my own relationship with nature. Affinity and passion are perhaps quite obvious, but the other elements are applicable too. That intimacy, the sense of knowing nature really well, knowing what she's going to do next, knowing some of her secrets. This leads to care and affection, holding concern for nature's wellbeing and understanding our part in a reciprocal relationship that serves both parties. The desire to nurture and be nurtured in return. And then there's trust. I do trust nature. Not in a naïve, irrational sort of way – she's indifferent to everything and everyone and can bring with her pain, hardship and discomfort. I find nature's apathy to be one of the most beautiful things about her. But I trust in her rhythm – her ebb and flow and reliability. And in her ability to teach me lessons. Of course, there's attraction, too. The way summer-green tendrils of River Water-crowfoot whirl and ripple in the dawdling flow of a clear river. Gorgeous. The way

A NOD AND A WINK

a Kestrel preens her tail, slowly running a smoky feather through her notch-and-toothed beak until she reaches the black-tipped end, releasing it with a flourish and a flick. *Undeniably* hot.

But is it *love*? Science is poking a cold bony finger in a spot somewhere between my shoulder blades, repeating the question with a frown. And I don't have an answer. This is still up for debate. We find it hard to label precisely what love is between humans, let alone applying it to the way we feel about non-human life. We do know that it's a suite of connections and processes, squirting a concoction of chemicals into our brains that then makes us feel things. Serotonin and dopamine, oxytocin, oestrogen and testosterone. The things that send the butterflies fluttering, that make the pupils widen and cheeks flush. All of this can be measured.

'I think we love it because we know it's ultimately linked to our survival. And evolutionarily, our curiosity and affinity with nature has paid off.' At this, Nadia paused, bending down to pluck a trio of bright green hearts – Wood Sorrel! She nibbled the shamrock-esque leaves as she talked, relishing the apple-skin tang they released.

Nadia explained that being drawn to nature means we're paying attention. When we're in tune with our surroundings, aware of the smells around us, or the sound of birdsong or rustles in the leaf litter, then we're more likely to notice danger and find food. To love nature seems inevitable because in doing so, we're more likely to survive.

What we feel about nature might seem like something intangible, like clutching at smoke. But *why* we feel it –

that's something different. Nadia was describing an intrinsic affinity with nature that's bound into our bones, woven into our DNA. This is the biophilia hypothesis – literally the 'nature loving' hypothesis. It theorises that humans have an innate attraction to life and living things, that we're drawn to it and seek out connections with it. We find it rewarding in its appearance, forms and shapes. In the way it sounds, the way it smells. We find pleasure and beauty in the patterns of leaves, the light on the lake and the clouds in the sky. And that's useful to us. Because when you're attracted to something, you want to get closer to it. Affinity instils a sense of nosiness – we want to observe, to learn, to understand. And, in a truly animalistic sense, the more we know about nature, the more likely we are to survive. We know which plants are safe and which ones make us sick. We know which insects are harmless and which ones you're best avoiding. We understand the warning calls of the birds in the trees, telling us of something sharp-toothed and dangerous sneaking around the corner. The theory of biophilia suggests we inherently love nature and it's *because* of that love that we've made it this far.

Whilst this explains the wider human relationship with nature, it doesn't necessarily fully explain our own individual relationships. Perhaps something so personal doesn't need to be measured and quantified. After all, it is unique for each of us. A potion made from all sorts of ingredients – experiences and circumstances and preferences all bubbling away together in a cauldron. Just as our romantic relationships and friendships have their individual quirks, so too do our individual relationships with the natural world. I certainly

A NOD AND A WINK

feel like I have my own in-jokes with nature, the little nod and wink Nadia described.

Nadia continued, 'Nature always makes me laugh. It makes me feel safe. It's consistent and unrelenting. It always shows up, no matter what I look like or how unkind I am. I think life is about building a relationship no matter what because, ultimately, we're going to have to cohabit with nature in spite of everything.' She paused suddenly and hunched over, folding herself almost in half to look at her left ankle. I made out a tiny black dot – a single freckle on her shin. Except it wasn't a freckle. Nadia flicked the Tick away before it latched on, denying it the tasty blood meal it desired. She started laughing. 'See! Nature tries to give you Lyme disease and you still love it! So maybe it *is* love.'

Maybe it is. And perhaps the magic of it lies in the fact that this thing isn't tangible – you can't measure it. This feeling, this affinity, is a key element of nature joy for many of us. I might not be able to define it, I might not be able to plug my brain into a machine see it light up with answers – but I'll always be able to say 'I bloody *love* toads'.

The trunk of my favourite Oak tree on the Isle of Bute twists like a corkscrew. I like to imagine the acorn they grew from revolving like a spinning top, the newly emerged sapling twirling around like a ballerina as they reached for the canopy. I picture their crackle-barked trunk eventually settling into a pose of perpetual spiral, twisted like a piece of fusilli pasta. We stood at their feet, gazing upwards at the coiling, curved creature, taking every part of them in.

I refer to the tree as 'them' for two reasons. First, Oak trees don't fit neatly into gendered boxes (not that much does) but using 'it' seems so impersonal for a being of such character. 'They' seems very fitting for the mighty life form in front of me. Secondly, the Oak is not just an Oak. One of my favourite things about my favourite tree is that they're not alone. They're an amalgamation of lives, a ship carrying countless passengers in a green forest sea. Down one side of the oak, the north-facing side, sweeps a cloak of mosses. Every fissure and crevice is filled with their green springy plumpness. How many species, I've no idea. And looking up into the canopy, each branch is spangled with Polypody Ferns, jutting out in sprigs with wide-toothed silhouettes like chunky combs. There's a word for these plants that live on other plants – epiphytes, meaning 'upon' and 'plant'. Amidst all of the epiphytes are other lives, scuttling and sliming and crawling ones. This woody ship had many souls aboard.

As Nadia and I stood below them, gawping upwards, a plaintive *mew-mew-mew* wheezed its way down from the highest boughs. I squinted in the green-gloom light and spied a plump of pink – the colour of apple blush – bobbing lazily amongst the foliage. Another *mew-mew-mew* and a dustier-pink plump appeared, following the brighter mewer ahead. Bullfinches!

The ballerina Oak sits at the bottom of Barone Hill. At a measly 160 metres it's not a mountain, but it sticks its head high enough out of the woods for you to see right down to the sea from the top. I have nicknamed it Mount Bullfinch as I *always* see Bullfinches there. Maybe it's the same pair I see each time – perhaps the couple we watched lazily flitting in the oak, pretty in their duo of pinks. But whether there are just two or many more, I just know it's a place where I regularly spot them and it always brings me joy. My bird app describes Bullfinches as 'neckless' and 'sluggish', which I think is a bit mean – they're simply adorably pudgy and in no hurry at all.

A short amble later and the roof of the woods melted into open sky, still thick with smoky grey clouds. We gazed out over Loch Fad to our right, bordered each side by a bobbled Oak woodland that looked a bit like clumps of broccoli. It stretched away from us until it hit the horizon, where again the jagged silhouette of Arran's mountains towered. Closer to us, the sky fizzed with movement; slick silhouettes of Swallows and House Martins swept through the air and close to the surface of the water, their quips and chatters filling the air with loveliness.

Nadia's words on nature joy and nature love were still reverberating around my skull, but I also wanted to ask her about the flip side. We both agreed we feel love for nature but how do we feel about the state of it? About knowing its plight and witnessing it for ourselves?

'Love's so uncontrollable. You don't choose it, do you? So, when you love nature and you see it being hurt, it *is* like heartbreak. When I think about break-ups that I've had, when I've just cried and cried and cried, I would say that's a really comparable feeling. There's nothing you can do about it, other than feel the pain.'

Heartbreak! Of course it might sound cheesy on the face of it – but isn't heartbreak one of the biggest, most intense emotional experiences we face? It can come from teenage romance, or your first big love, or the adoration of a celebrity

LOVE IS A TOAD

(the dawning realisation at the age of 15 that Brandon Flowers would never fall in love with me was *true* heartbreak), but it's also so much wider than this. To me, heartbreak is that horrible feeling when it all comes to an end and you feel as though you've been punched in the tummy, as though you can't breathe. There's a deep ache, and you might feel it as dull and heavy, or hot and piercingly sharp, and everything seems grey and dreary, like you'll never be happy again. On the days that nature grief really gets to me, that's what it feels like. A big, blue sadness. A sense of loss, of hopelessness. When I see a patch of Cowslips obliterated, when a familiar Oak is felled, when I see a prickly casualty at the side of the road, my heart does hurt.

Nadia sighed. We paused on the wide track so that our line of sight reached right down the loch. Standing still, watching the surface of the water quiver with the fall of mizzle, she went on to point out that you can often see the damage being done to nature as a mirror held up to society, how the things that hurt nature are hurting people too, which adds to that sense of heartbreak.

It felt as though Nadia had taken a jumbled mess of thoughts in my brain and reordered them into something that made sense. When you step back and look at the bigger picture, it's easier to see how these things are inextricably linked. The pain and suffering of nature is connected to the pain and suffering of people. The systems that cause and perpetuate inequality and oppression are rooted in things that also affect nature – a relentlessly growth-based mindset, exploitation, disregard of wellbeing and an assumed entitlement to extraction. It's like trying to pull

A NOD AND A WINK

yourself free of some Bramble that's snarled itself into your jumper; everything's hooked and barbed on to everything else, and it starts pulling at threads and unravelling when you try and unpick it. A big, tangled mess.

We cast our eyes to the skies as we chatted, looking out for a gangly winged silhouette. The Ospreys had been back for a month; by now, a couple of females were likely to be incubating their eggs. A few days earlier I'd been eye to eye with a male as he 'pip-pip-pipped' above me before swooping into the shallows to grab a fishy gift for his mate, the loch water cascading off his monochrome plumage. But not today. Perhaps it was too wet even for an Osprey. Nadia lowered her binoculars, and letting them rest on her chest she continued.

'The way that we understand grief does include ecological grief now and so we should see it as the same as any other grief. It's now part of us. And it's heavy and it's constant, but then so is joy and love!'

Ambling onwards, we turned away from the loch and trudged up a gentle slope. Our boots thudded along the path as we walked, squelching in muddy grass and slipping over rain-polished stones.

'I now know my heartbreak can exist alongside love, whereas previously I thought, *How can I enjoy anything?!* I used to feel like I shouldn't find joy when things were so bad.' Nadia laughed. 'But now, the grief and love are constantly dancing alongside one another because I've figured out they are inseparable.'

Nadia's words helped me to picture this as a dance, as two threads intertwined and flowing along together, dynamic and moving. Like a tree carries Ivy, wrapped around its trunk as it

LOVE IS A TOAD

grows and reaches for the canopy, I too know I can hold both at the same time. I know I can feel the joy of the Swifts who returned screaming and wheeling to the skies just last week, whilst also carrying the sorrow of their decline, knowing that the skies are quieter than they used to be.

'I do have genuine feelings of hope,' Nadia continued, 'and it doesn't mean I'm *only* made of hope; I'm made of lots of other parts. Hope and despair are both there, but I'm also made of sorrow, grief, anger, joy. I'm made of all of these things. It was when I stopped hating people, that was when the hope could come in.'

We trundled back towards town, the thick globules of rain having soaked us through to our knickers. Nadia took a deep breath, drawing in the cool and delicious May air that smelt of lushness and life and wet things.

'It's constant work. As a species, we've been gifted with complex brains, which allow us to have all of the joyful moments we've talked about.' She paused, before smiling. 'So, I'm afraid it's the pay-off, innit?'

The verges hugged us; they were leafy and enlarged, the vegetation swelling out of the earth with the moisture. Everything around us exuded growth and expansion. We stopped at a patch of Hedge Garlic (a tasty spring snack) and I bent down for a closer look. It is the rule in April and May – you must always inspect Hedge Garlic (and Cuckoo flowers) closely, just in case a little treasure awaits. And bingo! There it was, a tiny speckle of orange, the same colour as apricots. The little dot was a single egg belonging to the Orange Tip Butterfly. It protruded from the stem in the shape of a rugby ball, adorned with ridges and bands in impossibly small detail. To see that tiny speck and to know a dinky life sat waiting inside – it's the stuff of magic. And finding them is half the fun of it – it's like a lepidopteran game of Where's Wally, spotting an infinitesimal dot of orange amidst a wash of green. I tore off one of the jagged-edged, floppy leaves, one without a little orange egg, for a nibble. The pleasant tang hit the back of my throat, a bit like horseradish. As I handed another leaf to Nadia, our field of view was interrupted by the flutter of an adult butterfly. A male Orange Tip, his wing tips the same shade of orange as the speckle we'd beheld, and his underwings patterned with moss-green splodges that completely disguised him when he landed upon some nearby Cow Parsley.

Nadia pointed and laughed. 'You know, we're talking about our feelings but butterflies could be the biggest grievers! We'll never know.'

Oh god, I don't even want to *begin* to think about sad butterflies.

CHAPTER 2

A Telltale Peep

Humanity | Misanthropy

AMY-JANE BEER
River Derwent, Yorkshire – 18 June

There was a sign. White background, black text, red border. It read 'DON'T EVEN THINK ABOUT IT.' Big bold letters, spelling out barking, authoritative words.

'THIS PLACE ISN'T FOR YOU. IT'S FOR ME.'

'KEEP YOUR FILTHY HANDS AND FEET OUT.'

'DON'T EVEN SO MUCH AS *LOOK* AT IT.'

OK, those weren't the *exact* words printed on the blunt, plastic notice. But they might as well have been. 'PRIVATE PROPERTY, NO TRESPASSING'. A collection of words seared into our collective minds. Generally printed in capitals, in a shade of red conveying *DANGER* or a shade of yellow telling you *YOU'RE IN TROUBLE*. Often accompanied by a vague threat of being prosecuted. This particular NO TRESPASSING sign was affixed to a tall wooden fence. The fence felt very new, with sharp edges and shiny bolts, built from thick, square posts. Smeared along the tops of each fence

LOVE IS A TOAD

post and rail was a thick, black ooze – like buttercream in a Vicky sponge – but I recognised it for what it was: sticky, staining, T-shirt-ruining anti-climb paint. A messy deterrent to miscreants, troublemakers, playing children and *bad people*.

'Look, there!' Amy pointed through the unfriendly barrier to a rope hanging limply from a tree. 'That was one of our swings. Lochy used to love playing in there, building dens.' I could still make out smooth tracks of earth snaking through the needle litter, worn by running feet. Amy sighed.

I met Amy-Jane Beer (fondly known as AJB) on the internet. It still feels a bit weird to make friends online. We were warned about it so much in high school in those early days of social media, MSN, MySpace. It's full of weirdos and predators, we were told. Yes, true – I've had more than one bloke send me pictures of his feet – but I've learnt it's also full of wonderful people. People like Amy, whose tweets about lizards and mosses and birdsong made me smile at my glassy phone screen. Amy's warmth radiated through the Twittersphere and it glows even more in person. On this muggy afternoon in June, wisps of her blond and pink hair framed her face like fern fronds, eyes twinkling with life and a smile like a hug.

We were bumbling along in the cool of the woods. It was cloudy but the air was warm and thick, almost viscous or textured when you sucked it in through your nose in a deep inhale.

A short while earlier, I'd jumped down from the bus into a lay-by, the roar of traffic on a busy main road ringing in my ears as the double-decker pulled away. Following the small digital map inside my phone, I peeled off down a surprisingly rural-

A TELLTALE PEEP

looking lane, drizzled in dappled green light and lined by swollen, lush verges. I soon came across Amy's home, where she lives with husband Roy and 12-year-old Lochy. Walking through the door, I marvelled – every surface seemed to be adorned with nature treasures, from feathers and skulls to shells and fossils. My fingers itched to pick them all up, give them a good ogle and a sniff. Over lunch, Lochy pulled several more treasures from the freezer – I stroked the inky feathers of a lifeless male Blackbird, and admired a Great Tit's tiny beak up close, fingering the thorn-sharp tip and relishing the slight discomfort of it digging into my skin.

After lunch, filled with the delicious simplicity of bread and salad, we headed off with our swimming togs stuffed in a rucksack. As our feet thumped on dust and tarmac, high-pitched sounds poured from the trees above – a concoction of wind chimes, dropped teaspoons and little bells. Even as we nattered, I subconsciously processed the songs, making out the avian language of two different voices. First, a Treecreeper's, those jingling, descending notes finishing in a little flourish that doesn't quite say 'oi'. I pictured their dinky, mottle-feathered body as it scooted up the tree bark, like a little hook-beaked mouse. God, I love Treecreepers. Behind their chiming, I picked out an even more piercing song. A piping tinkling on loop. The song of Goldcrests is heavenly, almost literally. Raining down from above, often from a dense and dark canopy of conifer, their voice reminds me of magical creatures, a showering of shimmering gold fairy dust. Both of these birds are tiny and so easy to miss by eye. But get your ear in, learn their music, and you realise you're very often in their company.

LOVE IS A TOAD

The mugginess of summer clung to our skin, but the spring whiff of wilted Wild Garlic still remained in the air. As we chattered and wandered, Amy kept darting off into the undergrowth, defiantly yoinking up fistfuls of young Himalayan Balsam, trying to keep the invasive and soppy-sweet flower at bay. As she scurried around and tugged at their stems, she radiated the vitality of a child, a bundle of never-ending energy.

After a short while we reached *the fence*. 'It's so sad, I used to bring Lochy in here all the time.' Amy explained that new owners of the woods were the fence-erectors. Walkers, wanderers, den-builders, rope-swingers – everyone was now to KEEP OUT. The new fence corralled anybody entering the trees along a rigid, narrow footpath. Here you could walk, but *only* here.

I understand that it's not 'our' woodland. I suppose the owners can do what they want with it, right? But haven't we all found joy in places we technically shouldn't be? Lots of us have pushed boundaries, explored and wandered past the lines and borders that dictate where we're 'allowed'. I grew up trespassing before I even knew what it was – it's just something we did.

I still own the map of my childhood playground. It's folded up, tucked away in some dusty corner of my head. If I unfurl it, smooth out the creases and wipe off the dirt, I can see the entire span of my little realm. The cluster of goopy ponds in the cow field (they inexplicably stunk when you pulled your welly from the clag of sucking mud). The upright, rotting trunk of an Oak tree, hollow and coated in a thick cloak of

A TELLTALE PEEP

Ivy you could use as a ladder to haul yourself up. The big smooth grey rock that breached the surface of the river at low tide. My Uncle Tim once told me it was a whale and I believed him for a *bit* too long. This was a small space – all contained within a field behind the semi I grew up in – but in it I could run and climb and paddle. I was free to play out and only come back when my belly gurgled.

In this outdoor realm, we would play. My little sister, Sal, and my little brother, Fred – we were a trio of siblings who possessed an increasingly rare thing: free rein. My best friend Archie was another. Most of the other kids in the streets around us had stricter limitations on their wandering – not allowed past a certain lamp post, road or other landmark within sight of their homes. But for some reason, our parents let us wander. There were, of course, limits to where we were 'allowed', but these would be pushed and disobeyed, as children so inevitably do. Together, we had the independence and autonomy to roam.

Roaming! It's something so intangible, something without a defined purpose. You can do it on any scale, in any direction. It's an activity that's chock-full of possibility. Roaming, adventuring, aimless wandering; all fuel children's minds like sunshine fuels Dandelions. Being free to roam meant being free to climb, to swim, to poke and prod and nosey at any creature I could find. Free to observe and to test. To learn to avoid Nettles and Brambles and Red Ants. Free to push limits – and to reap consequences. To get cuts and bruises and scratches and bites, and for it to not matter.

The nineties meant another thing – my childhood was also pre-mobile phone. Such an alien concept now, isn't it?

LOVE IS A TOAD

To be uncontactable. To be reachable only by the nearest house phone. If you were in the middle of a field, you were cut off. No pings in pockets, no vibrations, just the Daisies for company. A childhood without phones meant 'knocking on' – running down the road to Archie's, banging on the door and breathlessly asking, 'Is Archie playing out?' At the risk of sounding grumpy, I am convinced it also meant a different relationship with boredom. When we played outside, we had no distractions. No videos, memes or music in our pockets that could steal our attention. And that meant nosiness could flow uninterrupted. Logs were to be lifted, ponds to be sifted. Trees were there to climb and mud was to be thoroughly squelched in – preferably with bare toes.

It might seem as though I am romanticising but then in hindsight, mundanity often *is* quite romantic. Ordinary moments of simplicity and contentment are something we tend to look back on with fondness. Spending hours on end outside in the summer holidays could generate boredom, yes. But it didn't end there. When boredom appears, energy starts fizzing out and overspilling. It becomes other things: restlessness, probing, naughtiness, curiosity. Ruining your best clothes with a mud-slinging fight. Building treehouses in private woods. Crossing the River Douglas on the rusty (and dangerous) old pipe bridge. Trespassing in wheat fields (especially naughty) or playing with boisterous baby cows.

In recent years I've found new playgrounds. The stretch of willowy greenness down by the river under the busy main road; the patch of grassy scrub behind the retail park where I saw a Snipe and a Barn Owl. Lots of us have these local spots of sanctuary, somewhere you head to for a bit of peace,

A TELLTALE PEEP

headspace or to burn off overspilling, fidgety energy. When that sanctuary is taken away from us, or access is revoked, it hits like a personal loss.

Together, Amy and I gazed at the hanging rope swing, dangling still and out of reach. It's hard not to think about the cumulative nature of this loss – scraps of space and land being snapped up and closed off. People being squeezed out of places of play, woodlands emptying of laughter. The swing summoned memories of the best play, the sort that leaves you with filthy fingernails and aching muscles and grazed knees. I mentioned to Amy how sad and scary it is that the sparkle of play can be lost as we grow up.

'Yes! I remember in childhood where you suddenly want to grow up, and you want to race to be an adult and be taken seriously!' She laughed as she spoke. 'But getting into outdoor sports, climbing mountains and then kayaking – which are basically play – that was really important for me. Because it set out elements of play as a routine part of adult life. There's so much about growing up that robs us of that spontaneous joy and that's really sad. So I totally have made a conscious effort to let that back in and to sort of . . . um . . . re-child.'

Re-child. I loved that – and she was *so* right! You see, Amy is a badass who oozes fun. A writer, naturalist and biologist, she's also mad keen on an adventure. She hoiks up mountains and spent years throwing herself into the bubbling white froth of thundering rivers in her kayak. She camps on her own, something I'm scared to do myself, and explores and noseys around with all of the energy of a kid at play. I toyed with this

LOVE IS A TOAD

concept – of these activities being an adult form of play – in my mind and I liked it. It seemed to cast them in a new light, full of fizzy excitement and giddy silliness.

We left the woods behind – its coolness, a faint whiff of sweet, planty growth, and its dappling, quivering light and shadows. Ahead of us, we faced a slightly rickety-looking level crossing framed by a white picket fence. We crossed it, thankfully hearing or feeling no rumbling of an engine, and on the other side I spotted a familiar, fluffy-looking plant protruding from the scruffy edge of the tarmac. Mullein has thick, stodgy and soft leaves, sort of like a cuddly toy's ears that you want to thumb absent-mindedly. Looking at the plant more closely, I could see it was decorated with lots of green, sludge-like pellets: little dots of poo. The poo-makers were there too – small caterpillars, only a couple of centimetres long but starting to show their colours, their smooth cream skin tinged with the slightest hint of mint green and adorned with splodges of yellow and black. Very satisfying splodges they were too, as though they'd been dabbed with enthusiasm – no pretence of precision or elegance, just blobbed on. Black and yellow, black and yellow. They were the caterpillars of the Mullein Moth, a creature I'd only seen a couple of times before. Their clown-like jazziness as caterpillars is in contrast to the subtlety and modesty of the adult moths, which look like a neat piece of twig or woody plant in streaks of dark and sandy brown. We crouched together in a sort of admiring silence, enjoying the colourful little poo-makers, their entire world upon the leaves of the Mullein.

Perched on our haunches, Amy told me how she'd recognised the need to re-child when it came to her starting

A TELLTALE PEEP

to write about nature. Those elements of play – of fun, exploration, adventure – didn't marry up with the scientific style of writing she'd learnt to follow early on in her career. I remembered this feeling well from school – the pressure to write formally and seriously in a scientific context, no room for fun or silliness.

'Back then I was studying biology – I was training to be a scientist. And if you want to be a scientist, it's about being rigorous.' Amy put on a gruff and bossy voice, 'It's all "this is the methodology, and these are the rules". And of course, all of the rules are there for good reason but it means you're reined in. And I was *so* desperate to do well at it. To be taken seriously as a young woman in the scientific world and nature world.'

We trundled on a little, my outstretched hand tickling the Buttercups and Hogweed as Amy continued. 'And so, with my nature writing, I was trying to perform what I thought a naturalist was. I couldn't grow the beard, so I had to mimic that style. Science is a highly structured process of attention-giving that relies on rules. But trying to structure curiosity is a bit like trying to structure love. A structured, restrained kind of curiosity or love can never be enough on its own. There's no room for spontaneity or flights of fancy, ridiculousness, hilarity, rage! It took me until my late forties to be brave enough to say what I thought. Because I didn't think my voice was one that would be listened to or respected. Or was worthy. I didn't feel that I fitted in.'

I knew exactly what she meant. Amy was describing a way of showing love within the rules that science defines, one which speaks a language of scientific names and order and organisation. Important, yes, but not the *only* way to talk about nature.

'I remember realising that there are people studying nature and working with and communicating nature who aren't scientists. It was like a revelation! And it was ridiculous that I was just not aware of the arts as a way of celebrating and exploring nature. That's where the activist's voice has come from because, suddenly, I'm not trying to conform to expectations.'

Amy's words soothed me, like the comforting warmth of a hot brew, her words giving voice to thoughts I've had myself but have never been able to quite articulate.

On the other side of the tracks, the path we followed faded to an end in a blur of Nettles, Brambles and lush undergrowth. There was a coolness in the air, a thickness and density that tells you you're near a body of water. We'd reached the River Derwent, a jumble of Willow and Alder lining the banks.

The thing with the Derwent is that you're not technically allowed to access much of it. Like most of our rivers in England and Wales, large stretches of the green winding channel are out of bounds to the public who might want to paddle in canoes or kayaks, and the rules around wild swimming are even murkier. So not only were we taking a rather soggy path, but we were about to trespass as we did.

AJB and I stripped down to cozzies, stuffing our clothes in a floating bag that'd keep our stuff dry. She entered first, confidently stepping into the watery realm she knows so well. My feet sunk a few inches into thick, sucking mud as I stepped down to the water's edge and I felt the delicious

A TELLTALE PEEP

squidginess of it forcing my toes apart in a sort of riverine massage. Lowering myself into a slow, calm current, I entered a realm of greens – every green under the sun. The bright, zesty greens of summer vegetation still mid-growth. Darker, shade-casting greens of the tree canopy – blob-round Alder leaves and whip-thin Willow leaves. Even the water was green, a swirl of emerald eddies and khaki currents. Both riverbanks were cuddled by trees which draped and overhung and jostled for space. My skin goosebumped as I slunk below the surface into the cool water, contrasting with the still mugginess of the air.

As my toes extracted themselves from the clag beneath, I pushed myself out into the open and the flow. I'm a confident swimmer – my mum and nana took us to the swimming baths every weekend as kids – but I could still feel a tickle of trepidation. As my legs kicked me outwards into the opaque water, neurons started fabricating a weird concoction of threats below the surface. When I was swimming in the canal once as a kid, my mum had warned me of the dangers of jumping into places where people might chuck stuff. 'There could be bikes, trolleys, or a piano!' she'd warned. The bizarre image of splintered wooden legs and algae-coated monochrome keys flickered back into my mind as I tried to float as close to the surface as I could.

We set off with a slow breaststroke. Amy swam confidently and smoothly, carving through the water in the calm way an Otter might. Though Amy told me that she hadn't learnt to swim until the end of primary school. Swimming was something her mum wasn't keen on, despite having swum in rivers and lakes in her own childhood.

LOVE IS A TOAD

As the culture changed to focus on the importance of children's safety, Amy's mother became increasingly anxious about the risks she perceived in more adventurous outdoor activities.

It's funny how something so enjoyable and natural-feeling is quite a scary concept to lots of us. It was for me. Whilst I've always swum, it was in the 'safe haven' of a pool or maybe the flat, calm sea on a hot summer's day. For some reason, swapping either of those for a river, lake or loch felt wilder, riskier. The first time I swam in a quarry, I felt ripples of nervousness in my belly and kicked a little bit harder and more urgently than I normally would. But when you think about it, risk is an inescapable part of existing outside; it's not necessarily a bad thing, especially when you consider we're essentially just being an animal in its habitat.

In that moment, I felt like one. A million tingles peppered my skin, which was coated in a satisfying film of algal ooze. My muscles worked in a rhythmic, pleasing manner, stretching and contracting through the water. Breathing through my nose, I snuffled up the earthiness and wetness, the rich and moist scent of life – a soup of riverine scents just waiting to be interpreted. In a deep breath of pleasure, I expressed my contentment within the sensation of feeling enveloped by your environment, body just being. Swimming outside just feels *right*.

'Yes! You totally feel that you belong; you're doing the same thing as every other living thing is doing in that environment. Being immersed in it takes you away from a lot of stuff – grief, worries, anxiety. When you're just in nature, it's manageable. Because you're not also dealing with all the

A TELLTALE PEEP

other things that we get stressed about, like whether we were on time, whether we remembered everything we're supposed to do.'

She was right – I hadn't thought about my overflowing inbox or otherwise boring life admin once this morning. I was too busy feeling stuff, concentrating on sensations and sounds and smells.

Ahead of us, a flickering of dark mini-shadows sputtered and sparkled over the surface of the water. At certain angles the light caught them and in that fleeting moment they beamed iridescence – a flash of Magpie blue or a glint of bottle green. Banded Demoiselles! Bulging and beady-eyed damselflies, they're a perfect potion of exquisite beauty and extreme cuteness. Think Puss in Boots from *Shrek 2*. On a warm summer's day you can bear witness to a showy and captivating dance between sexes. The dark and shiny male – who you'd think was made out of brass, if brass was peacock blue – has wings adorned with inky-black splodges that flash and flicker and coax your eyeballs in their direction. And the elegant female is clad in a metallic emerald so polished you can almost see your reflection upon her body. It's entirely impossible to decide who's more fabulous of the two. They scooted and flitted around us, teasing the surface of the water with their dangling, fairy-like feet.

It was so peaceful, even the birdsong was relaxed. A wistful, summery Blackbird perched in a dead tree on the bank was letting his voice pour from his beak in a slow trickle that lacked the hormonal oomph he might have had just a month ago. We continued nattering about it – the sensations and deliciousness of it all.

LOVE IS A TOAD

'That feeling of awareness and using all your senses to appraise the situation is *sooo* good. And that's one of the things I love about being out by myself. I walk alone a lot and go out at night by myself.'

To be outside somewhere by yourself can be exhilarating and exciting. I've spent a couple of hours perched in the gnarled branches of an old Oak and enveloped by the busy grassiness of a meadow, just watching the wild world do its thing. It feels peaceful and unpressured; there's no need to carry conversation or worry about words. Those moments are magic but being on your bill can be a bit intimidating.

I asked Amy if she was ever nervous being outside on her own. She described that all-familiar anxiety many women experience when wandering solo – clutching your keys in your fist, knuckles tense, blade protruding between fingers, a makeshift weapon often carried after dark, for fear of predators of our own species.

'We're told to be afraid of each other but we must remember we're not natural enemies of one another. Because actually, if you were in real trouble in a wild place, the thing you might most desperately hope to see would be a light coming towards you in the dark.'

Her words hit home. I pictured myself stranded somewhere, perhaps in a tent in a freezing blizzard, feeling lost and hopeless. And then seeing the warm glow of a torch bobbing in the gloom. The joy. The relief!

'You know, I have to say, humans, they're one of my favourite species – if not my favourite species. I wouldn't want to be without them. I just love people. I enjoy being without them, as well!' Amy laughed. 'I wouldn't be with them *all* the time! My solitary time is really important to me but I wouldn't ever want to be without people.'

We slid through the water side by side, chatting as our pruned fingers stretched forward into the green, our feet frog-legging behind us. On the bank, a cracked and splintered Willow weaved in and out of the water. It looked almost like it had paused mid-topple, somehow not being swallowed by the hungry, sucking river. Shoots sprang from its half-submerged branches, reaching upwards, away from the wet and towards the light. Swimming amongst its many limbs felt wonderfully tangled and jungly. On one of the cracked boughs a male Blackcap perched, a small warbler, dapper in grey with his sleek and dark little hat. As we passed him, he moved – not flying but almost trickling down branches towards the water, like a slinky descending a staircase. His jumbled, cluttered song of whistles and scratches reached across the surface of the water. What a treat. His was a voice that used to meld with the background chatter of birdsong but was now familiar to me – a voice I could recognise like I can a good mate's. And it was *people* who'd taken the time to teach me to recognise that birdsong, *people* who'd enabled my interpretation of avian language. People who were kind and patient and interested, who enjoyed sharing joy and encompassed all of the wonderful things about humanity.

For every hostile, cold or unapproachable person I've encountered in the nature world, there has been another who was the opposite. The pages of this book are full of them – naturalists, enthusiasts, nerds and nosey folk. They're people who light sparks, share knowledge and radiate unashamed joy. They hand you gifts – a parcel of information on an

LOVE IS A TOAD

outstretched palm like a shiny acorn or some magic beans. It is people who embody all of the beautiful things it is to be human in a wild world: storytelling, community, play. When you share nature experiences with fellow humans, beholding other living beings and gawping and whooping and hugging, you experience a moment of mutual nature joy that's unlike anything else.

On that muggy June afternoon, in the middle of a river, we shared one such moment. As we swam, it *felt* Kingfishery. A wide expanse of water coupled with the hint of Minnows' shadows, flickering in the green light dappling through a woodland canopy. There were plenty of overhanging, perchable branches. A Kingfisher's paradise. And then, we heard it. The telltale peep. You hear it distantly at first, tickling at the edge of your mind before your brain has properly processed what it means. Then louder, and louder still. Practically yelling, it rounded the corner, piloting between branches and zipping inches from the water's surface. A zooming halcyon rocket, the epitome of streamlined. *Pee-pew. Pee-pew.* It flew over our heads in a pointy-fronted, squeaky and electric blue blur. Wow. Kingfishers are always, *always* followed by a fizz of giddy joy. We beamed mid-breaststroke, relishing the fleeting encounter in all its fabulousness.

My muscles felt cold and slow, but in a good, satisfyingly tired sort of way. We'd swum nearly a whole mile downstream, and as we manoeuvred around another fallen tree, the arched stone bridge we were aiming for came into view. Amongst the thin, blade-like silhouettes of the Willow's leaves, another form hung. An ugly shawl of tatters and shreds, it was a long sheet of black plastic, the sort that bin liners are made out of. Amy told me she suspected it was wrapping intended for silage, which had made its way into the river. About half the litter she pulled out of the Derwent was the usual stuff – crisp packets and pop bottles – but the rest of it was that of industry, the waste discarded from farming and fishing.

We'd soon breaststroked our way under the bridge and as we emerged from its shadow, I spied a smattering of yellow in the water up ahead. At first I thought it was more litter – it was that bright sort of yellow that denotes snacks. Tasty things! But no, not Quavers packets – it was something much more joy-inducing: a whole patch of Yellow Water-lilies, their massive, chunky flowers protruding from the water. This little floral flotilla was ever so satisfying to look at – a flat raft of splayed pads, their outline conjuring associations with Frogs and nursery rhymes. Then there were the flowers. I'd only recently learnt they're known as 'brandy bottles'. With their whiff of sweet, sickly liqueur, they do in fact remind me of something cheap and knockoff I'd have swigged from a bottle in the park as a teenager.

We paddled from the lilies to the bank and climbed out, taking the friendly hand of an Alder tree whose roots tumbled down like wooden steps to the water's edge. On a stretch of grass we shivered and towelled and dressed in the slightly damp clothes pulled from our dry bags. As we sat on our soggy towels, teeth chattering, a group of teens ambled down from the bridge, heading for the water's edge. A gaggle of boys and girls, all piss-taking and shoving and laughter. They brought drinks and snacks – pickled onion Monster Munch, excellent. Budweiser, even better. We watched as they stripped down

LOVE IS A TOAD

to their cozzies and tried to build up the courage to jump in. A girl took the plunge first – swinging from a rope on the tree's branches and clumsing into the water in a not-as-cool-as-she-hoped splash. It wasn't the hottest day of June, making their activity choice even more admirable. After a while, the braver members of the bunch headed back up to the stone bridge, egging each other on till one of them leapt into the water from a height. It was good to see their energy bubbling, teenage play, risk-taking and showing off. We sat and smiled.

I remembered being moved along when I was a teenager for just hanging out. And I can imagine some folks might think of the group as an annoyance, feeling an urge to quash energy and dampen fizz. Kids being noisy and dangerous, kids spoiling the nice scenery, kids leaving their trash on the riverbank. I think you encounter this attitude across society, but to me it feels particularly rife in the conservation and outdoors sector. How nature reserves are for the right sort of person, behaving in the right sort of way. How *we* know best and you – *you* – filthy townie, don't understand any of it. Of course, there are lots of things that make people feel hostile to others sharing natural places. Pollution and litter and mowing and flailing and felling and literal shit pouring into the life force of our beautiful rivers. And it's an understandable, deeply human reaction to see these things, look around at our peers and point a finger. It feels good to have someone to blame, right?

I've felt these things too. When you know that a nature reserve is the last refuge for a Curlew for miles around, it hurts to see a person let Buster off the lead and flush the

A TELLTALE PEEP

bird out of its nest, leaving its eggs exposed and vulnerable. When a stretch of river is a spot of tranquillity and peace for you, it breaks your heart to see pop bottles and condoms bobbing along on the current. And it's easy to see how this sort of acute grief for nature manifests as misanthropy. Over the years, I've muttered under my breath about these *idiots*, rolling my eyes and feeling the anger bubbling inside me. But I think we have to be careful where that anger takes us, how it makes us think and feel about others – something I said to Amy as we huddled and hugged our knees for warmth on the riverbank, the kids whooping and laughing as they threw themselves into the water.

'I see this rage leak out everywhere but it tends to be directed towards other people rather than the system. That is the problem, and it's where misanthropy comes in.' Amy smiled. 'And I get it. If you are a person trying to do your best for a patch of land that you feel that you are a guardian of, and you feel that your custodianship is benefiting the wildlife there – that's a powerful thing. But I just want to say, "Love, you're not going to live long enough to protect this forever. So who's going to care for it after you?" If you shut people out, if you blame them as individuals – individuals who just want to go for a swim . . .' She gestured at the joyous ruckus in front of us, a group who were technically trespassing '. . . that will be your legacy. And when you're gone, all your work may be undone anyway. Whereas if, as a society, as a culture, we can move to a position where we all feel that sense of custodianship and we all feel welcome, future generations will take up your mantle. And we can all do it together.'

LOVE IS A TOAD

Amy smiled and looked out over the river, absent-mindedly playing with the grass we sat on as she spoke. She continued to explain how she thinks fortress conservation – a term used to describe an attempt to protect nature by putting a fence around it and shutting people out – is doomed. In this model, everything outside of the fortress of protection gets trashed and as a result, it becomes harder for people to connect with what remains. This has been the dominant conservation model for decades and whilst it's an important lifeline for some of the most vulnerable plants and animals, it is not working well, nor is it enough to turn things around. The whole idea of fortress conservation – the belief that to help nature we must create protected areas devoid of people and the 'disturbance' they inflict – makes people feel excluded and problematic. It leads to othering and judgement, picking out some people as 'good' for wildlife and some as 'bad'. It instils a certain amount of self-loathing too, that kind of intimate misanthropy – seeing ourselves as bad by our very nature. And whilst the protection of these areas might act as a sticking plaster, it's not a long-term solution.

Let's come back to that Curlew in the nature reserve. She's settled on her eggs – four of them, speckled and splodged and perfect. She's the only Curlew for miles; none of her kind have bred in the fields near here for a decade. She sits enclosed, a fence of silver wires and zapping currents encircling her as she broods. A person walks past and sees her curve-beaked silhouette from a distance. But they don't know her name, what she is or why she's special. They've never seen a Curlew before. This fence might help her raise

A TELLTALE PEEP

a chick or two, keeping sniffing snouts and snapping jaws away for long enough to let the eggs hatch. But she's isolated and exposed. What about the next year? And the next?

Amy had come across this point of view often. On a tributary of the Derwent, a local fisherman claimed that if someone wanted to swim in the river then they should buy a piece of it. She sighed at this attitude, exasperated. 'He's obviously devoted a lot of his life to caring for this stretch of river, for which I wanted to say – thank you! That's great! But we need more people to be doing that, and to have that sense of responsibility and belonging. And he just totally rejected that.'

I felt Amy's sadness, that a person who'd taken so much solace and peace from being in a beautiful space felt like it couldn't be shared with others.

'So many of us have this belief that people are a problem, rather than understanding it's the *system* that's a problem, and it's a problem that people can help with. We *need* people to help with it – that's the only way out of this.'

We're not going to heal our fractured relationship with nature and land by hating each other. If we keep people at arms' length – taking the 'keep out' approach – it's not going to do anything to bring people closer to nature. If people don't feel they belong in nature, that they're *of* nature – the soil, the trees, the flowers, the rivers – how can we expect them to give a crap? Yes, individuals do bad things, but I really believe there are bigger, systemic reasons as to *why* these things happen – it's not a simple case of 'bad people being bad'. These systems are complex and ingrained, systems of exploitation, oppression and greed. They have stewed and

LOVE IS A TOAD

composted over centuries into the soup of conditions we currently find ourselves in – ones that are bad for a lot of people and for nature too.

Let's think about the 'L word' – litter. It's the bane of ramblers and anglers, twitchers and farmers, and just about anybody who thinks of themselves as an 'outdoorsy' person. The stuff is everywhere. Wotsit packets in hedgerows, Snickers wrappers on the beach, Coke bottles bobbing in the flow of a river; there's literally tonnes of it and more appearing all the time. It's gross, disgusting, depressing. What sort of person litters?!

I do. There – I admit it. No, I don't chuck my chocolate wrappers at the side of a footpath or leave behind an explosion of ugly detritus after a picnic, but I do buy things in single-use plastic. I shove as much as I can in the recycling, like I'm supposed to do, and some of it I chuck straight in the bin. And that's the end of it. Except it isn't. In all likelihood, some of my rubbish, the very items I've handled, have ended up in the sea, or choking up a river, or fluttering through the streets. Somewhere 'else'. Somewhere we ship our rubbish off to, where we keep no tabs of what happens to it, making it another country's problem. And then there's the fact we've built this single-use system in the first place. As Greenpeace have said: 'The problem isn't that people aren't recycling enough. The problem is that there is still far too much throwaway plastic being produced.' So much plastic, that we can't cope with it, and it ends up spilling out into the environment. The bottom line is that in all likelihood, *all of us* litter. Suddenly it becomes clearer that this is a systemic problem – a de-prioritisation of an environmental issue by

A TELLTALE PEEP

our government and a long-standing cultural disregard for the people overseas who have to deal with it.

On top of this, much of the fury and outrage surrounding litter tends to focus a stereotype that litter consists of individual, personal items. Discarded fag butts, Maccies wrappers and sports drink bottles. But we forget, or perhaps don't notice, that a large proportion of rubbish and clutter in the natural environment is from industry. Fishing nets and rope strewn across beaches, fishing wire wrapped around the beak of a helpless Cormorant. Reams of plastic twine and shreds of bale wrap fluttering in the wind and clogging our rivers – like the stuff Amy and I saw as we swam.

When I see a crisp packet, a feeling bubbles in my throat – anger, annoyance, disgust. But I think it's too easy to direct that at others. In reality, these things are a result of a system we all live in, and the colourful plastic we mush into the earth under our walking boots is an ugly and enduring reminder of that. We live in the era of ultra-convenience, of ravenous overconsumption. A time when the spectre of capitalism will come up with a purchasable solution to a niche problem you didn't know you had, and it'll hand it to you on a platter, packaged in plastic, whilst whispering phoney greenwashing promises in your ear.

Another gripe and grumble of the nature sector is the concept of disturbance: the actions of people interrupting wildlife to its detriment. Dogs off leads, flushing out a flock of roosting Knot on a beach, or scaring our Curlew off her nest. People walking in places they shouldn't, getting too close to things. Adders, Nightjars, Little Ringed Plovers, Bluebells – we hear about these things being disturbed all the time.

LOVE IS A TOAD

But does a Fox not disturb? A Sparrowhawk, a deer, a cow? Even a Hedgehog can rootle through the undergrowth and upset a Skylark, maybe even scoff her eggs. Disturbance is a fact of life in an ecosystem full of interacting species that want to eat, breed and compete.

Yes, the scales are out of kilter. You could argue that the volume of people is too great, that there are simply too many unruly poodles on the loose, too many feet thumping the footpaths. But it's more nuanced than that. Firstly, why is our wildlife so vulnerable? A creature like our lonely Curlew, confined behind her fence on a farmer's field, is effectively stranded on a desert island. If much of the landscape nearby isn't Curlew-friendly, then she's marooned. If a Fox pushes its way through the fence and snarfles her eggs, where can she go to try again? To put it another way, if the local environment hasn't got the dynamism, the complexity or the variability to provide a plan B, C or D for the Curlew, what hope is there? A healthier ecosystem would give wildlife these options – the flexibility to shift and move when conditions aren't right, and the resilience to keep trying. But our landscapes aren't flexible, they aren't thriving, they aren't dynamic. And so there she'll sit, behind her palisade of metal and currents, and maybe, just maybe, she'll succeed. Two fluffy-bummed, gangly-legged youngsters might hatch and, against the odds, they might make it. Evading the whirring blades of the combine and the chomping jaws of the Fox, they might reach adulthood. But in a land that's been de-curlewed, where can they go to attempt to nest themselves?

Secondly, there's the fact that the severity and distribution of this disturbance is undoubtedly influenced by

A TELLTALE PEEP

the current state of access – our very human laws and rules that dictate where we can and can't go. It's a well-observed phenomenon; people tend to flock to the same honeypot places. Type 'where to walk near me' into Google and you'll get page after page of the same five suggestions. You only have to visit Windermere or Castleton or Holkham on a sunny summer's day to see this deluge effect. And whilst tourism and destination guides are the face of this issue, they're not the cause. The truth is, there's only a certain amount of countryside we're actually allowed to access, especially in England. Public rights of way – footpaths and open-access land – make up a tiny proportion of the total. When people can't disperse, their impact becomes concentrated; it's like using the focused jet of a power hose when we could have the light spatter of a sprinkler. It's no wonder that under this system of access, wildlife feels the pressure of us in high numbers. But we must remember – Curlew numbers haven't plummeted because we let our dogs off the lead or because we got too close. Disturbance isn't the cause of wildlife decline – it's just another pressure on top of a lofty pile of problems.

A human wandering through an environment shouldn't be any more disturbing than any other species. We tend to assume the impact of our presence is negative. We use words like disturbance, pressure and damage. But people in a landscape can be a good thing – humans can work in a reciprocal, restorative and two-way relationship with nature. People do it all over the world. We are, after all, an animal in an environment, and animals and environments interact – surely nature is just one big disturbance event?

LOVE IS A TOAD

I can't blame any of us for being saddened or angered when we see individuals doing crap things – it's a natural reaction. But I think our energy can be redirected. It's the systems that enable these behaviours that are the problem. The ones that make it possible for a company to pump millions of gallons of sewage into a river. The ones that offer a bottomless selection of snacks and drinks and vapes and just about anything wrapped in ugly discardable packaging. The ones that make it possible for a single person to 'own' 100,000 acres of land. There's plenty to be angry about here but I don't think it's the people drinking bottles of pop.

The shivering had wrapped its dull, aching fingers around our bones. We juddered and shuddered. So we decided to go for a landlubber's wander to warm up the muscles. Peeling away from the busyness of the bridge, we slunk through grassland and trees, surrounded by an ear-soothing low hum of insect activity. We headed downstream, gentle eddies forming swirls like snail shells on the surface of the water as it slugged alongside us. I felt very in my body – barefoot with aching muscles, and my goosebumpy, slightly river-slimed skin. Every now and then, the air was punctuated with the crunch and crumple of a dragonfly passing us, banking in a zigzag on a mission to gobble insects we couldn't see.

We reflected on our riverside chat as we pattered along the path of cool, compact earth. Amy continued. 'Of course, whilst it's ugly, I do think this misanthropy is born of the grief we feel when we see nature being lost or damaged. And grief is not an overstatement of a word. It is like a bereavement, especially when it's related to place and home.'

A TELLTALE PEEP

We'd both experienced that sensation today – the strange juxtaposition of a glorious Kingfisher flying by tattered rags of plastic trailing in the current. Swimming in a green, watery realm of gorgeousness, knowing it's probably full of excess nutrients from agricultural run-off, and that the next time it rains it'll likely flow brown with sewage. How are we supposed to deal with it? And how, when faced with all of this crap, can we remember our humanity?

I asked Amy these questions and she launched into a story about an interaction she'd had a couple of years ago. On a trip to join Nick Hayes from the Right to Roam campaign for a paddle, she'd taken a short detour to visit an old childhood home. Outside the house she'd lived in throughout her teenage years had stood a large, beautiful Oak tree.

'I loved that tree; it was just my friend.' Amy smiled.

Oh god. I could see where this story was going. Sure enough, when Amy returned to the house, only a stump remained. Her brow furrowed under the wisps of her hair and I could feel the sadness in her voice as she described how she'd sat in her car and sobbed. She was still crying when she met Nick and she handed him her phone with photos of the razed tree. He quickly spotted some little green shoots sprouting from the stump, and insisted the pair return to the house after a paddle down the river.

We stepped under looping tendrils of Ivy, which hung like garlands from a wonky Alder, half-fallen across the path as though it were mid-stumble. The path we were ambling down coiled towards the water, bringing us very close to the bank. In the shadows of the green something sizeable stirred. A Heron, moments earlier frozen and statuesque, spread its paddle-like wings, all gawk and gangle, and took off with an air of floppiness.

'I couldn't just go into the front garden because the new owners were in, so I went and knocked on the door and I explained who I was,' Amy continued. 'I said I was really sad to see the Oak gone and the new owner told me he thought it was sick – it kept dropping all this sticky stuff… which of course to me was evidence of how much life it was supporting, *ahh*.' She sighed and I felt her exasperation ooze out of her like the sap out of her Oak tree. It's possible the 'sticky stuff' could've been explained by something relatively harmless – perhaps it was honeydew from aphids in the canopy or sap oozing from a canker and creating a small invertebran waterhole. It seemed such a shame to have lost such a beautiful creature.

'Anyway,' she said, breathing deeply as if to physically dispel the frustration. 'I was very calm and asked if I could take some cuttings from the sprouting twigs around the stump, and he said yes. And it turned out some of them were seedlings! So now I have three of them that have survived and they're growing up, which gives me hope. We got back in the car and Nick said, "Well, I think that went really well, given what we look like." He was wearing these multicoloured patchwork trousers and a bandana. I said, "Yeah, you're dressed as some sort of clown-pirate." And he looked at me and said, "Well actually, I meant that you've got goose shit on your face!"'

The path we followed wove an intricate, wiggly loop through the woods and meadows, so that we found ourselves walking upstream, back towards our starting point. We

A TELLTALE PEEP

soon reached the spot on the riverbank where we'd hauled ourselves out and huddled on the grass. The kids were gone. It was calm and serene – no more music, whooping, laughing. Scattered on the riverbank were the remains of the fun: bottles and their caps, plastic wrappers, a lurid disposable vape. We ambled over to the scene and gathered up the detritus – a couple of handfuls worth – to put in the bin we'd pass on the way home.

I wish they hadn't left their litter. I really do. But at the same time, it didn't cost the two of us much time or effort to pick it up. And thinking about it, I believe it's part of our duty to do these sorts of things. When you have the privilege of getting to be in beautiful spaces, collective care for the land and nature must come into play. There are *huge* problems we must surmount. So many ways we need to restore, heal, fix our relationship with nature. But I feel like tolerance for each other is a good starting point. For people, who are ultimately great, even if they can be a pain in the arse. People who chuck a crisp packet over their shoulder, or cast down a bottle in anger, or drop a fag butt – and who might never have seen a Kingfisher zoom by or felt the coolness of a river's cuddle on their skin. I'll pick up their litter. I don't mind, not really.

DO BEETLES FEEL GLEE?

at her mad tale. I remember being hunkered down below the Oak boughs, a mucky finger fiddling its way into an empty fairy hat, so I could feel its suction against my skin, my mind trembling with images of beautiful and sinister little pixies. A concoction of emotions, fearful and curious. Who were these little people? Why did they want to steal children? Could they ride snails like ponies and butterflies like aeroplanes?!

The hidden space and its fairies is the earliest memory I have of an interaction with Oak, a plant that now feels deeply rooted in my core. It's as though I swallowed an acorn as I crouched in the shadows and its leafy tendrils have lived inside me since. The Oak still stands there, at the back of the garden at number 23, long after my grandfolks have transformed into soil and memories. An individual organism I've known my whole life, and she'll hopefully outlive me too.

If the Oak before the Ash,
Then we'll only have a splash.
If the Ash before the Oak,
Then we'll surely have a soak!

The Ash must've come into leaf first this year. We were soggy before we'd made it 20 metres into the woods. It was the sort of mizzly rain that's suspended perpetually in the air, coming at you from all directions even when there's no wind. Walking under the canopy, we were also subjected to dense drips, plopping from layers of Oak leaves on to the head, soaking the scalp, running down the nose and tasting fresh and delicious

LOVE IS A TOAD

on our lips. Oak leaves in the middle of July have a very specific hue of green – it's darker and more light-absorbing than the bright, limey and soft leaves of spring. By midsummer, the leaves have thickened and hardened; taking a closer look at them reveals all sorts of nibblings and blemishes, evidence of other creatures living amongst the boughs and bark.

Only a short distance in, the sound of the road was absorbed by a curtain of dense greenery and lushness. The forest felt tall as well as deep, with towering, sturdy trunks of Oaks rising from the undergrowth on every side, branching, stretching and reaching. Indy towered next to me too, a just-turned 18-year-old with limbs like limbs, though he was more reminiscent of a slender Willow whip than a stout Oak.

It felt good to be back in Sherwood again. These were the woods where Indy and I had met, only a handful of years ago. I'd spied him standing outside the visitor centre one morning, nervous, glancing at the door, only 14 years old. His hand rested upon a bag that was absolutely plastered in bird-themed pin badges. He'd signed up to volunteer in the forest and soon enough, he'd chucked himself into practical management and leading guided walks for visitors. From the very start it struck me how personable he was; Indy can chat as eagerly and warmly to an 80-year-old as he can to an eight-year-old. In the few short years since then he'd erupted in height, as teenagers tend to do, and on this soggy day in the forest he was even sporting a bristling beard. He knows paths through the forest intimately – the wide, official sandy ones, and the curled and winding off-the-map ones. As we walked, he'd peel off suddenly, taking lefts and rights and seemingly ploughing straight into the undergrowth,

DO BEETLES FEEL GLEE?

following the sort of track you can't really see until you're pattering along it.

Indy grew up in the woods, a proper wild child, in a house owned by the Thoresby Estate in Nottinghamshire. Surrounded by old Oak woods, towering rows of pine plantation and sweeps of open heath, he had a big and bushy playground as a kid. He'd explore these places on foot or by pedal, running and cycling through the woods on his own. After stumbling into bird-nerdery, he'd become familiar with the area's feathered residents; he has an uncanny ability to imitate a Robin or a Woodlark simply with a whistle. A couple of years ago, his folks got turfed out of the house they rented at the whim of the landowner and had to move a little further away from the places he knew so well. Indy still headed down to the woods whenever he could and as we nattered, he told me how he felt about growing up in Sherwood Forest.

'I know I was really lucky, and I think about that more and more since we got kicked out of our old house and moved into one of the local former mining towns. Obviously, I'd love to still be living right there. It was the absolute best!' Indy smiled as he spoke, and I imagined he was picturing his many encounters with Goshawks, Nightjars and Bramblings. 'It was brilliant. I had a Honey Buzzard on the garden list, for God's sake! And at the time people would say, "Aww you're so lucky," and I was like, "Yeah I know." But now I really *know*. I really don't take it for granted.'

I can only imagine the excitement of seeing a Honey Buzzard. I'd first heard of these birds only a few years ago and couldn't quite believe they were real. Buzzards, yes. But *Honey* Buzzards? After the sweet, sticky, oozing stuff? Nah, fictional. Surely? I learnt these birds of prey sort of resemble common Buzzards, but rather than scoffing bunny rabbits and carrion, they instead use their sharp talons and hooked beaks to guzzle insects. Honey Buzzards skulk through woodlands, following social bees and wasps back to their nests – which sounds like a tricky enough task in itself. I once spent hours chasing a female Leafcutter Bee to and from a patch of Buddleia; she was cutting perfect circles from its leaves to seal her nest with. It wasn't easy and I imagine I looked quite weird legging it back and forth, staring furiously at the air in front of me.

Anyway, back to Honey Buzzards. It's not actually honey they're after; they are partial to a juicy bee or wasp grub. Their legs and faces are adorned with tough, scale-like skin, impenetrable to stings, and their nostrils are thin and slit-like, removing the opportunity for furious and defensive critters to burrow up them. They're elusive woodland and glade dwellers and I'd never seen one.

It makes sense that Indy had seen one; he has an incredible knack for noticing things – picking up on the tiniest sound or movement that gives away the presence of something feathered.

'Why birds?' I asked him.

'Growing up out here in the woods felt very isolating a lot of the time. My school was a long drive away, and I never really had any play dates, it was just me. So I discovered birds and figured out there's plenty of them around and they're such an easy thing to observe and interact with. They're one of the easiest bits of wildlife to tackle, so I got stuck in!'

Fair enough. Getting into watching birds simply because

DO BEETLES FEEL GLEE?

they're there felt like a good enough reason to me. It's funny how we're surrounded by birdlife, wherever we are – the Mallards on the canal, the Pigeons and Peregrines of the city, the Blue Tits by the bus stop – but for many of us, they remain unnoticed until some sort of catalyst comes along. Perhaps somebody points something out to you, or your brain tingles in a moment of curiosity, or you simply spy a particularly handsome Magpie. It's one of those worlds that quickly swells from something tiny to something *huge* when you open the door. I remember thinking all small birds were brown and mousey. Flicking through the pages of a bird book (admittedly after getting that job with the RSPB, ha), I was baffled and tantalised by the array of colours on the pages in front of me: the scarlet of a male Crossbill or the sunshine-yellow bum of a Grey Wagtail. And don't even get me started on Bee Eaters.

We heard a distant Crossbill as we ambled through the drizzle, its metallic voice sounding like a small hammer plinking away upon a rock. We'd entered the deep woods – a part of the forest that feels wide and spacious and stretching. Woodland pasture of this type is unusual; you feel enveloped and sheltered by the canopies and trunks of Oaks, yet you can see quite far in any direction. The Oaks themselves were astounding. Some were vertical giants, towering and sleek, with trunks like pillars topped with a splayed garland of lush, lobed leaves. Others were lumpier and frumpier. The really, *really* old ones were gnarled and wizened, with crooked, twisted branches and pot-bellied waistlines. They look like wisdom itself carved from wood.

Over time, I'd grown to know individual trees here well,

LOVE IS A TOAD

becoming familiar with them like the one at Grandma and Grandad's. They had names – given to them by rangers, volunteers and visitors over the years – Medusa, Twister, Potbelly and Stumpy. Standing in the company of an ancient Oak tree humbles you to the very core. There's a delicious sense of insignificance that rains upon you when you meet a being so magnificent and aged – some of the characters in these woods are over a thousand years old. All of your worries and trivialities dwindle as you gawp at their boughs, formed slowly and confidently over centuries. On this particular day in July, the trees almost steamed with humidity and wetness. The rain had turned their wrinkled, fissured bark a dark chocolate that absorbed the murky light of the day.

As the two of us wandered, our eyes unthinkingly scanned the world around us. On the path ahead, a steaming and flat pile of slop caught our attention simultaneously.

'Ooh. A poo with suspicious holes in it! Has something gone in there?!' Indy was squatting on his haunches before I could blink, bringing his nose dangerously close to the wet pat in front of us. 'You can dig in first. Look, here's a stick, perfectly placed for a good poo dig.' He handed me a slender and rigid twig, smiling under his wet hood. I crouched beside him and started to prod, teasing the mush of brown grassy goop apart in the most holey areas.

Can I recommend a wonderfully weird activity to do on a sunny summer's day? Take yourself out for a wander where there's some big animals. Somewhere with grazing ponies, a small herd of cows or perhaps some deer. [Note: Ideally these animals won't have been exposed to lots of anti-worming meds, which tend to be bad for invertebrates.] Next, see if

DO BEETLES FEEL GLEE?

you can find some of their poo. The fresher the better. Think thick, moist and – ideally – still steaming. Hunker yourself down, get comfy, apply suncream and just *watch*. That pile of poo might reveal itself as a buzzing hub of Dung Beetle activity. I once spent an afternoon on a heath in Cannock Chase, Staffordshire, doing just this – lying on my tummy and gazing fondly at the soft, ice-cream-scoop lumps of a horse's droppings. I witnessed beetle after beetle after beetle zooming in from the surrounding area, diddy little brown ones and chunky, black heavy ones. As they approached the pile, their glinting wings snapped shut into their cases and the beetles dive-bombed into the moistness like kids hurtling off a diving board into a pool. Do beetles feel glee? On that day, I would've put money on it.

The pat in front of us was sizeable; it must've come from the lumbering Longhorn cattle that graze within the forest. 'Wow, it's fresh! What a colour. It's like, khaki green.'

I had to admire the boy's enthusiasm for poo. I reached the base of the hole with my woody tool and spied one tiny, beetly bum, burrowing away from the light. It'd gone before I could get a good look at it, carrying on with the all-important business of rummaging through crap. Dung Beetles are all about poo; their entire life cycle is dependent upon it. Poo is always proximal – depending on the species, they'll dig tunnels through it, under it, or near it, and both adult beetles and their larvae eat the stuff. Mmm.

We wrenched ourselves away from the gross source of nosiness and made a beeline for the back of the woods. Taking a turn, we walked out into a more open area of forest, a spot we call the heathy ride. This sweeping glade is a favourite spot of mine within Sherwood – in spring, the subtle song of Redstarts rains down on you from lofty Oaks and on a hot summer's day, you're likely to hear the cackling of a Green Woodpecker, laughing with gusto in between bouts of scoffing ants.

From the ride we headed further north towards Budby South Forest, an expanse of lowland heath and the altogether quieter sister of Sherwood. In mid-July, the heather was hinting at the impending colour bloom of August, with a tease of amethyst and a trace of warmth amongst the greyscale of woody shrubs in the rain. It was in this open space of heath and big skies that I heard and saw my first Woodlarks – which sounded just like Indy's whistle. Streaky birds of browns and creams you might easily overlook (I've learnt to challenge those habits), but whose song sits in your chest, eliciting beautiful images of clear, cold water tumbling over time-smoothed pebbles. I've walked the sandy paths of Budby at night, listening to the alien chumblings of Nightjars and stumbling across Glow Worms and their green neon bums in the dark.

There were no Woodlarks singing nor Glow Worms glowing in the middle of this soggy day in July. Indy and I trundled along wide, sandy tracks. Neither of us bothered to avoid puddles in our sandals, using the tepid pools to wash the sandy grit from between our toes every few steps. On a drier day, these paths would be places of anticipation and potential; hot summer sun shining on a sandy patch of earth normally means there are all sorts of goodies waiting to be spied. At Budby, we knew to keep an eye out for a suite of sand-burrowing critters and a wider web of other critters

DO BEETLES FEEL GLEE?

associated with them – all have evolved to take advantage of this pliable, malleable substrate.

We slowed as we squeezed through a kissing gate and Indy toed at some tiny burrows in the ground as he waited for me to follow him. He reminded me of myself in these moments – always prodding and poking at something, the inquisitiveness just oozing out of him – and it sounded like he'd been that way for a while.

'I've just always had that kind of classic nosiness you have as a kid, I guess. I remember when I was younger, there was a pile of logs in the garden. I'd lift them up and there'd be ground beetles and woodlice and millipedes and *all sorts* underneath it.' He sounded excited about it even now. That feeling when lifting up a piece of deadwood, the potential and possibility – it's even better than opening a box of chocolates.

'I used to have a little notebook that I would take with me and I'd just draw what I saw, little sketches of stuff that I didn't know the names of. I didn't have a phone or a camera or anything, so I'd just draw things to help me understand them.'

It was an adorable image. And it felt familiar – that kind of energetic hunger you have when you're little, driving you to search for things and watch them do stuff and try to work out why they're doing it.

Indy continued, 'I guess I've always been one of those annoying kids who asks loads of questions. Seeing something and just wanting to know more about it. When I'm watching wildlife, I'm like, *Who are you?! Why are you doing that? What're you up to?* Kind of like that spider-hunting wasp!'

The spider-hunting wasp. Blimey. I *must* tell you about the spider-hunting wasp. Just over a year before this soggy day in July, Indy and I were walking along the same stretch of sandy track on Budby. It was one of those warm days in late May when the sweetness of spring sits on the tongue and busyness surrounds you: growth, movement, activity.

Mystery Lump

It was the quivering that caught our attention. The wing-flicking, bum-bouncing, antennae-twitching quivering. A black speck on the floor, so easy to overlook, was about to gift us one of the most exhilarating hours of the season.

We froze and watched. Scuttle . . . pause . . . scuttle . . . pause. Just what was going on? To investigate required a face-down, bum-up approach. We lowered ourselves slowly on to the compacted path so as not to notify the creature of our gargantuan presence. Getting closer, I recognised the black scurrying form in front of me. A wasp! A spider-hunting wasp!

I'd read about these wasps in books and online. They were almost mythical. Their life cycle is fascinating and morbid and alien, and here I was watching it unfold in front of me.

She was busy. I say 'she' because it's only the females who carry out the frankly badass task of spider hunting. She was toing and froing, tickling the earth with her antennae every time she paused mid-scuttle. We watched her for a few minutes, the grit and gravel jabbing dimples into our skin through our clothes. We stayed quiet and breathed gently, not wishing to disturb the scene as we watched intensely. And then, we noticed the lump. A few inches away from her

DO BEETLES FEEL GLEE?

zone of scampering lay a plump brown nugget. A mystery lump. What on earth was it? A small pebble? A pellet of rabbit poo? And then we noticed the legs. A spider, all scrunched up, apparently dead. But in the world of invertebrate drama, all is not as it seems . . .

You see, the wasp had already hunted her spider. She'd searched, stalked and located her victim earlier, pinning them down and injecting them with venom. But this isn't a deadly venom — at least, not directly. It has the effect of paralysing the spider, keeping them alive yet unable to twitch even a leg. But why? This spider wasn't her dinner. She may be a spider-hunter but as an adult, this wasp feeds innocently on the nectar of flowers. The frozen, stupefied spider was sourced for her young.

We lay belly-down on the hard earth, buttons and buckles digging into our tummies. I think to fully appreciate these things, you have to get down, dirty and eye level with the drama — that way you don't miss a thing. By now, the wasp had stopped scuttling and had picked a spot. I don't know what she could sense about that spot — was it the compactness of the soil? The moisture content? The crumb? Whatever it was, she liked it. The digging began.

And there was so much digging. Whirring away, a Looney Tunes blur of legs, little piles of soil appearing as she descended. A tiny miner. A hymenopteran bunny. She dug, and dug, and dug. As she got deeper, she'd disappear for a minute or two at a time before resurfacing to dump some soil; all the while, her prey sat paralysed beside her.

Eventually, she decided her burrow had reached perfection. In the earth underneath us now lay an excavated

LOVE IS A TOAD

chamber with a tunnel to the surface. The wasp emerged one more time and focused upon her plump, motionless spider. Grabbing it, she reversed back into her tunnel, pulling her treasure with her. If you've seen the old Jumanji *film (spoiler), it's a bit like when the baddie bloke gets sucked into the board game at the end. Bum first, the legs of the spider squeezed around its face, it disappeared down the hole one tiny tug at a time. In the depths of her excavated pit, she would lay a single, teeny egg upon the still-alive spider, which would soon hatch into a hungry wasp larvae. Here, beneath unsuspecting feet, that larvae would scoff and grow, scoff and grow, feasting upon a fresh, juicy arachnid. Morbid. Hideous. Wonderful.*

Indy and I had watched the whole fantastic ordeal play out before us, our phones and cameras arranged around the site of the hole like paparazzi on a red carpet. In the silence after her final descent, the energy was palpable. In the days afterwards we scoured the internet, identifying the species – Anoplius viaticus, *aka the Black-banded Spider Wasp – putting a name to her and reading about the fascinating chain of events we'd witnessed.*

We reminisced about it in the rain, laughing at the memory of our dusty tummies and sore hips, stiff from an hour of wasp watching. When I think about it, it was curiosity that fuelled this experience, that lit a spark and made us think, *What's going on here then?* This was the force that drove us to spend all that time watching, waiting and observing.

Indy reacted to a noise up ahead, a *dink-dink-dink-dink* ricocheting through the muffle of the rain. It sounded like two

DO BEETLES FEEL GLEE?

marbles, or perhaps burnished pebbles, being clinked together in the palm of your hand. We soon realised we were surrounded – every time there was a *clink* in front of us, another *dink* answered from behind. Then we saw the smart white collar, bright like a light in the dim of the drizzle. A Stonechat! A bird with all of the warmth of a Robin – big, round, dark eyes and a plump, rotund belly. A flittering and zooming between stands of heather and clumps of Gorse made it apparent we'd stumbled upon a family of them – three young and the adult pair. Begging, feeding and flitting. Heavenly.

'I love asking why,' Indy said. 'I'm not always fussed about knowing what everything's called. Like, I know I've seen that plant before but I don't know what it's called.' He gestured to a clump of greenery by his feet and shrugged. 'It's not massively important to me; I just love looking at stuff. That's what I really enjoy!'

Me too, god. I love giving into that force, relinquishing control of my wanting mind and letting go. It is to 're-child' again, giving into that nosiness, just as Amy had described. It's a sensation we all remember, something I believe would be good for many of us to recapture, cupped like a butterfly between soft palms. To see a beetle trundling along and follow it because – why not? What are you up to, little beetle? Where are you going?

For me, being in a curious state is inextricably linked with wildlife – it's led me to some of my most submersive moments of pure nature joy. And, let's be honest, giving into this nosiness feels good. It gives us that sense of indulgence, putting aside other more 'productive' activities (if there are such things) to simply observe and to wonder. To allow yourself this time

LOVE IS A TOAD

to ponder and speculate, to wonder and to learn – it's what treasures are made of.

I see curiosity as an energetic state to be in; it's expansive and it opens us up. When we're being curious, we're reaching out. We connect with things and graciously accept new knowledge and new experiences. And when I submerge myself into a nosey state, a good sesh of prodding, poking and ogling, I find I lose that sense of self and start to connect with everything else.

We'd naturally slowed to a lazy amble, by now soaked through. A deep, particularly muddy puddle forced us to the edge of the path, where we squeezed up against a small Oak. As the leaves brushed my sodden jacket, I noticed some of them were a funny shape; their tops weirdly curled up and slightly browning. Hmm, what was going on here?

As I had learnt at the bottom of my grandfolks' garden, Oaks are guaranteed to yield treasures. Lots of the leaves on this individual showed the signs of other life – nibbles, webs and growths. And then there was this strange curling. I could see it on quite a few of them, the outermost lobes of the leaves rolled up and around themselves; they looked like a short cigar or a spring roll. Amidst our bafflement, a slow, lethargic movement caught my eye. A shiny dot of red. A small weevil, the colour of cherries. It looked like a beetle from a children's storybook, its beady eyes bulging aside its little black head and a rounded, hunched back. It reminded me of a tortoise in its form, speed and bumbling movement. Could this be the culprit?

We bent in for a closer nosey at some of the dried, small curls on the leaves. They were quite squat and stubby, a bit

DO BEETLES FEEL GLEE?

like a barrel, and upon closer inspection were very deliberately crafted – tightly coiled and folded shapes, complete with a door at the end. The sight was new to both of us. An unknown creature, unfamiliar and exciting.

We had *so* many questions and I typed several of them into Google later that evening, nice and dry and sitting with a brew on the sofa. So, who was this? The little beetle was apparently called the Oak Leaf Roller: a weevil that does what it says on the tin. Definitely the culprit. But what were the little curls about? What business did a little red weevil have with rolling up Oak leaves like rugs? I read that the female Oak Leaf Roller uses Oak leaves as a sort of protective swaddle for her eggs. She'll select a new-ish leaf, one from that year, and use a combination of her mandibles and the toothed edge of her leg to cut along it, splitting it in two down to a point. Then she'll scuttle off on her beetley business for a bit, waiting until nightfall. This gives time for the leaf to wilt, making it more pliable for the next step. After dark, she'll return to the cut leaf and after folding it slightly, will lay an egg inside. Then she'll start the rolling, tightly folding the leaf from the tip towards the stem, before taking the edges and tucking them inwards. Think of rolling a burrito; you want it to be nice and snug, and for nothing precious to fall out. The roll will remain attached to the tree for a while, drying out a little in the summer sunshine, before it detaches and drops to the ground, where it'll stay till next spring. Inside the tightly packed tube, the egg will hatch into a larva and spend the next ten months in a state of munching or snoozing before pupating into an adult beetle the following spring.

LOVE IS A TOAD

It was exactly as Indy had described: in a moment of nosiness we'd been whisked away, totally distracted and fascinated in equal measure. And the curiosity hadn't stopped after we left the weevil to her business; when I found answers online that night, I sent them excitedly to Indy, relishing the new knowledge I'd gained about a beast I hadn't even known existed just a few hours earlier.

We watched her for a few minutes more and I gently held one of the rolls between my fingers, inspecting it more closely. *I wonder how she sticks it together? I wonder if different weevils have different rolling techniques?* The questions came tumbling out of both of us as we shivered in the mizzle; asking things we'd probably never get answers to.

'That's one of the best things about curiosity, those unanswered questions!' Indy said. 'And what I love about all of this is that nobody knows everything. Just dipping your toe in, knowing just a little bit, asking questions about how it works – that's all I need really.' We both un-hunched and left the weevil to her plodding. A little life ambling onwards, going about its day.

'There are so many different worlds you can delve into, you know – plants, birds, bugs, bees – it's never-ending. And I think that's a really nice thing to get lost in, even if you're a novice. I don't mind if I'm wrong and I might never find out. I just love trying to figure things out!'

I liked Indy's perspective. And I think he's right: it's not about knowing everything, it's just about being open to learning, to observing. Like love, curiosity is likely to be linked with our survival. Affinity with nature drives curiosity, and by asking questions, testing and watching, we come to

DO BEETLES FEEL GLEE?

know nature better. We know the plants and insects; we can follow trails and identify scents. In being nosey about nature we become more intimate with it and we learn about our place in a tangled mesh of other life.

Indy talked about all of the different things you can delve into in nature. When you do just that – jump in with gusto – it unlocks so much. If you can learn to be unashamed in that nosiness, despite the judgement of some, there's a whole bounty of joy awaiting. I believe nosiness is all it takes to be a naturalist, really. To be a naturalist is not something that requires a qualification; there isn't a certain level to reach, against which you're being measured. It is simply to be someone who looks at nature, who observes and connects with it, who submerges themselves in it. To be a naturalist is to ask questions. And we all do that. So, I believe every single one of us is, fundamentally, a naturalist. It's what it is to be human.

Like the leaf roller, any insect we stumbled across moved sluggishly in the cool and the drizzle. Indy and I weren't too speedy ourselves. As the path we followed wound closer to a road, the borders of heather transitioned into a tousled verge of greenery and flowers. Grasses intertwined with pink-topped Willowherbs, the yellows of Agrimony and St John's Wort, and the altogether more muted bobble-tops of Plantain.

We soon crossed the busy road, thumping across the wet tarmac into a narrow strip of woodland, winding our way along a slender and extremely slippery path. We each took it in turns to slip and judder, arms flailing and feet scrabbling for grip on the smooth, compact mud. Above our heads, a Green Woodpecker cackled, seeming to laugh at our inelegance. At

LOVE IS A TOAD

one point, I nearly stacked it as I attempted to step over a particularly monstrous slug. It was huge, its crinkled back shiny with sliminess. After I caught my balance, I bent over and gave it a gentle tickle. It's back hunched up, looking like some sort of mollusc-buffalo hybrid, and it proceeded to wiggle back and forth in a slow-motion effort to look as intimidating as possible.

We pushed on, skidding our way along the path as it started to climb slowly upwards. Soon the trees opened up into grassland and we huffed our way up on to a plateaued hilltop known as Thoresby spoil heap, an artificial mound formed from the waste material from an old colliery. It's a strange formation, rising suddenly and awkwardly upwards, a significant jut in an otherwise flat landscape. Even though it's only a small hill, it's still the highest point for miles, and the view from the top is big and expansive. The once-bare spoil heap has been left to grow into a lovely tangle of grasses and flowers, and so we took a seat, nestling down amongst the bobbing yellows of Hawkweeds and Ragwort, plus the soft pink heads of Hare's-foot Clover. The air constantly bubbled and tinkled with song raining down from the grey clouds above. A hand to the brow and a heavy squint revealed the culprit: the fluttering silhouettes of Skylarks, belting out their never-ending music over their grassland domain. Delish.

We'd not been sitting long before the energy in the air suddenly shifted. A skittering of warning calls rang out in the grassland, seconds before a sleek silhouette zoomed past us. It seemed quite big, was it a Goshawk?! The bird locked on to a target: a Meadow Pipit. It chased it briefly, rocketing upwards.

DO BEETLES FEEL GLEE?

'A Sparrowhawk! See, a Goshawk would never do a spiral that quickly, they're much more considered.' Indy smiled with satisfaction. The pipit escaped and the Sparrowhawk floated away, dropping over the brow of the hill and down towards the forest. I hoped it'd find some lunch down there.

The view from our spot made Sherwood seem simultaneously vast and tiny. We gazed down on a bobbly topped expanse of trees. From way up on the hill, you couldn't pick out any of the colossal, ancient characters that make up the forest — trees like the Major Oak, Twister or Medusa — they all just blended into the textured deciduous carpet, stretching out below us. But, whilst those individual trees all melded together, the expanse of the forest was limited by harsh borders.

'I only came up here for the first time about two years ago,' Indy said. 'It's a big spoil heap from a mine. When I was a kid, I'd see bulldozers up the top of it every day. I sort of forgot about it until the work stopped. And then one day, mid-July, I climbed through a hole in the fence, came up here and sat down, and it was the weirdest thing. Because I've walked this forest forever and it seems like such a massive, extensive area. But when I climbed up here, I was like, *Gosh, it only reaches to there!*' Indy gestured at the landscape ahead of us, pointing at the rigid boundary where Sherwood ended. The wood itself looked bushy and thick, and the landscape around it clinical, neat and straight-lined. Forestry hugged two edges of the forest, its orderly rows of conifers contrasting starkly with the jumble of deciduous trees next door. Another edge was bordered with farmland, all neat and uniform. In the same way you can cut shapes from card with a scalpel, Sherwood looked like an isolated island, a scrap left behind after everything else had been sliced away.

Indy carried on. 'I was just so surprised at how tiny the forest looked. You can see the amount of fragmentation and the edges. The forest feels massive when you're down there, and it feels especially big standing under the ancient Oaks. Some of them are like massive, great cathedrals towering over you. But then when you're able to look down on them like this, you can just see how vulnerable it is. How small it is.'

At that moment, sitting on the hilltop, the seemingly great forest was reduced to a small patch on a huge quilt, fleeting and delicate. And this was just one place, one example of isolation and vulnerability. Zooming out from Sherwood, we mused over the bigger picture of nature's decline.

'It's such a big issue; where the hell do you begin? I see it all over social media, and it can feel so overwhelming, but also sort of numbing. I find it hard to find the drive to keep fighting sometimes, even though we obviously have to, for the spider wasps!' Indy smiled. 'It feels like we're wasting time, and we're wasting energy, talent and passion. I find it difficult to know where to focus my energy and I feel no sense of control – very confused and powerless.'

I imagine quite a lot of us can relate to that feeling, as though everything's out of our control, every problem big and sprawling. It's quite terrifying. Powerlessness feels like the right word here – when there's all of these big forces in play, and time is racing by, we can feel like we have no agency within the bigger picture.

DO BEETLES FEEL GLEE?

For me, the sensation of powerlessness is a key element of nature grief. It comes from the realisation that we can't prevent the loss of nature single-handedly; as an individual, I'm unable to stem the flow of destruction. In the face of countless problems, our individual efforts can feel as though we're holding an umbrella up against a tidal wave – you're trying but you simply haven't got the resources to hold the big wave back. That we live in a system that contributes to these issues only compounds the sensation, adding guilt and shame to the sticky potion.

Indy had described a familiar moment of transition. The dawning realisation that things aren't right, a moment when the childlike state of curiosity and optimism seems to fall away, like petals falling from a flower. Now, stepping into adulthood, Indy told me about the expectations he's felt as a teenager, dipping a toe into the conservation sector.

'People keep saying, "Oh, young people will solve it." But how long have we been saying that?!' Indy played with the vegetation at his feet absent-mindedly, tugging at the damp grass as we watched more Skylarks rise and sing their way into the air. Organisations ask for input from young people, he explained, but they never take any suggestions or ideas on board.

'We try things like going to the climate strikes, and then the media gets angry and says we should all be in school. And then some of the nature organisations are too afraid to go to a climate march because they're scared of the bad press. So we end up going on our own,' he sighed.

Indy was right. Placing the weight of this monumental task upon the shoulders of some undefined generation is simply kicking the can of responsibility and accountability down the road. And that weight is heavy too, a big burden for young folks to carry.

Many of us also feel powerless in the places where we're trying to take action and there are reasons why some people might feel that more than others. The bulk of these changes to nature – its loss and destruction – have happened very quickly, a comparatively tiny blip in the yawning chasm of time. In a just a handful of centuries, capitalism took hold in Western societies, and as its grappling fingers of domination and industrialisation colonised countries across the world, biodiversity suffered. And it suffered here first. When we think of the forces and attitudes behind these actions – the pursual of growth, exploitation, acquisition and control – we can see how they are applicable to Britain's relationship with nature. We can also see how they affect people. Plenty feel disempowered and excluded from the conversation. In these systems of inequity, your age, your class, your race, your ethnicity, your gender or sexuality, if you're neurodiverse or have a disability, might make you feel less empowered to speak up.

If you can't access nature – physically wiggle your toes in the grass, climb the trees and swim freely in the rivers – then you're also disempowered. And that feeds disengagement, helplessness and apathy. Problems this complicated require long-term solutions, and they're something that all of us need to contribute to as a collective effort. At this point, we need to consider who might feel the most lacking in power amongst us and then hand it to them.

Empowering more people in this big old task ahead means

DO BEETLES FEEL GLEE?

we can shoulder burdens together; it increases our resilience and helps us work with care and empathy. It helps us process our personal grief collectively. It is just. Hearing and listening to more voices brings different perspectives, and new and exciting ideas.

'Yeah, you need that range. At the moment it's just one bracket, one chunk of society that's involved. We *want* to contribute. We want to say stuff. We have points of view that those in power don't have and will never have. And so do lots of other people!'

Another skittering of warning calls interrupted our chat (nature doesn't care for politeness) and Indy and I spun around to see what was going on.

'Ooh, there! That's a Gos! That's a Gos! Ahh, it's huge. Wow! Did you see how full its crop was?!'

The bird that cut through the air in front of us was definitely *not* a Sparrowhawk. Moving with determination and a confident steadiness, it soared past us low to the ground in a smooth, unflapping motion. We saw its side profile clearly, including a full, rounded crop (a pouch birds store food in before digesting it). The Goshawk had had its lunch. It banked slightly, ignoring the mild panic it caused amongst the pipits and Skylarks, and dropped below the skyline. We had quite the view of it, looking upon its back as it cruised down the hill before disappearing into the thick green of the forest below. We watched in a state of exhilaration, staring at the treetops for a while after it had disappeared.

'I love this place so much,' Indy sighed, hugging his knees as he gazed down across the forest, now lit by tickles of sunlight poking through the clouds. 'It's infuriating sitting up here, seeing it all, and knowing there's nothing I can do right now to help.'

Spotlights of sunshine illuminated the dimpled forest canopy below us, falling into dips and sweeping over the highest treetops as the clouds rumbled overhead in the wind. In the distance, we could see a smoky sheet of cloud pouring from the sky – the next band of rain on its way. I looked down on the patch of woodland and imagined the mad array of life bustling away in there – Redstarts feeding their fledglings, the buzzing of a Hornet's nest, the slow spreading of fungi's tendrils through the soil and deadwood. The gentle breathing of a thousand ancient Oaks, souls who've stood in the same spot for nearly a millennium. How magic and beautiful it all is.

'Oh . . . hello, who's that?' Indy brought my attention back to the grass in front of us. He pointed at something – a tiny speck of orange clinging to a grass stem. A Small Skipper Butterfly, wings the colour of marmalade and totally bejewelled with tiny droplets of rain. We marvelled at its tininess, its soot-black eyes, dotted like beads, and jaunty, jutting antennae punctuated with dark blobbed ends.

'I love their eyes. What do you reckon a butterfly can see?'

'Look at those antennae, what do you think they can detect?'

'What's the difference between the skippers again?'

Aha – curiosity.

CHAPTER 4

Hoardyceps

Flow | Fear

CHANTELLE LINDSAY

Coulsdon Common, Greater London – 18 August

Hoardyceps

It was a particularly smooth one, with thick and rippling edges, like splashes of cream. It had a slight curve and one side of it was fuller than the other. It was adorned with splodged bars, soft fuzzy margins blending from the colour of time-worn bone to the dusty brown of slightly stale chocolate. As soft as velvet and as dull as muffled smoke. I slid it from under the crunch of seaweed and saltiness, dried by the sun. What a feather! A Curlew's, with its iconic horizontal stripes, each side slightly out of sync with the other as they kissed the off-centre vane. It twizzled deliciously between my fingers, almost pirouetting as I admired it from every angle. I lodged it firmly in the tightest part of my ponytail, pinching the shaft between my fingers like a quill so as not to buckle its delicate form.

LOVE IS A TOAD

Ooh, what's this one? Convex in profile, mimicking the gentle curve of my spine as I bent to pluck it from the sand. Black all over – at least at first. I held it to the sunshine and it sparkled with an understated iridescence of greens and blues that reminded me abstractly of mermaids. The curved shape led to a pointed tip, a quintessential triangle outlined in a subtly darker fringe. It framed the iridescence like a jewel set in metal and I imagined looking at lots of them up close, arranged in orderly layers across the back of the Shag it came from like fish scales. Mmm-hmm, you're coming home with me.

By now I'd acquired quite the tuft, an eclectic clump of feathers protruding haphazardly from my hair bobble. Striped ones and straight ones and bent ones and tiny ones with strangely long nibs. The find of the day was a Diver feather – either Black Throated or Great Northern, I'm never sure. It was a little feather, two inches at most. It was soft and curled, a bit like a Quaver but significantly less cheesy. A body feather that yielded easily to my petting finger, it had none of the rigidity of a tail or flight feather. It was a deep black with a moderate shininess to it, and at the very top, either side of the vane, sat two little spots, bright white and square like headlights. The feather had eyed me up from the strandline, nestled between drift twigs and crispy Bladderwrack. Gorgeous.

And ooh, what's this one?! Oh god. I couldn't stop. Another feather. Another one. Just one more. A buzz of contentment seemed to be rattling gently around my skull. A tingle in the scalp, a sparkle somewhere behind the eyes. My toes dug into the sand, feeling its caress and coolness. The air tasted

HOARDYCEPS

and smelled delicious, sucked in with greedy, soul-satisfying breaths. The tangled strandline stretched ahead of me, like a seaweed-filled scribble scrawled along the beach. I couldn't tear my eyes away. Time ceased to be, and my footsteps and mind flowed without pause or flicker. Step, step, feather. Tuck. Step, step, feather . . .

When I get stuck in a flow like this, I like to imagine I've been infected by an innocuous fungus. I've inhaled its spores and it has infiltrated my mind, spreading its mycelium throughout my brain until it controls my every thought, every movement. I call it 'Hoardyceps'. In the same way its Cordyceps cousins force ants or moths to climb high and emit their spores, Hoardyceps forces me to, well, hoard. The compulsion to collect is exclusively nature-based; it makes me seek out natural treasures and slip them into my pocket. Pebbles and seashells, fallen leaves and feathers. Once the fungus has infiltrated me there's no hope. I must seek. I must collect.

Walking down the beach on a sunny evening, I felt the tendrils of Hoardyceps tickling at the edges of my mind. There's no point in resisting. I surrendered. Just one more feather.

'I looked at them, their little faces, and I thought, *I bet you've never had a concert before!* So I did it. I just started dancing and singing for them. I think they loved it, don't you?!'

We beheld the huddle of blank faces in front of us, bearded and bristled and staring with square-pupiled eyes. A couple of them munched something absent-mindedly. Chantelle threw her head back and laughed – the kind of laugh that fills your own chest with warmth. The tiny hairy goats didn't react one way or another.

Chantelle is *exactly* the type of person to put on a spur-of-the-moment performance for a herd of goats. When she talks, it's always in animated, vibrant gushes, and she's absolutely hilarious. She's one of those people who just *sparkles*.

Leaving the density of the woods and walking into a grassy clearing that morning, we'd stumbled across the gathering of dinky goats – about a dozen of them. Chan walks past them often and it was clear she'd developed a wonderfully weird attachment to them. I could see why – their bog-eyed and wiry faces were undeniably gorgeous. *Perhaps they expect a performance from me too*, I thought, imagining myself attempting to juggle or stand on my head.

Standing there in the open, I could feel the heat of the sun on my neck. My thighs were absolutely boiling. My weather app had promised rain but it had clearly told a blatant lie – the day had turned thick and muggy, and my leggings were uncomfortably warm. I cursed myself for not wearing the shorts I'd eyed up in the morning. I'd got the train to Chantelle's house a few hours earlier and we'd walked from her door straight to the nearest patch of bushy greenery. The sign on the corner said Coulsdon Common and we took a wide grassy path that led into the green shade of the trees beyond.

Being in the woods in August is a delicious thing. There's that very specific temperature of air; it's moist and soothingly cool. It's the time of year when the birds have chilled out – everything's a bit quieter and less urgent. Even the trees seem relaxed. On the path, almost at our feet, a small brown smudge scurried past in a blur of fur and tiny feet.

HOARDYCEPS

'Oh, hello!' Chan greeted the little vole with a wave. It froze for a second, as if it had been caught doing something it shouldn't be, and then spied the two giants towering above it. Two little beady eyes took us in for a second and then it dived into the undergrowth in a blink. I smiled at her interaction with it and she laughed. 'I always wanted to talk to animals!'

God, me too. I think lots of kids dream of it, right? To be able to talk to a pet. To hold a conversation with the birds. To tell secrets to a snail or share jokes with the Ladybirds. I vividly remember wishing I could find a Hedgehog and befriend them, telling them I wished them no harm, I just wanted to hang out. It's such a natural urge when you're young – and if I'm being honest, I don't think it's ever gone away. I still natter away to passing flocks of Long-tailed Tits. I still whisper compliments to spiders.

Chan still does it too – be it goats or voles. Growing up, she was the youngest of three and had struggled for a while to find the thing she loved being and doing, until she got into this whole *nature thing*.

The first time I met Chan in 3D, I listened to her speak about her work to a room full of young folks. Her words that day were chock-full of enthusiasm and love, and we'd chattered excitedly together afterwards. Before that, in the 2D, online world, the thoughts and words and poetry she'd shared had really resonated, making me laugh and cry and tap heart-eyes emojis into my phone. A couple of years later, it was an honour to be joining her on a bumble around her local patch.

Coulsdon Common is a hotchpotch mix of dense, old

LOVE IS A TOAD

woodlands and expanses of meadows and grassland. Nestled between estates and other green spaces in south Croydon, it's a lovely place to wander around. I felt cosy and enveloped by greenery as we criss-crossed multiple paths, zigzagging this way and that. We stopped at one dusty crossroad, two paths intersecting, creating an X of compacted earth. The X forked around a colossal Oak tree – a beautiful creature standing confidently upright, as if in the middle of a dramatic and flamboyant pose. Chantelle rested a hand on the crackled bark of the thick trunk.

'I'm very drawn to plants. I love trees *so* much. Like standing under this one here and thinking, *What have you seen?!*' She looked up fondly at the twists and kinks of branches above us. I saw a familiar expression in her gaze: admiration, peacefulness and awe.

The tree was broad and chunky; their trunk was several hugs thick and I reckoned they must've been at least three or four centuries old. It's quite humbling meeting ancient beasts like this one. A creature who's stood in the same spot for hundreds of years, maybe over a thousand. I want to ask them questions. *What have you witnessed? Who's lived in your boughs and branches? Tell me all the things you remember!* Imagining the breadth and bounty of potential answers is so exciting. It's quite possible that if you've rested your own hand upon the bark of an ancient oak, you might've touched the very spot where a wolf once pissed. Isn't that brilliant?!

We wandered under a concoction of canopies, the sunlight breaking through varying from smattered speckles to big pooling blobs depending on the type of tree and the way it held its leaves. The humidity of the air had a distinct whiff

HOARDYCEPS

upon it, the comfortingly earthy smell of wood rot, sweet and fusty in equal measure.

We nattered away as we walked, not really paying attention to the direction or route. More than once we realised we'd walked in a circle, accidentally retracing our own footsteps. I imagined our route mapped out from above like messy squiggles of calligraphy, looping around and criss-crossing with an air of mild chaos. It was nice to have nowhere specific to go, no map to follow.

'You know what I love?' Chan smiled. 'That you don't have to be a certain way when you're in nature. I feel like it just accepts me as I am – it doesn't actually care! It blesses me without me asking, like just now I can feel the sun on my back and it's *exactly* what I needed.' Her words were soft and gentle; you'd struggle not to feel touched by them. I loved her perception – that the indifference of nature is in itself one of the most comforting things about it. No malice, no intention. Just a beautiful sort of apathy.

Chan continued, 'When I'm in nature, it's not demanding anything from me. I know that I'm a part of this beautiful world, and I'm just *being*.' The emphasis on her last word exuded a palatable sense of relief, that feeling of just letting go. 'Being present, being here, being now. I don't feel the need to dwell on yesterday, on tomorrow – I'm safe.'

At this point on our wander, we'd stumbled across a clearing in the trees. I again imagined it from above, appearing like a plunge pool amidst the snug Oak canopies. The space opened up into a wide grassy meadow, fringed with bushy clumps of Nettles, Cow Parsley and Brambles. Wherever we looked, our eyes were enticed by flitters and

LOVE IS A TOAD

flickering; it appeared we'd stumbled into the realm of the butterflies. Around the edge of the clearing, Speckled Woods danced in the shadows. Gloriously uncolourful and defiantly beautiful, Speckled Wood Butterflies have *such* a vibe. You'll see them in one of two states – either lethargically basking in a splodge of sunshine on a leaf, as if they absolutely can't be arsed, or in an apparent state of rage. We watched one male dare to infringe upon the patch of another. The territory holder, previously chilling in a pool of dappled light, suddenly exploded. A dramatic clash unfolded in mid-air, a swirling tornado of colliding wings, beating and flapping in a frenzy of lepidopteran politics and outright war. I'll never not find fighting butterflies hilarious, their stereotypical delicateness and beauty juxtaposed with fury and ferocity. Further out in the open glade we spied the lazily fluttering forms of Gatekeepers, another of the brown-and-gorgeous butterflies. As we watched them dance languidly, I asked Chan about the state she'd touched on – that sense of being present when watching wildlife.

'So for me, being present in nature is about noticing. It's about allowing the time for just being. I really like sitting still in a space and feeling everything around me – the grass under my feet, the sky above me, the sycamore tree to my left, the bumblebee to my right.' She smiled and gestured as the chunky bee rumbled past, filling the air with its telltale hum. 'It's that feeling of being held, of knowing that there's something next to you, something above you, something below you. And in those moments, I'm not thinking about my to-do list or big worries about life, it just flows!'

It just flows. Chantelle was describing a state that felt deeply familiar. The simplicity of spending time outside watching wild things and becoming totally absorbed in that act. It's a state of fluidity, one in which your body, hunkered down into the moment and the mud, merges with your thoughts, everything flowing smoothly like the burbling of water down a stream, surging from pool to pool in an unbroken cascade of clear liquid. In these moments you feel animalistic, your mind focused and trance-like, beyond the reaches of distraction. Your senses heightened, everything is seen and felt and heard and smelt in unison, each perception melding into the next.

This feeling isn't the same as being in a state of relaxation; it has momentum and an energy. It has a focus. And it's an actual thing in science. Known as the flow state, you might call it 'being in the zone'. It happens when you're so deeply involved in a task that you almost forget yourself. Time disappears and you become completely absorbed in the thing you're doing. This could be anything – running, painting, reading or scraping the goop off of a particularly handsome Fox skull. It's about the sensation rather than the activity.

I find myself in this state most often when I'm interacting with nature. It feels like the most natural form of intense concentration, something innate. And it's a huge component of the nature joy I feel. Some of my best 'wild moments' have been when I've reached this state of presence and flow. Poo-gazing, or wasp-watching, or lying on my back in the woods at dusk watching the silhouettes of bats zoom inches from the tingling tip of my nose, feeling the whoosh of the air pushed over my skin by the power of their beating wings, tiny and delicate and strong and perfect.

LOVE IS A TOAD

Flow state is linked closely with skill; it happens when we're engaging our brains on some sort of task, be it physical or mental, that challenges us, that requires effort and motivation, but something that's not *too* difficult. A goldilocks sort of task. And thinking of us as the animals we are, it makes a lot of sense. This kind of state benefits us. It'd be useful for lots of the things we would have previously needed to do to survive. Like foraging for food, our minds locked on the task of scanning our surroundings and identifying tasty plants, berries and bugs. Or hunting – concentrating entirely on chasing and catching our prey. We'd enter it when crafting and making (and many of us still do), our brains rewarding us when we achieve something and do it well. I reckon it's why those nature-collecting activities, the Hoardyceps ones, are particularly entrancing and enjoyable – they feel like the sorts of things our brains crave. In those moments I'm in a true state of flow, present in the moment and focused only on finding the next feather.

A pair of Gatekeepers flopped lethargically around our feet, moving with a lazy dither rather than an energetic flutter. The glade was peaceful and still. Insects were caught in the sunlight like fizzling sparks and a gentle breeze tickled patches of Nettles, sending ripples through them as though their fuzzy, hairy leaves were the surface of a shallow pool.

I told Chan about my feather-hoarding tendencies and she nodded along. She described how, when she enters that state and plugs into nature, she starts to feel creativity flow. 'It inspires me. Nature is the muse; wildlife is the muse!'

I knew Chantelle had a creative flair from her beautiful words and poetry she'd shared on Instagram. She told me she'd written poetry throughout her life, starting when she was little. She'd had poetry published in young people's anthologies and dreams of sharing her work more widely one day. There was a particular poem she shared a while back. Short and sweet, it had really resonated with me when I clapped eyes on it at the end of a long and frazzling day. She told me she'd written it when she too was feeling brain foggy and burnt out.

'I knew I needed to be on the ground; I needed to be held. So I found a spot under a tree and lay down. I was looking up at the sky, feeling my weight being held by Mother Nature, being nurtured, letting the tears fall. And that poem just came to me because it was exactly how I felt. I feel like I can be my rawest when I am in nature, when I'm plugged in – I find peace amongst the chaos.'

Amid all the chaos,
I find peace on the ground.
And in how the trees sound,
and for a moment I feel unbound
by the constant round and round.

Chan spoke the words softly, repeating them with a gentle rhythm as we passed under the boughs of another magnificent Oak. Dappled leaf-light danced across our bodies as if cast by a mellowed disco ball, covering our skin with a mottling of sunshine and shadow.

Finding this flow feels like an intrinsically positive and enjoyable thing to do. It also feels like an antidote, a deliberate and valuable thing we can immerse ourselves in when there's

LOVE IS A TOAD

so much else pulling at our attention. Many of us live in a world that provides constant stimulation: gigabytes of information being funnelled into our brains, like stuffing a sleeping bag into one of those impossibly small sacks. Our nerves are zapped by noises, crowds, flashing lights and adverts telling you to *buy this crap or you'll never be happy*. Most of us have little electrical and glassy-faced gremlins living in our pockets, tugging at our attention as though they're attached to us by thread, tempting us with distractions of headlines and dog videos and bottomless scrolling. Could this thing – this flow, this presence – counteract all of this? And if so, how do we find it?

I asked Chantelle about this. How do we cultivate that wonderful state, like coaxing a Dandelion into growth from between the pavement cracks? She had a great answer. 'Well, my heritage is Jamaican and I've been to Jamaica twice in my lifetime. The first time that I went, one of the locals said to me, "You know, we can always tell when people aren't born in Jamaica. Because of how fast you walk. Slow down!" And that has always stuck with me!'

I'm certainly guilty of this, scuttling and scurrying around with all of the hurry of a Weasel. I think I need to channel more slug in my life.

'There's so much beauty in slowing down.' Chan continued. 'I had the same feeling when I lived in Spain for nine months. As soon as I got back to London, everyone's rushing, everyone's got somewhere to be, zipping past each other. And when that's happening you're not noticing the little things, the beautiful things.'

Oi-oi-oi-oi. A cheeky, indignant noise boinged downwards

HOARDYCEPS

as we passed beneath the boughs of a tall, straight-trunked Oak. Scanning the canopy, Chan spotted the dinky, angular silhouette of a Nuthatch, shuffling its way up the bark. I always think that Nuthatches look like they're whittled from the very wood they scuttle upon. Their plumage is smooth and neat, as though it's been painted on to a sanded surface, their black eyeliner the finishing touch, applied with the flick of a wrist.

The tree was busy. As the Nuthatch scurried out of sight, a commotion caught our attention: a clacking call and a scuffle of black and white. Two Magpies were bickering and birring their way from one tree to another. Chan and I paused, watching them interact in their cheeky corvidian language. Scrawking, twitching tails, bows and bobs, all communicating something. What, I wondered?

'You know what I love so much about the natural world? The instinctiveness of it all.' Chan smiled as we watched the Magpies threading and weaving through the treetops. 'How when you watch something like a Magpie doing its thing, you can see that they are so reliant on their instincts. Because they have to be! They have to be in tune with themselves. If they're not noticing the subtle differences in the wind or the rustle of the grass then something might get them. That's something I want to try and lean into – to rely on my intuition.'

I understood what she meant; I too want to learn to trust my gut more, to lean into my body and feel those instincts, picking up on subtle cues and fully engaging my senses. I love watching it happen in other living things – that innateness of actions and interactions. Like the way a male Goldeneye Duck can't help but be sexy and display when a female swims past, throwing his white-cheeked head back and emitting a guttural, involuntary creak (if you haven't seen this before, you must google it, it's hilarious). Or the way a Garden Cross Spider builds her web on autopilot, pulling silk from her spinnerets like a spool in a sequence of actions: spin, pull, attach, repeat. I love how this is always going on all around me; it's so reassuring.

The Magpies disappeared into the green of the woods continuing their conversation, their harsh scrawking fading slowly. We carried on along the path, heading towards a wall of sunshine that indicated the edge of the wood. Sure enough, the trees opened on to a wide and grassy slope – the top of a small hill overlooking some of Coulsdon Common and the neighbourhoods around it. A wide, mown path drew us across the meadow, winding through tufts of long grasses and wildflowers.

'Watching something like those Magpies is a reminder that I'm part of something greater, that there's stuff going on outside of my microclimate, my head, my heart. Life is going on and that's really comforting to me.'

As Chan spoke, our line of sight was interrupted by a sleek zooming. A Kestrel – a ginger-backed female – soared smoothly over the meadow before catching suddenly in the air, a bit like an avian handbrake turn. Her beady eyes locked on something scurrying in the grass. As she hovered, her stare was so focused she appeared to have a furrowed brow. We both stopped in our tracks to watch her.

'Like watching this Kestrel, just hovering and diving, doing her thing. I know that even if I'm not OK right now – even if everything doesn't *feel* OK – I know it will be, because

HOARDYCEPS

outside my window, life is just going on. It's still resilient. It's still persevering. It's still pushing on.' Chan paused, staring ahead at the streamlined bird as she pondered further. 'But I am scared. Fear is a big part of the grief I feel for nature.'

The Kestrel broke her focus suddenly, her potential lunch clearly having made a scuttle for it. She glided away in an effortless, air-slicing way and started scanning the base of a hedgerow at the bottom of the slope.

Chan explained how she fell in love with trees when she used to work for the Great North Wood Partnership with the London Wildlife Trust. But her job also brought fear with it. 'At work, I've had to fell Ash trees because of Ash dieback, just hoping I'm doing the right thing for the natural world even though it feels wrong.'

My train had passed some sickly Ash trees on the way to meet Chan that morning, their skeletal branches standing stark against the rest of the summer greenery.

'And I worry. I worry I'm not going to be able to seek comfort in the natural world, that these things are going to be gone because we've messed it up. I worry that someone in the future who needs to feel the sun on their back or needs to hear the birds in the trees to make them feel better or like they belong, that they're not going to be able to have that. I feel sadness when I think about it, and I'm scared.'

The lump in my throat felt as big as the vole we saw earlier. Chan had described a feeling I expect lots of us have experienced, worrying about the state of things and looking at the horizon with a sense of trepidation and fearful anticipation. When we're surrounded by loss, it's only to be expected that we'll try to peer into the future, looking for

LOVE IS A TOAD

answers like a sort of forecast. I feel it myself – when I cast my eyes across bare landscapes, when I notice the silence of the hedgerows, when the Swallows don't return – it's a deep sense of unease and anxiety, a chest fluttering and thoughts racing at a million miles an hour. It's obvious why we feel like this. It's hard to not be afraid when we're faced with an onslaught of headlines about loss and destruction. As we comprehend the scale of suffering, both of nature and people, of course we feel terror rise in our throats.

Chan and I paused as we gazed over the meadow, our eyes glittering with tears. It's simultaneously emotional and reassuring to know somebody else has felt the same way as you. We'd stopped by a vibrant clump of Common Knapweed, buoyant in a delicious fuchsia, a colour that seems to entice life from all around. Hoverflies, wasps, skipper butterflies . . . nobody could resist the allure of a hot pink. Not even us. We hunched over the busy flower heads, admiring the hairy-bellied behind of a female Leafcutter Bee, her tummy coated in bristles the colour of dandelions. I was thinking about what Chantelle had said and I asked her how she deals with the fear when she feels it bubbling.

'It's weird. Because sometimes, although I know it's not OK right now, I believe it *will* be. And then other times, I question it. It's not OK right now and *will it be*? Even though it's strong and persevering, will our natural world be OK? Are we going to be able to protect it?'

Another bee hustled in on the Knapweed – a Honeybee, possibly – and nudged the Leafcutter from her flower head in a bossy, elbowing sort of way. If bees have elbows, that is.

When I was a child, protecting nature used to feel simple.

HOARDYCEPS

I remember kneeling on the hard, gritty tarmac of the school yard, gently wrapping a Seagull[1] in my school jumper as small stones dug into my bare knees. The feathers on their wing were bloodied, their beak agape with fear. The bird had been brought to me held upside down by their legs by a usually cocky lad, who now looked quite tearful. He and his mates had taken to throwing stones at the large flocks of gulls that would descend on the playground every break time, looking for scraps. For the first time, they'd actually hit one. Now, my significantly uncool reputation as 'animal girl' had finally paid off and I swaddled the bird in navy-blue polyester before tucking it under my arm and heading for the school office, where I'd ask them to call the RSPCA.

This is what I thought protecting nature was: the literal act of helping an animal. But things don't feel the same as they did when I was thirteen. Now, protecting nature feels both nuanced and overwhelming. It feels complex and ungraspable, like trying to pick out plasticine that's been mashed into a carpet. Between moments of hope where it seems like change is possible, colossal waves of fear loom over me frequently, threatening to block out the sun and come crashing down at any point. But, as Chantelle reminded me, it's OK to feel both.

'I know it's contradictory but for me that polarity is so much a part of the grief. And nature's like that – there's the polarity of the beauty and the ugliness. The chaos of nature and also the peace of it. You can find all these spectrums in nature and they help me feel a little less crazy because

---

[1] I know there's technically no such thing as a seagull, you bird nerds.

I know that chaos and peace can exist at the same time. So I can believe and hope it'll be OK, and still be scared that it might not be.'

The sun felt warm on our skin as we stood in the open, a light breeze coaxing the grasses and flowers into a gentle dance. It's funny, I knew exactly what Chantelle was getting at, even though I'd never really considered it before. I could see now that it's totally possible to carry these two different thoughts at the same time: to hope that nature will be OK – to truly believe in its resilience and ability to bounce back – but also to fear that it won't, that things might not turn out all right. I've often felt my mind flip-flopping from one thought to the other and back again, on loop a bit like a Chiffchaff's song: *chiff-chaff-chiff-chaff*, 'it'll be okay – no it won't – yes it will – no it won't'. These feelings are confusing and heavy; hope is a very natural human emotion, but fear is too. Chan had showed me that it is OK to carry both at the same time.

Whenever I was afraid of doing something as a kid – talking in front of the school assembly, doing a race on sports day, climbing a really big tree – I'd tell my mum I was scared. Like a catchphrase, her response each time was guaranteed. With firmness and a smile, she'd always say to me, 'Well, do it scared then!' Now, after talking to Chan, I see Mum's words are applicable to the crises we face. How I must persevere even when my voice trembles and my knees quiver. We must fight for the changes we need to see nature and people thrive, even when we're uncomfortable, even when we're scared.

The welcoming touch of sunshine invited us to sit, and

so we ambled off the path and nestled down amongst the peaceful bustle of the meadow. On our backs, we watched the clouds dawdle overhead, their forms and shapes shifting imperceptibly: one minute a crocodile, the next something more fish-like.

'You know, when you're lying back in the grass and looking around, things just don't seem so pressurised. They don't seem so important.' Chan sighed. 'I woke up yesterday feeling a massive mix of emotions: grief, fear, gratitude. All of that, all in one. And when those big emotions come up, I just feel like nature takes away the pressure. It's just everything.'

Lying there with the fresh tang of grass and Hogweed tickling the nostrils, it *was* everything. Relaxed, peaceful, chill. A dark speck, solid and chunky, buzzed clumsily out of the air and landed with a mini-thud on Chantelle's forearm. A bug – a shieldbug! Its bronze-brown body had jutty, pointed shoulders, like an 1980s jacket complete with shoulder pads, and it was outlined in a neat, chequered border. Right in the middle of its back was a little dot, the same bright orange as the juiciest of tangerines.

'Oh, hello! Who's that on my arm? Hi, little shieldbug! Wow, look how bright that orange is!' The red-legged little beast scuttled its way up towards her elbow. 'Whenever something lands on me, I wonder what it means. Like, you chose me! Are you my spirit animal?!' Chantelle laughed as the orange-bummed being rumbled along her skin.

I later learnt it was a Forest Bug, a sap-sucker, fond of guzzling the sweet juices of Oaks and other trees. It made sense that we found it so close to the woods we'd walked

LOVE IS A TOAD

through. Chantelle lifted her arm, holding her friend up to her face to have an ogle, eye to beady eye. She smiled.

'I just fucking love nature. I'm so grateful for it. And I really want it to stick around.'

CHAPTER 5

Pincushion of Opportunity

Complexity | Loss

NEVILLE JONES
Dee Estuary, the Wirral – 12 September

A Life Inside a Life Inside a Life

A squiggle. A tiny, delicate scribble. Reminiscent of ink, penned in a flamboyant flourish with the nifty flick of a wrist. It zigzags back and forth between two veins of a single Beech leaf. The leaf is nestled amongst countless others upon the forest floor, in a terrestrial sea of caramels and marmalades and beautiful, unnameable shades of brown that contrast and blend together simultaneously. This particular leaf is the sort of warmish brown that burns orange when you hold it up to the sun, the soft, downy hairs along the papery edges illuminated in a way that reminds me of eyelashes. Around the squiggle, a small part of the leaf remains a bright green, mixed with splodges of yellow. It looks almost like the traffic light lollies my nana would give us in a paper bag when we were little.

LOVE IS A TOAD

The squiggle, strictly confined between straight, parallel veins – only half a centimetre apart at most – tos and fros in a satisfying way, like how you might absent-mindedly doodle between two lines in a notepad. Towards the middle vein of the leaf, the squiggle is skinny and fine. As it moves further away towards the edge it becomes thicker, with each turn of the doodle curvier and larger, like the mark of a felt tip. Against a backdrop of September sunlight I can see through the squiggle – and I can see it's got stuff in it. Frass. Poo.

Squinting harder and bringing the leaf up to my nose, I follow the scribbly signature to its fattest end and . . . there! Unmistakably, I see the form of a minuscule sausage-bodied creature. It's a caterpillar and it's living in between *the layers of a leaf. A tiny body, sandwiched between membranes, and an even tinier head, pulsating with regular, rhythmic munching. I see now that the squiggle is the caterpillar's tracks, the route it's taken through the leaf during its short life of scoffing. I can see where it started, an egg smaller than a grain of sand, a pinprick on the leaf's surface. From hatching, the eating had begun and, like a real-life version of* The Very Hungry Caterpillar, *I could trace the growth of the little chomper through both the fattening of its tunnel and the increasing volume of peppery black poo that filled it in its wake.*

I remember the first time I saw one. Not literally – but the first time I saw *one. Noticing bone-white wiggles and curves etched into a Bramble leaf and asking the question, 'What exactly is that?' Typing a jumble of words into Google, I'd found out. Stigmella aurella – a tiny species of moth. The similar markings I'd seen on Beech leaves belonged to*

PINCUSHION OF OPPORTUNITY

other moths: 'Beech Dots', Stigmella tityrella, or possibly Stigmella hemargyrella. I felt like my eyes had been opened. Suddenly, I went from not knowing they existed to seeing them everywhere: squiggles on Bramble, Honeysuckle, Oak and Birch. Some were chaotic, like an angry scribbling out of someone's name. Some followed rules, sticking between veins or tracing the perimeter of a leaf. And some of them were practically works of art, fine, flamboyant handwriting in an invertebrean calligraphy.

A tiny caterpillar, living inside a leaf. A wonderfully elaborate, yet simple and obvious strategy. Concealing yourself from predators by enveloping yourself inside your own food source. How bloody clever. But the cleverness didn't end there. Looking closely at that brown Beech leaf, with a zigzag squiggle surrounded by green, I could feel questions forming in my mind. Why was it still green? What did it mean?

This is where it gets deliciously complicated. Let's go back to the trees. The changing colours of autumn are familiar to us — that melting of the greens of summer into golds, coppers, rusts. This change is called senescence and it happens in autumn when trees switch off the production of plant hormones called cytokinins. All well and good, unless you're a caterpillar living inside said leaf and you need to eat a little bit more of the delicious greenness before you're ready to pupate. Enter Wolbachia. Wolbachia are a group of bacteria that live inside the caterpillar that lives inside the leaf. A life inside a life inside a life. The relationship between this bacteria and the caterpillar is fascinating because the bacteria affects the caterpillar's labial glands, which is where its spit is made.

LOVE IS A TOAD

Mmm. Now, the clever bit: Wolbachia makes the caterpillar ooze cytokinins in that spit. Picture those minuscule jaws munching away, the saliva juices flowing, seeping into the surrounding leaf tissue. The cytokinins in those juices keep the area around the caterpillar green for long enough for it to finish scoffing and pupate. This relationship between insect and bacteria effectively stops autumn in its tracks. And all of this plays out in the rustling leaves under your feet, every year. Proper magic.

'I could cry about it now!' The words hung in the air as we gazed upwards, seeing the drowsy flaps of the silhouettes above us, glob-winged and chunky. A noise toppled down from the grey mizzly sky as we watched; it was alien, electronic, textured. Like the sound of several voices all talking at once through a synthesiser or a robotic sample from a nineties dance track. It seemed to vibrate gently in a way you almost feel in your throat. *Peeeee-wit*! A high-pitched, gurgling screech followed by a flourishing little pip. Really weird and utterly heavenly. The dollop of Lapwings, perhaps 20 of them, fluttered over us dreamily.

'In terms of birds, the ones that I miss most emotionally are Lapwings.' Nev's facial expression melded joy and sadness together in an all-too-familiar way. He squinted at the grey-but-brilliant sky and we saw a couple of the birds peel off in a twirling, elaborate loop-de-loop, *pee-witting* as they danced downwards.

'Sometimes, I can feel tears welling up in my eyes. I'm a very emotional person! I feel it when I think about my grandchildren. When I contemplate what has happened in my own country

PINCUSHION OF OPPORTUNITY

– it does make me angry and I feel the tears coming.' Nev continued watching the birds until they disappeared out of view, perhaps landing again after a spook by a Peregrine Falcon. Then, sitting across from me on a damp, slightly slimy picnic bench, he looked me in the eye. His face crumpled into a huge grin, the northern warmth radiating from every inch of it. I love the way Nev talks – emphasised, considered, slow – friendliness oozing from every word and expression.

'So yes, I miss Lapwings. And you don't replace them. No matter how hard you try. You're a beautiful girl but you're not *that* beautiful!' He laughed and leant forwards, clasping his big weathered hands around mine on the algae-covered tabletop. There was the other thing I love about Nev – his cheekiness. He's like a twinkle in the eye in human form, always ready to tease and piss-take in the gentlest way. The sweet inkling of autumn hung in the air, cool and mulchy. I inhaled it, drawing it deep into my lungs.

Only a few hours earlier, I'd been hoiking my bike up an escalator in Liverpool Central station, ignoring the rules and risking a painful tumble as I rushed for a train. A short journey later and I was on the move, wheels sloshing through puddle after puddle as I pedalled down a cycle track along the Dee Estuary, heading for a nature reserve nestled in the muddy armpit of the Wirral. I chained up my bike and headed to the main hide at Burton Mere, the flush and warmth of exercise still thumping in my chest.

I spied Nev as soon as I walked in. He faced away from me and it'd been a year or two since I'd last seen him, but I recognised his mac-clad back as he peered through the big glass window overlooking the estuary. As he turned around,

LOVE IS A TOAD

I was greeted with a bursting smile, the sort that enfolds someone's eyes in creases and provokes one in return.

The massive windows in front of us were framed in chunky wood and seemed to have a persuasive, pulling effect, tempting you closer for a look across the landscape. We stood there for a moment, gazing over sweeping pools, dotted and sliced by grassy islands and embankments, bordered by the quivering and towering walls of golden reeds. In the very distance, almost like the wallpaper at the back of a colossal room, stood the very human silhouettes of industry – stiff structures to do with steel and power and cement.

Everywhere I looked, my eyes caught movement. To the right, a Kestrel hung suspended in a quivering focus, her entire body trembling around her motionless head as she glowered at the grass below. Further back, a cluster of white forms caught my eye. A bunch of Cattle Egrets were haunting some Welsh Carneddau ponies, motionless amongst the herd. One perched upon a pony's rump, looking gangly and awkward as the horse munched away unperturbed.

Closer to us, a thick and velvety silhouette broke over the reed beds, sending a quiver and a flutter through the birdlife on the pools. A female Marsh Harrier, gliding as if in slow motion, gently tilting this way and that as she cast an eye over her domain. Such underrated plumage: a matte, silky brown, a little bit like the delicious dusting on a chocolate truffle, topped with a caramel cap, the feathers on her head and face a warm honey colour.

Inside the hide, I could tell everyone's attention was being pulled in one direction, binoculars and scopes tugged to the left as if by a magnet. I lifted my own binoculars and ogled

PINCUSHION OF OPPORTUNITY

a little bird with an ever-so-slightly curved beak wading in the muddy shallows. It was a Curlew Sandpiper, picking and probing at unknown invertebrate morsels in the silt.

We left the centre and slunk outside. It was unquestionably autumnal – wet and cool, and the vegetation was that dark, end-of-summer green. It had a distinct droop, as if starting to bow before the oncoming era of decay and retreat. We wound our way along narrow paths, enclosed in reeds and feeling sheltered and protected by their looming, tuft-topped silhouettes. A wooden rail beside us hosted several Garden Cross Spiders, suspended in their bike-spoked webs along with silk-bound tasty things and scattered, sparkling dewdrops. We bent down a little closer to take a look, admiring the chunky, splodge-adorned bum of a female, gorgeous in all its chestnuts, creams and mahoganies. I whispered compliments to her in my head.

'My love for nature is definitely an aesthetic and appreciation thing,' Nev said, ogling her elegant eight-legged form, which bobbed subtly in the breeze. If you looked a little closer, you could see a cluster of reflections around her, shrunken upside-down images of the reeds and hogweed behind her, suspended in droplets. I asked Nev how he discovered his appreciation for other life.

'It's a slippery slope, isn't it? It started off with birds. My parents discovered this interest that I'd got – a fascination more or less. And they bought me *The Observer's Book of Birds*, which cost three and sixpence!' Nev beamed at me, standing up to continue our wander through the reed bed. He explained how his parents, from a small working-class mining village, weren't particularly intellectual and didn't have any books in the house. When they'd gifted him his little bird book it had opened his eyes – a young boy turning the pages to read about things like the Great Crested Grebe.

'I read its name and I thought, *What the hell is that?*' Honestly, I had no idea! Anyway, that was the beginning of it all.'

I remembered my own first encounter with a Great Crested Grebe – or, at least, the first time I consciously saw one. It was another bird I hadn't known existed until I was an adult. I saw a pair of them in all of their splendid breeding finery approaching each other in the middle of a large pond. They're both fabulous and ridiculous-looking, with funny, feathery tufts splaying from their heads like some sort of momentous shock has occurred. As a form of flirtation, they flamboyantly fling pondweed at each other. A wonderfully weird bird, the Great Crested Grebe.

We continued down the boardwalk, our footsteps eliciting a satisfying rumble from the weathered wood, carrying us over land otherwise too soggy to traverse. I love walking amongst the towering reeds. It's disorientating in an exciting way, a bit like wandering around a maze. With your vision obscured, sound suddenly becomes more useful. The music the reed stems make as the breeze caresses them is gorgeous – a sort of soothing, hissing whispering. The soundscape of a reed bed in spring is particularly brilliant. The backing track of rustling foliage is joined by all sorts of other sounds too: the cries like that of squealing pigs give away the presence of Water Rails, Sedge and Reed Warblers who seem to compete with each other in a game of 'who's got the scratchiest, roughest song?' If you're there early in the morning, you might just feel the deep, fluty boom of a Bittern reverberating in your ribcage. Now, in September, the reed bed spoke through the voice of Cettis Warblers – their boinging song belted with vigour from the depths of the reeds, finishing as abruptly as it started.

Burton Mere has plenty of reed beds. It's a bit of a hotchpotch of habitats: old woodland, with gnarled Oaks and Bluebell carpets in the spring; lagoons and pools, wet and muddy and full of birdlife; soggy meadows where Avocets and Lapwings breed. Nev knows the place really well; it's why he chose it when I asked him to go for a wander with me. He knows lots of RSPB reserves well, actually, having been a long-standing member and volunteer for many years.

Nev signed up as a member in 1966 – for an annual subscription of one and a half guineas – after mulling over the decision for a while. At first, he'd been under the impression that an organisation like this wasn't for people like him, that it was full of 'fuddy-duddies'. But, after delving into their magazines and reading about the RSPB's work, he'd begun to feel a sense of camaraderie with others who shared his concerns for wildlife.

Not long after joining, Nev had dipped a tentative toe into volunteering. He wasn't really sure what he wanted to do at first but had a go anyway. He started off organising events to raise funds for the charity. Pulling together a film screening with his wife Sue proved successful ('We worked like stink! And we caused a traffic jam – 850 people came!'). By the time I met him at Coombes Valley, he'd had a go at all sorts: leading youth groups, guided walks, meeting and greeting, and practical work parties. One of his most recent roles, based at Sherwood Forest, involved him dressing up as a medieval forest-dweller, telling tales of Robin Hood to enthralled children. It must be brilliant visiting the reserve and being welcomed by Nev's massive grin. You can tell he loves it too.

'One of my favourite things about all this is meeting people like you. Young people!' Flatterer. 'Sue says to me, "You know, when you go to Coombes or Sherwood, I can tell you've had a really lovely time, not because you're in the woods, but because you're meeting young people!"'

We rounded a corner and boardwalk gave way to a gravelled path, which appeared to be covered in a scattering of little lumps and bobbles. The previous week had seen a deluge of soggy days and the moisture had tempted the molluscs out. Slugs and snails peppered the ground ahead of us, pushing slimily through the grit and forcing us into a game of stop and start, pausing regularly to sidestep someone glistening or shiny-shelled.

The flowers of late summer were still knocking around, the five-pence heads of Tansy and the ten-pence heads of Fleabane infusing the verge next to us with cheerful splodges of yellow. We soon rumbled up to a picnic bench. It was sitting in the grass just off the path and nestled close to an Alder that looked a bit like a hand – five chunky stems reaching up and out, knuckled like fingers. Intertwined with its lower branches and hugging its trunk were other plants: the thorned arches of Dog Rose, tufts of fragrant Meadowsweet and Hogweed seed heads.

'Shall we sit?' Nev gestured to the bench, greened by moss and dampness, and we settled down in the cool air for a natter. We'd not been there long before the lollop and *peewits* of Lapwings interrupted us.

I thought Nev would be the perfect person to chat to about loss. Only two weeks earlier, he'd turned 84. Born on 1 September 1939, Nev had grown up in a world of war; he knew nothing different until he was six years old. Over the course of his life, he's witnessed an ongoing and widespread loss of wildlife, one that's crept into every nook and cranny of the isles we live upon. The silencing of birdsong, the felling of giants, the slow smothering of life in all of its scuttling, fluttering, growing and swimming forms. I could only imagine what things might've been like when he was little, what ordinary but wonderful wildness Nev might've seen on a regular basis.

I absent-mindedly thumbed a blob-silhouetted leaf of the Alder next to us. Whilst running my finger over a medley of small nodules (possibly caused by mites), I noticed a tiny humpbacked button of iridescence perched upon the stem. It was an Alder Beetle, its rounded, gumdrop bum looking like some sort of emerald pearl. What followed was one of those moments of weird wildlife realisation, when your eyes zoom out and you become aware of a presence you were previously oblivious too. The Alder tree was absolutely *plastered* in beetles. And lots of them were in the middle of coleopteran coitus, paired up in comical piggybacks and bumbling around rather lethargically. As I pointed them out to Nev, I asked him about the changes he'd seen over the years.

'In my lifetime, I have seen a *massive* loss in insects. When I used to drive at night, it was like a snowstorm!' Nev held up his hands, wafting them in the air as if to mime being stuck in a blizzard. 'If you went on a car journey in summer, you had to clear the dead insects off your windscreen before you set out. But you don't have to do that any more. Beautiful, aren't they?' He paused, looking at the copulating couple closest to us in all of their metallic finery.

'And this might surprise you – House Sparrows. There were millions!' Nev's eyes popped as he emphasised the volume of these familiar bickerers of eaves and hedges on terraced streets. 'You used to drive out into the country and in every farmyard you went by, there were flocks and flocks of House Sparrows. And Tree Sparrows!' he sighed.

Whilst House Sparrows are still a well-known feathered face, I hadn't seen a Tree Sparrow myself for a couple of years. There used to be a small bunch of them along a track a couple of miles into the broad, flat cabbage-lands near home. But their homes of bushy Hawthorn hedges had become the focus of an intense flailing operation and I hadn't seen any there for ages.

'Now you go out for a day's walk and you see a single Treecreeper and it livens up the day, it's wonderful! But then I think to myself, this is a *dearth*. There should be so much more.'

A dearth. He was right. You can find wildness and wild things anywhere. Of this I am a firm believer. Life lives in the gutter, like the little tufts of Procumbent Pearlwort (yes, a real plant's name!) you see protruding from between bricks and slabs, the dinkiest of flowers dotting the pavement. Life lives at the bus stop – the Funnel-web Spider peeking out from her lace-webbed tunnel in the corner. It lives plastered on to walls or nestled within them, in the form of lichens and

PINCUSHION OF OPPORTUNITY

mosses, woodlice and Ladybirds. I've witnessed it plenty of times. Life singing at 3am. A Blackbird doused in the melting orange glow of a street light, belting his heart out as I listened transfixed, many pints in and wobbling in my heels on the cobbles. A moment of strange, drunk serenity. Of meeting wild things in unexpected places.

But it's hard to deny that when you go for a walk in most places, there's a sensation of emptiness. A heavy, belly-deep instinct telling you something's missing, something's gone. I've witnessed loss myself and I've only been knocking around for three decades. No time at all, really. The dwindling Tree Sparrows, yes, but lots of other things too. Some losses are tangible, a categorical, measurable decline you see with your own eyes. The Cuckoo that sang in the cow fields behind the house where I grew up. Gone. The ponds at the top of the village, the ones that bustled with Fire-bellied Newts and the rustle of a hundred dragonflies. Gone. The butterflies adoring every Buddleia, every Bramble. Gone.

God, the butterflies.

I have a vivid memory of playing in a bit of scrappy wood near my cousin's house on the edge of town shortly after my grandma died. I would've been 13, my cousin Charlotte (the best name said in a Leyland accent: *Shaah-luh*) a year older. Legging it around in the early autumn sunshine, we hoiked over a fence into a field, ducking under a border of Hawthorns and a wizened apple tree. A couple of steps ahead of Charlotte, my knees nearly buckled with shock when the ground below the tree seemed to detonate, shattering into pieces of colour and hysterical fluttering. I'd unknowingly disturbed a storm of Red Admiral Butterflies who'd been slurping the fermented juices of mould-crumpled apples dotted amongst the grass. There must've been a hundred, flying off in every direction. The moment stunned us. Knowing that Red Admirals were my grandma's favourite solidified the event in my memory. I've never seen butterfly numbers like that since.

I might not be able to back up all of these examples with numbers (although, actually, I probably could) but these are all things that I've noticed, things that I've felt. They're the sorts of losses that leave you clutching and grasping, trying desperately to hold on to the sand as it pours through your fingers. And yes, this is just one person's experience, witnessing loss on a small scale. But so many of us have our own examples and our own stories to tell: a local park tarmacked over, an Oak tree felled down the street, pavements sprayed with weedkiller. If we zoom out and extrapolate these instances, we can see loss occurring all over the place. And it all adds up. We're witnessing death by a thousand, or a million, cuts. Lots of little wounds totting up, painting a bigger picture of pain, sickness and injury.

Together, over time, all of these cuts become visible on a landscape scale. Gradual alterations to the places we live, wander and roam. Fields growing bigger and bigger as they merge, creating enough space for colossal combines and their huge turning circles. Hedgerows being battered, cut back or outright disappearing. Ponds being filled. Trees being felled. Entire woodlands gone. Skylines simplified and views emptying. Year by year, it feels as though we witness more neatening and tidying and straightening. The homogenisation of the landscape is something I've personally noticed since the nineties, its texture, depth and tangle fading

PINCUSHION OF OPPORTUNITY

away. And life seems to be fading with it, places becoming quieter, cleaner, emptier.

For me, the sensation of nature's loss spans time. When I dwell on the things lost in my short lifetime, I can't help but look further backwards. I want to see how things *were*, to put my eye to a tiny peephole in a fence and steal a glimpse of the past beyond it.

Let me explain what I mean. Let's say that peephole gives us a view into the 1950s. If you and I were to peer through it, we might see an abundance of wild things we're not at all familiar with. The sort of things Nev described: colossal flocks of birds, insects on windscreens. There's the moth clouds my folks told of seeing outside their bedroom windows as kids, the descriptions in old bird books of Turtle Doves in every hedgerow. It would probably astound us, the two strange peepers from the future, to see the sheer volume of life that there used to be.

It's hard to process and imagine it. And because of that, it's easy to underestimate the volume and abundance of life that we've lost. I think about the numbers of those Red Admirals when I was younger, only twenty-something years ago, and it's easy to picture it as an abundance relative to today. But that was already depleted. It's likely that someone in the fifties would've seen those numbers under the apple tree and thought, *What, only 100 butterflies?!*

Nev has witnessed a whole lifetime of loss and has a measure of it much greater than my own.

'That shifting of the baseline is going on all the time. I've just been reading Francis Kilvert's diaries, written in the early 1870s in Clyro, mid Wales. He wasn't writing about nature, he was just writing about his job and stuff about the village, local characters. But nature gets mentioned. And every now and again he says something like, "I went along to see old Mrs. Roberts at the church, and on the way there were two Land-rails in the field." And I realised he's talking about Corncrakes! Apparently there were Corncrakes everywhere then.'

Land-rails. It's a name for the Corncrake that we don't really use any more – like a Water Rail (a streaky, sneaky wetland bird that paddles around reed beds) but on the land. I've seen a grand total of one and a half Corncrakes in my life. The full one was on Bute, the year I moved there. Cycling to the beach on a clunky, rusty bike, I'd been puffing and pedalling at speed when I heard the telltale creak of its call. Short and sharp, a sort of squeaky rasp, it sounded like a cheap alarm clock or someone running a fingernail over a plastic comb. Skidding to a halt, I hung around until I spied it, its head sticking out of the bushy verge, rasping into the sky. It was the first one recorded on the island for well over a decade. The half a Corncrake came a few years earlier. I glimpsed the tiniest hint of bum as it disappeared into the grass, creaking away – barely a sighting, really. This one lived on South Uist, one of a few Hebridean islands where these funny field scamperers cling on. This was a bird that was common and it's now normal to think of them as a coveted rarity, something to get excited over.

Nev mentioned shifting baselines – full name 'shifting baseline syndrome' – which is an interesting concept. It's defined as 'a gradual change in the accepted norms for the condition of the natural environment due to a lack of experience, memory and/or knowledge of its past condition'. It means that whatever the conditions are like when we're young, we accept as normal. This is the 'baseline' against which we measure any future changes in wildlife or the environment – be they declines or increases. If we've no understanding of what came before our own memory, or that of our parents or grandparents, then it's difficult for us to conceptualise what things might've looked like, what 'normal' might've been in the past. We see this quite a lot in data from the conservation sector: declines in bird numbers are often measured against an arbitrary date – generally when modern recording efforts and standardised surveys began. For example, the website of the British Trust for Ornithology tells us that 'since the early 1980s, Cuckoo numbers have dropped by 65 per cent'. But what about before that point? What if the numbers of Cuckoos in the early 1980s were already severely depleted?

Lee Ray, author of *The Atlas of Early Modern Wildlife*, has looked into this in detail. Trawling through archives and compiling observations from all sorts of people, they have managed to paint a picture of some species' abundance and distribution as far back as the 1600s. The archives Lee used tell tales of White-tailed Sea Eagles occupying the skies around the coasts of Britain and Ireland, and one account describes a mass beaching of Orca in Northumberland. This record, dating back to 1734, tells of a pod of 60 'grampus' (a brilliant old word for Orca and big fish) grounding themselves – a number that's greater than the total number of Orca thought to be swimming in British and Irish waters today.

LOVE IS A TOAD

It's hard to imagine the abundance Lee's research outlines. The species recorded tend to involve the big and snazzy species, creatures people notice (or that people dislike, or like to eat) like Orca, Wild Boar and Wolves. They did look at species relevant to people's daily lives – like fish stocks and some wild plants. But I can't help but be curious about the everyday 'mundane' wildlife, the stuff in the background. Can you imagine what the wildflowers looked like in 1734? And the numbers of the invertebrates that crawled and buzzed along them?

Our imagination, or lack of it, is important when it comes to picturing and comprehending the scale of this loss. Nev began to tell me of a lad he used to play with when he was growing up, during the Second World War, who was a few years older than him. He remembered chatting with this friend at a time when food was rationed, who told Nev he had it easy. Nev had no idea what ice cream was and had never tasted bananas or pineapples. His friend had eaten them all before the war and had then witnessed them disappear, whilst Nev hadn't understood there was a 'before'. He told me he believes many of us think about wildlife in the same way.

Whilst I can rationally understand the concept of 'before', and I can read historical records and anecdotes that tell me about the abundance of species in the past, I find it quite difficult to comprehend. It's like my brain can't form the picture, as though I'm trying to clutch and grasp at something as intangible as smoke. The reality is that we live in an era of normalised depletion. We're all likely to be experiencing shifting baseline syndrome and so we all struggle to fully appreciate what's missing.

PINCUSHION OF OPPORTUNITY

That, for me, is part of the sensation of loss too. I grieve the things I've seen disappear over my lifetime; I walk around my home and the places I know well, and remember instances of destruction, encroachment, displacement. But then I also feel the loss of the things I never saw. And I find myself fantasising about them, struggling to imagine them. Picturing in my mind orchards full of anthills, their occupants gobbled by Wrynecks with their wonderfully bizarre tongues. I imagine shoals of fish so colossal you'd tire before you swam the length of them. I think of tangled, wet, temperate rainforests with trees older than castles and Nightingales blasting from bushes in every town centre. There's an alternative reality there and I can almost see it. I can almost taste it.

The sadness of what we'd been talking of seemed to cling to the dampness in the air. We needed something nice to think about, and quick. As if on cue, we were treated to a backing track of a Cettis' song, belting out from the reeds behind us. The muggy air held warmth in its humidity and the insect life around us was still busy. A rustling crackled through the sky directly above our heads, sounding a bit like static. The crispy, crunchy sounds were coming from dragonflies, massive Southern Hawkers adorned with black, sky-blue and lime-green splodges. We followed one on its zipping, circular patrol around the clearing, watching it change its trajectory at an almost imperceptible speed.

Early autumn is the best time to see dragons, in my opinion. In summer, they're way too speedy to properly appreciate. Their little back muscles are warmed by sunshine and they're always on the hunt, wings a blur. As the coolness of autumn takes hold, they tend to chill out a bit more with a slightly lazier flight, a few more rest stops. The hawkers pause to perch more often, so you can get a proper gander at their patterned tails and beady eyes. And the darters, they suddenly seem fearless. Hold out an outstretched hand and they'll quite often land on you, seeming to grasp it gratefully as though you're gifting a bit of relief for their busy wings.

The hawker we watched snapped at something invisible in the air, a tiny meal perhaps, and then proceeded to divebomb the Alder beside us. It homed in on some more prey, pursuing it with fury and focus, almost loop-de-looping in the high-speed chase of some unidentifiable insect. Another snap, something gobbled and then the dragon soared away through an arch of a thorn-adorned stem. And from that stem protruded a rather bizarre tuft. Bright pinkish-red, the colour of radishes, it splayed outwards in a mad, frazzled way. It appeared distinctly thorny with lots of shaggy-looking barbs, sort of resembling a spiky pom-pom.

'I just love this plant – Dog Rose – because it looks beautiful!' Nev exclaimed.

It does look beautiful. I love Dog Rose's fabulous claw-like thorns, embellishing the stems like sharks' fins. I love their flowers too – pale pink and not too garish. Though they'd all gone by now and vivid red rosehips were growing in their place. Nev's attention then turned to the bright red tuft.

'But then this gall is even more beauty on top! It's one of those aesthetic things; it's a pleasurable thing to me. Just to know its name – a Robin's Pincushion. Brilliant!' Nev reached over from his spot on the bench and fondled the tuft, petting it like a little creature. It yielded to his touch; it didn't look sharp or spiky at all. His face seemed thoughtful as he stroked the scarlet clump. 'The world is in a teaspoon, isn't it? Almost the entire life of a universe is in a plant gall.'

Nev spoke slowly and with emphasis. It felt like wonder oozed from his every word.

The Pincushion of Opportunity

I'm going to take a moment here to tell you a little bit about Robin's pincushions. If you haven't seen one before, it's as I described; a bright red bristly growth you find on different wild roses, like the Dog Rose and other species like Sweet Briar. Look closely at one and you'll see what a tangled explosion of loveliness it is. Dense, hairy barbs in a delicious combination of lime green, cherry red and raspberry pink. The colours of lollipops and slushies full of e-numbers. Give one a tentative squeeze and you'll feel it gives in to your probing fingers; they're surprisingly spongey and squidgy, despite their prickly and fearsome appearance.

The Robin's pincushion gets its lovely name not from the bird but from the folklore surrounding Robin Goodfellow, a fairy or imp of the woods. Its other name, the Bedeguar, means 'windblown'. I suppose it does look a little like a tumbleweed.

Robin's pincushion is a type of gall, this being an unusual swelling or growth on a plant. It could be on its stem, twigs, leaves, flowers or roots. Galls are caused by an interaction between a plant and another organism, which stimulates the plant in a way that causes it to distort abnormally. These other organisms can be invertebrates (like aphids, mites

LOVE IS A TOAD

and flies), or they could be fungi or bacteria. In the case of the Robin's pincushion, it's a wasp – Diplolepis rosae. *But* Diplolepis rosae *isn't your typical wasp. They don't try to pinch your ice cream, nor do they wear black and yellow stripes. They're absolutely tiny, only a few millimetres long. You'd barely notice one.*

The female wasp will locate a wild rose and proceed to lay her eggs inside the leaf buds, using an ovipositor (egg depositor) thinner than hair. Here, some kind of invertebrean magic takes place (OK, maybe it's chemistry) that causes a wonderful distortion to occur, resulting in a growth like the one Nev and I were looking at. The wasp (and her magic) basically forces the plant to do her bidding; it will deform and grow around her eggs, producing these fuzzy, fabulous pom-poms – a safe place for her young to grow and eat. If you were to split one open, you'd find up to 60 little chambers inside, each with a tiny wasp larva munching away upon the gall material. But that's not all you'd be likely to find.

Here's where it gets super grim, super nerdy and extra-complex. Buckle up, this is about to get as complicated as the little old lady who swallowed a fly. You see, by laying her eggs and so forming this gall, Diplolepis rosae has inadvertently created not only a Robin's pincushion but a pincushion of opportunity. The pincushion is both a safe structure and a good food source; it's formed of plant material that the young wasp grubs like to feed on and that protects them from predators like birds at the same time. But it's not just D. rosae *that wants to take advantage of these features, oh no. Those neatly parcelled little grubs – whilst relatively safe from avian predators – are a temptation for*

PINCUSHION OF OPPORTUNITY

other species and the nutritious gall material is an attractive resource too. And so, in this pincushion of opportunity, a tangled web of lives has evolved to interact, collide and exploit one another.

First up, there are some sneaky insects that like to exploit all of that jazzy, free plant material. Other species of wasps (things like Periclistus brandtii*) will come along after the gall has formed and deposit their eggs in its fuzzy tissues. Here, their larvae will hatch, munch on the gall for themselves and form their own separate chambers.* P. brandtii *is totally reliant on the existence of the galls in order to complete their life cycle. Species that exploit galls (or other things, like nests) in this way are referred to as inquilines – it comes from the Latin for 'tenant' or 'lodger'.*

*So now our gall has two species of wasp living inside it: the original gall-causing species (*D. rosae*) and a relatively harmless lodger (*P. brandtii*), who came along afterwards. So far, so simple. But that's not the end of this story. Because at this point, a whole other bunch of wasps comes in. Some of them, like little* Eurytoma rosae, *are predators. They will hatch from an egg laid inside the gall and begin a crusade of consumption. This species targets inquilines like* P. brandtii, *moving from one chamber to the next, gobbling up each larva.*

Then, we've got the parasites. There are ichneumon wasps, species like Orthopelma mediator, *known rather wonderfully as 'Bedeguar Botherer', and emerald-green chalcid wasps like* Torymus bedeguaris. *These focus specifically on* D. rosae, *laying their eggs directly into the larvae of the gall wasp, which will hatch and consume the young from the inside out. Other species, like* Glyphomerus stigma, *are a little less fussy and will parasitise both* D. rosae *and* P. brandtii. *Told you it was grim.*

But we're still not finished. The chain of complexity continues because even more parasites are involved. You see, the parasites have parasites themselves. Yet more species of wasps, things like Pteromalus bedeguaris *and* Caenacis inflexa, *can be 'hyperparasites' of the parasites, meaning they'll lay their eggs into* O. mediator, T. bedeguaris *or* G. stigma.

The bottom line is this: a plant is parasitised by a wasp, that wasp is then parasitised by another wasp, which is then parasitised by yet another wasp. And as if that's not enough, the 'pincushion of opportunity' can be taken advantage of by birds, who peck open the galls for a tasty snack, or – to add even more parasitism to the mix – it can be infected by a parasitic fungus called Phragmidium subcorticum. *This is a story of niches, of relationships, of opportunity and of complexity – an infinitely complicated tangle of life forms, all interacting right under our noses.*

Nev turned back to me, away from the pincushion. 'When I see things like this, I think of that old poem.' He paused, I assume for dramatic effect, before launching into a short bit of verse.

Big fleas have little fleas,
upon their backs to bite them.
And little fleas have littler fleas,
and so ad infinitum!

PINCUSHION OF OPPORTUNITY

He finished with a flourish, his lovely grin taking up most of his face. I'd never heard it before and thought it was a brilliant observation of the situation in front of us, and of nature's wonderful intricacy in general.

'I always say with nature, the more you learn about it, the more you realise you don't know. Your ignorance grows at a faster rate than your knowledge. And however fast your knowledge grows, your ignorance is ahead of it, all the time!'

Nev laughed.

That's exactly it. The more you look at nature, the more you witness. The more you witness, the more you learn. And the more you learn, the more you realise how much you've still got left to know, and how infinitesimal your knowledge really is.

I used to think that was scary. When I felt the pressure to become a 'proper naturalist' (whatever that is), I felt as though I had to learn as much as possible. I thought I had to know all of the scientific names, to be able to identify all the moths, all the wildflowers, all the birds and to know how they were connected. I've since realised that's a load of bollocks. I now see my obliviousness as an opportunity. It's something wonderfully humbling, and it's exciting. I find it reassuring to know that it's impossible to know everything, for any of us to ace the test. And it's so exciting to know that nature will always yield gifts and surprises when you let her.

Nothing in nature is simple. She's layered, she's nuanced, she's busy. And it seems as though nature likes being complicated. Be it the structural complexity of a feather or the socially intricate courtship ritual of Great Crested Grebes, we have endless examples of evolution's tendency to make things complicated over time. And each time I get to witness one of these things, to observe it and then understand it, I feel it zip through my neurons and blow my mind before I tuck it away like a treasure to be remembered later.

After talking to Nev, I could now see how this complexity is the exact opposite of the simplicity we see in a landscape of loss. Where there's complexity in an environment, life flourishes. Where nature can expand, build layers, connections and depth, she's at her strongest. Where there's complexity, there's opportunity.

I loved chatting with Nev about this sort of stuff. When he gushed about wildlife, his eyes twinkled with glee and his enthusiasm was contagious. 'You're never bored with nature! When somebody shows you something, like this gall, it's a gift of communication, isn't it?'

He was right. I too consider people's stories to be a gift. When somebody shows me something in nature – a flower, a critter or anything, really – and when they jumble a few words together to tell me about its name or its behaviour, or simply to compliment it, it's better than any material gift in the world. And we're lucky enough to live in a world full of intricate, beautiful, complex life. We'll never run out of stories to share. Isn't that fantastic?

'I always try to see the best in people,' said Nev, 'and offer love to the planet, to nature. All you can do is strive and work for a better world where people care for each other, care for other life and are loving. And if you do that, it will repay you, over and over again with joy.'

Nev breaks my heart. We smiled, full of that joy and a bit teary-eyed too. Our bellies rumbled and we both were in need of a brew. Just as we went to stand up, a man in some rather jazzy sunglasses bounded around the corner, emerging from the reed beds at a good pace.

'You know, it's so surprising how sound travels. I can hear you two laughing right up at the top,' he said, gesturing to the hill behind him.

Nev responded as quick as a dragonfly's snap, 'Sir, that's because my stories are so humorous!'

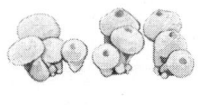

CHAPTER 6

The Granny Pine

Comprehension | Guilt

CHARLIE BELL
Braemar, Aberdeenshire – 1 October

The tiny, twirling, lime-green sausage was nearly up my left nostril before I noticed it. Suspended from something invisible, it spun around awkwardly as it dangled, looking like a bungee jumper post-jump, waiting to be hoiked up or cut loose. My clunky boots dug into the earth as I skidded to a halt, my eyes crossing in an ache as I tried to focus on the floating little wiener. A dinky caterpillar! Hanging from a silk thread finer than hair. The thread was so delicate, I wasn't entirely sure I *could* see it – only a subtle, silvery glint gave it away. The caterpillar's tiny, sucker-like legs flailed slowly as it swung and bobbed, levitating just inches away from my nose. I laughed and tried to show it to Charlie, who struggled at first to follow the direction of my finger as I seemingly pointed at nothing.

'Oh! Another one!' Charlie had spied her own little dangler in front of her. 'Ooh, and another!'

LOVE IS A TOAD

We'd suddenly found ourselves besieged by minuscule and seemingly floating caterpillars. Hanging at different heights – some above our heads, some at our hips, some at the perfect eyeball level for ogling – they punctuated the air all around us. One made it into Charlie's hair and I found another dangling from my glasses. It was like walking into a massive, harmless boobytrap. Charlie laughed as the heavily caterpillared situation became apparent. It was brilliant.

I'd seen caterpillars hanging from a thread before – hairy ones, brownish ones, bright green ones – but always on their own. I'd read about them in a state of nosiness, wondering why and how they ended up bungeeing from the treetops. It came down to two possibilities. The first was 'ballooning', a fantastic term for a process that has evolved to aid dispersal. The caterpillars of some moth species suspend themselves from incredibly fine silk threads and wait for a firm gust to come along and carry them away to a new food source. Very clever. Spiders do something similar, sticking their bum into the air and spraying silk threads upwards until they're whisked away on the breeze. It's ace to watch.

The second possibility is literally a form of lepidopteran abseiling – except it's motivated by impending danger rather than thrill-seeking. When faced with a predator in the canopy, some caterpillars are known to throw themselves from the foliage, hanging from a silken cord until the danger has passed, before returning to safety. I pondered which of these factors might have been the motivation in this instance as we watched them dangle. Of course, we'd probably never know. But whatever caused us to be plastered by caterpillars that day, I could understand it was something *awesome*.

THE GRANNY PINE

We ducked and dodged the peppering of 'pillars, and as we slunk away, I spied one stranded in a web of silk from another source. A small spider tinkered away, wrapping up a juicy green-sausage burrito. What a treat.

Woody fingers of Blaeberry prodded our trousers as we meandered down a narrow track and I couldn't help but think about the possibility of bloodthirsty residents dwelling amongst the foliage. I asked Charlie if she'd been unlucky enough to find many ticks recently.

'Um, I haven't found any. But then I haven't really been naked. So there could be lots!' She laughed as she ambled, pants tucked into socks, denying any potential latchers the chance to access so much as a centimetre of skin.

Charlie Bell is a human of loveliness. She's gentle and soft, quiet at first, but you soon encounter a sense of humour that sizzles. She walks and swims and scales mountains with pickaxes, and her eyes glimmer with wit when she pokes fun at you. She's just thoroughly pleasant to be around. I'd first met her several years earlier over a tray full of soil and snails. She'd been working for the Field Studies Council and I'd been an enthusiastic attendee of a subsidised mollusc identification course. We'd bonded over slimy-formed creatures and became friends afterwards.

After escaping the caterpillar boobytrap, she ambled ahead of me, her reddish hair protruding from her bobble hat. It was overcast and cool – the first day of October and autumn had already taken a firm grasp of the month with chilly fingers. The skinny path we took that morning drew us into the woods, pulling us between towering pines and away from the road. Gravity tugged at us as we wound down a

LOVE IS A TOAD

steep slope, the track under our feet formed from the spongey earth you tend to find in pine forests. The otherwise heavy thuds of our boots were dulled, kind of like the *whumph* of a feather pillow when you thump it. Lui Water, a tributary of the Dee, tumbled and gurgled alongside us. The river felt alive – it was swollen and unrelenting, thundering with the weight of recent rain that had poured from the hills, so that the noise filled our ears, a cacophony from all angles. Strewn in the flow were weather-bleached skeletons of dead trees, their worn forms no doubt providing precious shelter for wide-eyed young salmon.

'I brought you somewhere I know very little about – but I know it makes me feel good!' Charlie gestured to the river, carving through the lush pine forest around us. 'When I come here, it feels like the ecosystem is whole, and healthy, and right. It just feels *right*. And that makes me feel better as well.'

I looked at the forest around us and saw what she meant. There was just so much going on here. I felt like a kid in a sweet shop – my eyes pulled in every direction by wild goodies and treats. Shapes and forms filled the space, towering and stretching everywhere. Plants – both dead and alive – interacted in tangles and clashes; there were layers in both depth and structure. It was wonderfully complicated.

The Cairngorms are a place Charlie treasures and she had very kindly let me gatecrash a holiday with her partner. I'd met her in the village of Braemar for a wander in the woods of the Mar Lodge estate. Later on, Dave, Charlie's partner, was to join us and I'd assume my position as the nerdy third wheel for an evening of camping.

As we walked, I took deep, chest-filling sniffs, drawing

THE GRANNY PINE

the resinous scent of pine into my lungs and savouring the richness of it. The delicious smell emanated specifically from one of my favourite trees: hundreds of Scots Pines surrounded us, gorgeous in form, fieriness and fragrance. Pines (and conifers generally) are a funny one. I feel like for lots of us, our relationship with these hardy trees is distant and confused. We are familiar with rigidly organised plantations, the sort we see blanketing uplands, or out of the window on trains or motorways. These are places of straight lines, rows and neatness. Planted banks of Corsican Pine, Sitka Spruce or Larch, as orderly and square as a spreadsheet, and as gloomy as a damp cellar. Plantations are places of industry, they are commercialised forests, grown to feed an insatiable appetite for cheap timber. They might be casually labelled as woodland – we might even give them 'forest' in their name – but in the trees' uniformity of girth and height the life force of proper woodland is missing. There's no thrum, no buzz, no pulse.

But we do have some brilliant native conifers. There are three species you'll come across growing naturally in Britain, all of them characterful and beautiful. Juniper: a small and tough shrub adorned with cones that resemble dusty blue berries, emitting a sigh-worthy fragrance of black pepper and spice and gin. Then there's Yew, the thick and heavily needled trees that seem to defy time, living for millennia and entwined with tales of death and mortality. And, of course, there's Scots Pine, the builders and makers of Caledonian pine forests. As they age, Scots Pines redden, and the cool, dark base of their trunks melds into copper-coloured bark as your eye travels upwards, seeming to ignite the tree in a rusty hue.

LOVE IS A TOAD

The woodland Charlie had taken me to was composed of them in all sorts of shapes and sizes, dotted between Junipers and deciduous trees like Birch, Aspen and Rowan. Reaching the peak of a path wiggle, Charlie and I naturally paused, and I took a moment to absorb the scene in front of us. The sloped bank on the opposite side of the river trailed upwards, the varied trees and their foliage creating an abstract canvas of colour. It was chaotic and beautiful; the needle-green of the pines was interspersed with shivering splashes of warmer autumnal hues. Close to us, Birch leaves beamed in wax-crayon yellow, contrasting with the trunk's parchment bark and set against the blue sky above. One of the best colour combos of autumn, I reckon. Then, daubed sporadically in the fore and background, were sprays of the fieriest orange Rowan leaves. I love the colour of Rowans in autumn; there's a subtle blush to them, reminding me oddly of pink grapefruit. Best of all were the Aspens. As we stood, a breeze rustled its way downstream and the air filled with the excited whispering of their leaves. A few stands of these beautiful trees surrounded us, their foliage mottled with splodges of greens and browns amongst the warmest yellow. I bent down, plucked a fallen leaf from the ground and held it up against the sky. Its silhouette reminded me of a crab's carapace – symmetrical and wiggly-edged with a pointy tip, where the crab's face would go. This one was particularly splodgy: a yellow background with big brown freckles. The veins of the leaf were still lit up in the green of summer; it looked a bit like a photo taken with a thermal camera. And its stem was very flat, meaning it wiggled and fluttered energetically in even the lightest breeze. I looked

THE GRANNY PINE

up to see thousands of them doing the same on the quivering trees we stood amongst. Aspen has been given the nicknames of 'trembling' or 'quaking' Aspen – I could see why.

The trees became sparser as the valley opened up. We stared into the distance, down the Linn of Dee, the wiggling river framed by an apathetic shrug of mountains. Their curves, rising quickly from the flattened belly of the glen, were fluid and smooth. A little bit *too* smooth. Whilst this undulating upland landscape was undoubtedly beautiful, it didn't feel quite right. We looked at its rolls and lolloping arcs of browns and burnt maroons, soon to be streaked in ice and snow as autumn turned to winter. It had plenty of shape, sure. But the shape was lacking in texture. The vegetation on much of the slopes seemed only to be of heather height or below. There were very few trees. No Juniper, no Aspen, no Scots Pines.

'I've been visiting Scotland for as long as I can remember,' Charlie said as we wandered out into the open, crossing a bridge over the Dee. 'And as soon as you know what the hills are meant to look like, that's it. You can't unknow or unsee these things. You realise that the moors and the uplands aren't really meant to look the way they do. Like they do way up there.' She waved a hand, gesturing to the smooth glen ahead of us. It felt bare, a bit like a dog's belly that's been shaved before an operation.

It was quite a stark contrast. Behind us stretched Glen Lui. Dotted throughout the standard heather cover were lots of young trees. Baby Birch saplings of ankle, knee and hip height, their jagged-toothed leaves bringing shagginess and coarseness to the scene. Teenage Scots Pines with slender stems like skinny jeans and only a hint of that auburn bark starting to crackle upon their young trunks loitered all around.

When things feel this different, there's usually a reason behind it. Charlie said she thought deer numbers had been reduced on the estate, and so I looked into it. They had – at least, in some parts. It turned out that the two contrasting scenes we could see represented two different approaches to deer management. In one part of the estate, where shooters can pay to go deer stalking, the numbers of deer are allowed to be higher. More deer means a higher chance of a successful stalk, and if you're paying to stalk a deer, you want to get your money's worth. Another part of the estate, the messy, shaggy zone behind us, had a long-standing plan to bring down deer numbers. Since 1995, deer density had been reduced significantly in an effort to encourage the regeneration of Caledonian pine forest.

Deer are undoubtedly beautiful creatures. Sleek and mysterious, they used to seem to me almost mythical, a truffle-coloured shadow you see out of the corner of your eye, a rarely glimpsed wild beast of wild places. But their numbers have soared since I was a kid and I now see them very regularly. By their very nature, deer are munchers. Their soft, nimble lips make light work of anything they deem tasty – including the foliage of saplings. Over on the bare hills ahead of us, where there were a lot of them, that nibbling pressure had added up. So many teeth over so many years had played a game of whack-a-mole: every time a sapling pops up, it's gobbled. There were some trees on the slopes, of course, but they were all huge. Old and gnarled individuals, too big and too old to be affected by the chombling lips of Red Deer.

THE GRANNY PINE

They stood isolated and lonely in swathes of heather – no younger trees coming up to take their place, no new generation. The slope behind us, i.e. the low-deer zone, showed the impact of reducing that nibbling pressure. The Birch and Scots Pine saplings had managed to sprout and grow successfully without being munched to oblivion. The landscape was starting to get that sense of structure created by diverse medley of individuals, an assortment of ages from 'just out of the pine cone' to towering old veterans. It was so exciting to see.

The path led us over a time-smoothed wooden bridge across the Dee, its planks bleached and worn by successive floods, storms and winds. Next to the river it was considerably squelchier underfoot. Puddles of bog hugged the side of the path, threatening in some places to overtake it entirely. In these pools, the brightness of Sphagnum mosses shone green in the greyness of the day, bright and reminiscent of fresh things like limes and Granny Smith apples.

Charlie ushered me along, winding through thick stands of young Birch and hopping over puddles, clearly excited to show me something. 'Here we go!' she said, guiding me around a corner and gesturing ahead of us. 'Shall we go and see if we can meet her?'

Oh my lordy. The 'her' Charlie was referring to was a frankly colossal tree, a towering Scots Pine. A proper elder, an old and gnarled Granny Pine. She was a beast of beauty. She sprawled and reached, like the first stretch after a particularly satisfying sleep. Her skin was fissured and wrinkly with deep ravines raked into her flaky bark from base to canopy. She was the colour of cocoa dust and sun-baked mud, flecked with daubs of pale mint where lichens clung to her body.

LOVE IS A TOAD

Her splayed awning of dark, shiny needles explained the delectable scent of pine saturating the air. There was just *so much* going on.

I shuffled up to her trunk and leant in for a hug, wrapping my arms around her as if she was my own nana. Charlie joined me, her face resting nose-to-trunk as she stretched her arms around the granny's massive girth, admiring the rough, chocolate flakes of her bark with a hint of cross-eye. She explained how much she loves observing things on a micro scale, zooming in on the little world in front of her. Here she could observe other life, growing and scuttling and completely oblivious to anything else.

I zoomed in too. She was right: the bark of the granny was absolutely plastered with life. It was a perfect example of delving into that complexity I discussed with Nev; the more you looked, the more you saw. Up close, those pale green splodges revealed multiple species of lichens, some fuzzy, some lobed, and some flat and spreading as if buttered on thickly with a chunky knife. Between the fissures and cracks, life scurried and scuttled. Even in October, spiders sat waiting for an opportune snack and queues of Wood Ants streamed in different directions.

I zoomed back out and craned my neck to peer up into the granny's upper branches. As my eyes worked their way upwards, I could make out a shift in colour, a gentle gradient changing with height. It was that reddish hue Scots Pines gain with age, the cool grey-brown of the lower trunk thawing into bark the colour of rust. I pointed out the copper hue to Charlie with an admiring finger.

'Ooh, ooh, I realised a thing recently! Red Squirrels!'

THE GRANNY PINE

Charlie's eyes were wide and excited. 'Until you come somewhere like this, you don't realise why they're red. But then you see the colour of Scots Pines' bark and they're *exactly* the same shade of ginger as Red Squirrels!'

It seemed so obvious, but I'd never thought about it before. It was a fizzing moment of comprehension, an ecological joining of the dots. Simple dots, yes, but two I'd never scribbled a line between previously.

This sort of moment is something that's happened to me time and time again since nature started scuttling and wriggling into my soul. Mix together a curiosity and love for nature with pieces of information gifted from others and you get those *'ah-ha'* moments of understanding. It happens when you learn how two things interact with each other. Like how Blue Tits time their egg-laying so that the hatching coincides with a peak in caterpillar numbers, which in turn have synchronised their emergence with the budding of tasty spring leaves. It occurs when you understand why something is like it is. The way a Crossbill's beak overlaps wonkily, looking like crossed fingers, to enable them to perfectly prise apart pine cones.

Whilst I was still gazing up at the canopy above, Charlie's attention had redirected, her nose nudging even closer to the granny's waist. I snapped my eyes down to her viewpoint and saw she was watching the progress of the Wood Ants, streams of them trundling up and down the bark in orderly traffic. Charlie was enthralled by the busyness in front of her and I couldn't help but be drawn into it.

Wood Ants are proper ants. Rusty red, with a bulbous, chocolate-brown bum, they're quite attractive creatures and they're never not busy. Looking down at our feet, we saw that the floor flickered with their activity; every other ant seemed to be hauling something along – a woodlouse, a bit of bark, a pine needle. Two were even struggling with the corpse of a wasp between them. Just off to the side of the Granny Pine, the earth rose into a distinct swelling: a hummock with a rounded, smoothed silhouette, like a tea towel draped over a lump of moist dough. It was coated in needles in a sort of chaotic thatch and it glittered with even more ant intensity than the ground. This was the Wood Ants' nest, and we traced the line of traffic from the trunk all the way to its busy slopes.

'You know, I went on an ant course . . .' Charlie began. How delightfully nerdy; of course she did. 'And something the teacher told us blew my mind. Again, it's one of those obvious things, but he said that with ants, you almost can't think of them as individuals; a colony is like a super organism that operates with individual pieces. None of it works without all of those little parts, even though I can see each individual.' She raised her fingers to her head and mimed her mind being blown in a 'kaboom' sort of motion. 'I love trying to wrap my head around things like that!'

Charlie continued her gushing, telling me more about the rumbling little critters in front of us, reminding me of a bit of scientific fun.

An amazing thing about Wood Ants is that they can effectively squirt vinegar from their bums. Well, it's not technically vinegar, it's formic acid – which explains their family name of *Formica*. It's not technically their bum, either, rather a special type of orifice found in Wood Ants called their

THE GRANNY PINE

'acidopore' (love it). This vinegary-ness is a form of defence: when riled or threatened, they'll tuck their bums under their bodies, aim it forwards between their legs, and spray the threat with acid. It's an incredible (and slightly obscene) thing to see – mini spurts of liquid erupting from a needle-thatched mount, illuminated by sunshine. It's also an incredible thing to smell. Wave your hand over a bunch of angry Wood Ants and give your fingers a sniff – you'll be immediately transported to the chippy. I'm not the only one who appreciates it, either. Plenty of birds actively bathe in the stuff, stimulating the ants and their bum spray by sitting on anthills. Some theories suggest it's to help them groom or stimulate feather growth. Some say they do it to help rid themselves of parasites. Other folks have theorised it's simply because they like it – a form of self-stimulation that brings them pleasure. I quite like the idea of that last one. Charlie explained that the level of acidity they produce is enough to change the colour of litmus paper if it's waved above them. I'd never heard of this but the nerd in me definitely wants to try it.

Charlie's also got that nerdy streak when it comes to wildlife. She stood close to the granny, eyeballing the couple of ants that were wrestling with a wasp. 'I love knowing what species something is. It's geekery at its best, isn't it? But sometimes I think you just have to be like, "This is just a thing, and it's amazing." I don't need to name it; I don't have to look at it with a scientific eye.'

The duo carrying the wasp had got themselves properly organised by now and were efficiently lugging their prize towards the foot of the huge pine.

'I'm not saying we don't want scientific knowledge, because

LOVE IS A TOAD

we absolutely do, but sometimes you just have to think, *I'm just going to enjoy this moment – I can comprehend how beautiful it is without having to know its name and everything about it.*'

I love a bit of nerdery, with a good, thick dollop of geekery on top. Looking at the detail of something, letting that nosiness ooze and soaking up all of the information that emerges when you start prodding and asking questions. But it wasn't always this way. When I got my first job in conservation, at the age of 22, I didn't know the difference between a Blue Tit and a Great Tit. In fact, I'm pretty sure I thought they were called *Grey* Tits. In my interview, I was asked questions about Pied Flycatchers, Redstarts and Wood Warblers. I blinked – my best impression of a deer in headlights – and panicked. I worked in a shoe shop; I didn't even know the difference between common garden birds, let alone rare migrants of ancient Oak woodland. I bumbled through the rest of the meeting, masking my fear with enthusiasm, then I shook the managers' hands and left. Tears trickled on the way home, my cheeks burning with embarrassment.

A week later, as I was making my way through a delivery of clumpy school shoes, my phone rang. Hiding behind the bins on the roof, I struggled to understand the words at the other end. I had gotten the job. Through pure luck, mind – one candidate hadn't turned up and another had dropped out. It was either me or start the process again. And so I was given a chance and plunged into the deep end.

Ten months passed in a whirlwind of birdiness and nerdiness. I figured out you can use binoculars without seeing

THE GRANNY PINE

big, black splotches or your own blurry eyelashes. I saw for the first time birds I'd never even heard of. Wonderfully named species like Willow Warblers, Lesser Whitethroats, Grey Wagtails and Goshawks became part of my vernacular. One morning, in late April, I crouched by a gate in the heart of the wooded valley. You know those sorts of mornings, when spring's simmering and really starting to rumble? Life in the woods was busy – movement in every Bramble bush and birdsong clattering from the treetops. The Oak leaves were in the midst of sprouting in the canopy above, little tufts of lime-green lobes still soft and tender. It was the morning I saw my first ever Pied Flycatcher. A member of the aforementioned *'I've-never-heard-of-that-before'* club. I'd seen pictures of them in the visitor centre – beautifully two-tone, almost chubby-looking, with beady, dark eyes. Now, a male sat in front of me, perched upon a bony limb of a fallen tree. He sat and sang, and I marvelled at his smartness. Who knew all small birds weren't plain and brown?!

Discovering the wildlife was fascinating and bizarre; it was shiny and new, something wonderfully unfamiliar. But even more alien were the people. Naturalists – proper ones – seemed to belong to a genus all of their own. The birdwatchers used words like 'twitch', 'mega' and 'dipping', and they seemed to carry scopes with them wherever they went. Botanists conversed about plants almost entirely in Latin. I met one adorable elderly couple who specialised in hoverflies and wore matching sweaters. In this job, I encountered British natural history in all of its quirkiness, stiffness and competitiveness. A lot of these folks were wonderful and warm, taking me under their wings and gifting me their time and enthusiasm

– people like Nev. They patiently explained why the 'Kestrel' I'd seen was actually a Buzzard and they let me come in early and go with them to open the moth trap.

I love that there are people with such passions and fixations, who've asked all of the scientific questions and found the answers. People who've spent hours watching the feeding behaviours of Blue Tits, counting the number of caterpillars they bring to their young. People who've measured the length of beetles' elytra in fractions of millimetres or who've figured out that some lichens turn blue or violet when you pipette a bit of iodine on to them. There are people who've specialised in drawing the genitalia of micro-moths, for god's sake.

Comprehension of nature through the lens of science is great. It's how I met Charlie after all, back when I attended courses that involved counting the dimples on a mining bee's back (impossible) or comparing the caudal lamellae of damselfly larvae (don't ask). It's a type of learning about nature I've got loads of value from: I'm a champion Google-trawler and I adore my mini library of identification guides full of nerdy diagrams and keys. It's important, undoubtedly, but, as Charlie said, it's not the only way. And this type of learning doesn't feel like it's a main component of my love for nature or nature joy. A scientific relationship with nature tends to be a rather structured, rigid one; there's little room for softness, spontaneity or silliness, just as Amy had said to me.

In recent history, Western science has been worshipped as a superior form of understanding and learning; it's held in a higher regard than other types of knowledge. We tend to have this binary thinking that tells us 'scientific knowledge = good' and other ways of understanding the world around us are wrong or meaningless. But that's simply not true.

Scientific learning is simply one option, one tool amidst a whole toolbox of things we can use when we're learning about the natural world. Other items in that toolbox – things like art, spirituality, creative expression, storytelling – are all equally useful. These types of learning have helped our species navigate life for eons, allowing us to pass vital information from generation to generation, tens of thousands of years before modern science was even a thing. We're fundamentally a storytelling species; we learn about the natural world in lots of different ways and then we parcel that information up and pass it along to our kith and kin. And I think that's quite magic.

When it comes to nature, I feel like the rigidity of sticking solely to scientific learning can detach us from our bodies. We're effectively big sensation machines (with lots of goopy bits), and we can experience and learn about nature in a deeply sensory way, far away from books and scientific journals.

Let's take a look at Sticky Weed – the giddiness-fuelling plant with a hundred local names. Sticky Willy, Sticky Bobs, Cleavers, Claggy Meggies – all brilliant. You see, at the age of five, before I knew anything about wildlife – before I'd studied it or read any books about it – I could've told you what Sticky Weed tastes like. I could have described what it feels like to touch, the texture of its rough leaves on your fingers. What the snag of its little hooks feels like against a prying tongue. I could have described the sensation of nipping a little seed pod between your fingernails and the fresh smell of greenness it leaves behind when you do. I knew the best hedgerow to find it on the walk to school, and what time of year you could expect to see it poking out into the sunshine. In particular, I could have explained that the best tactic is to wait until your mate has their back turned, then you can gently brush the plant against their school jumper without them realising, stifling giggles. I could have told you all of these things without knowing anything else about it – except that to a five-year-old, it's called Sticky Weed. This is the type of comprehension that really fuels my nature joy: the stuff we know beyond words, the stuff we feel in our nerves, on our skin, our tongues.

I think it'd do us good to try to channel a little more of this joy and I think it's something we'll naturally return to if we change the ways people live and work in our landscapes. In a future where land access is equitable, a relationship with nature becomes a given. If people can be outside, working with the landscape in a reciprocal way, of course we'll get to know the other living things in that landscape. The structured, formal study of natural history isn't for everyone, but the softness of a daily intimacy with nature could be.

Charlie and I leant over my phone, our grinning faces appearing on screen as we took an under-chin selfie beneath the boughs of the Granny Pine. We stepped out from under her shelter and stood back, taking her and her surroundings in. Once again, I had that sensation Charlie had described earlier of things 'just feeling right'. It was hard to put a finger on it, as slippery as a slug after heavy rain, but I think that feeling of 'right' is a sort of subconscious comprehension.

THE GRANNY PINE

It is to feel the health and functioning of the interconnected scene surrounding you, tapping into a backdrop of hustle and bustle in a landscape full of other life.

Our moment of admiration was interrupted by a subtle-but-sudden dimming of daylight. We both became aware of the impending, pulsating storm cloud at the same time. In the distance, way up the glen, a sheet of dark grey rain discharged from the sky like thick, weighty smoke. It was time to scarper. We left the Granny Pine to her slow, tree-paced life and trundled onwards, back towards the denser woodland ahead of us and hopefully at least a little bit of shelter. The bare, dog-bellied hill seemed to loom over us as we walked. It looked sore and uncomfortable, and it kept pulling at my attention, as if my mind was bound to it by a thread.

'You know, I grew up feeling like a part of nature and that intensified as I got older, to a point where it was almost visceral. But by getting to know it I started seeing how damaged things were and that almost physically affected me, like a punch.' Charlie gestured to her stomach. I knew exactly the sensation she was describing. Those writhing, squirming tummy knots, the sort that leave you feeling as though the wind's been thumped out of you.

'There was a period when I found it very hard to be outdoors,' Charlie continued. 'I almost actively started avoiding nature. I couldn't see it and I couldn't be in it without feeling that grief. Because everywhere you go, even here, there's so much evidence of how we're impacting it.'

I understood. When you come to know nature, you're able to read it like words on a page. And just like with reading, it's not about the individual words – i.e. identifying a single species – rather, it's the connections between those words and the meanings they reveal. To read nature is to see the links between all of the living things that make up an ecosystem, to understand how they relate to one another, how they interact, associate and function. It's incredible to feel nature in this way but once you're able to, it also opens your eyes to her plight. To know when an ecosystem is healthy and functioning is to also recognise when it isn't. The scars and damage in a landscape become obvious, the loss and absence palpable.

'Going out in nature started to feel like poking at an open wound all the time,' Charlie continued. 'I'd think things like, *If I just worked a little bit harder at work, or if I did something else for nature in my free time, maybe things would be better.* It was that little voice in your head telling you if you just tried a bit harder, these things wouldn't happen. I just felt so guilty, all the time.'

Charlie's words hung in the air as we trudged over moist, peaty earth. The guilt. She had hit the nail on the head. On the face of it, the damage to nature I was witnessing felt quite clearcut and easy to label. I could get angry about pesticides, about pollution, tree felling or hedge flailing. But if I examined my feelings about any of these things more closely, turning them over like stones and peering at what's underneath, I could see a different emotion there. In some kind of Scooby Doo-esque reveal, Charlie had helped me realise that if I lifted the mask on those feelings – of anger and upset – I'd find out that it was actually guilt all along.

Guilt, and its heavier sibling shame, have followed me around for a while. I've felt it for all sorts of reasons. Guilty that my species does these things. Guilt simply for being a human because humans do bad things. I've felt shameful that I've contributed personally to this big old mess. Shame for driving, for buying plastic, for daring to eat those delicious halloumi fries. I feel like I'm always carrying this duo – guilt and shame. Like two lead weights sitting somewhere within my ribcage, reminding me of their presence with a gnawing ache and knotted stomach.

Charlie nodded as I explained, agreeing with me. She told me how she'd got to the point where every decision, action or purchase she made felt wrong, leaving her in a state of paralysis. Whether she was standing in the supermarket, mentally calculating food miles, or trying to work out the carbon footprint of her drink in the pub, the relentless worry and guilt became overwhelming. I must admit, it was reassuring to know I'm not the only one who's sitting in a beer garden fretting about this sort of thing.

Charlie has been quite open with me in the past about how this mindset affected her mental health. It got to the point that she was suffering from panic attacks and periods of despair. During this time, guilt was an ever-present emotion and it contributed significantly to her burnout. I can see why. Guilt is incredibly powerful. It's got to be one of the heaviest emotions we experience, a weighty mix of remorse, self-judgement and criticism. It's something that lingers; it sits inside us and can bubble to the surface unexpectedly and suddenly, taking us by surprise like an abrupt rainstorm.

When I was little, and I mean really little, maybe four years old, I accidentally killed a butterfly. They were a white butterfly; I'm not sure of the species but they were enchanting. It was in

LOVE IS A TOAD

the early days of my butterfly-catching escapades. I'd sneaked up on them, hands ready to cup around their splayed wings as they perched upon a plant. In the very moment I lunged, they erupted into a fluttering flight and the enthusiastic clasp of my palms collided with their little body, as delicate as paper. I vividly remember opening my hands to the crumpled and lifeless being, mortified at my own clumsiness. I felt so, so guilty. A sick feeling squeezed my tummy and I cried as I understood what I'd done. Like I was part of some sort of U-rated crime show, I hurried to hide the butterfly's body amongst the foliage, tucking it away under the plants and vowing to keep my murderous ways a secret forever.

In hindsight, I can smile about it – a four-year-old feeling like a criminal because of a simple accident. But I thought about it regularly throughout my childhood, the guilt nibbling away inside me as though my chest was full of the butterfly's own ravenous caterpillars. I didn't intend to harm the butterfly, I didn't mean to be so clumsy, yet I caused their death all the same. It was hard not to feel as though I was simply inherently bad because I'd done a 'bad' thing.

Charlie seemed to experience nature guilt on a massive scale, feeling complicit and shameful about her own individual role in the plight of other living beings. I've felt these things too. Trying to comprehend the impact of my actions versus the scale of the problem starts to feel like forcing an old computer to download a file that's too big; my mind inevitably ends up whirring, freezing and crashing.

But is it any wonder we feel guilty when we're unwittingly absorbing messages that tell us we should do? There's a pervasive and widespread narrative in our media and in our culture when it comes to the nature and climate crisis. It's one that tells us we're inherently bad. I think many of us in the West operate constantly within this mindset of guilt and blame. We feel guilty for our own actions and impact, and we judge our friends, family and peers by theirs. We measure ourselves and each other against some non-existent environmental scorecard: he drives a car; she took three flights last year; they eat steak every night for tea. It means you're accused of hypocrisy if you dare to question the way things are, just because you currently use those things or benefit from them. It's a culture that breeds judgement, mistrust and elitism, and does nothing to fix the bigger problems at hand (in these cases, a car-reliant society, underregulated air travel and damaging farming practices).

This culture of blame, and its resulting guilt, is no accident. There's a reason why the 'solutions' to the nature crisis are so often targeted at the individual. If you and I feel like the burden of change is upon our shoulders, it acts as a smokescreen and hides the real culprits behind the climate and nature crises. You can see this most clearly in the use of collective language. Within narratives and conversations around environmental issues, there's a widespread use of the word 'we'. To use 'we' in the context of these crises (for example, 'we're destroying rainforests at an unprecedented rate', 'we're polluting all of our rivers') lumps all of us in together. It makes each of us responsible; it makes our guilt collective. But are we all equally guilty?

Not all of us belong to that 'we'. Dare I say it – most of us don't. Unless you're the CEO of an airline, a PR strategist for BP or a weapons manufacturer, I would bet that you have good intentions and that you would like to see the current way of the world changed. To use the term 'we' in reference to all of humanity is to negate the massive disparity of power and influence that exists across the world, and, with that, deny the massive disparity in the impact and damage caused by different groups of people. Indigenous peoples living in hunter-gatherer communities in a forest do not belong to the same 'we' as the companies wanting to mine lithium from under their feet. You and I do not belong to the same 'we' as the oil industry lobbyists spending (and earning) millions to convince governments not to act on climate change. But collective language is powerful and so is guilt. If you can convince people that all of these problems would be resolved if they only tried harder, went vegan, stopped mowing the lawn and turned off the tap when they brushed their teeth, then you can obscure the true perpetrators in these crises.

The reality is that individual solutions to such widespread, systemic problems aren't going to work; you can't heal a deep wound with lots of tiny disjointed sticking plasters. This isn't to make excuses – and nor am I suggesting we don't (or shouldn't) make individual efforts when it comes to environmental and nature issues. There are things within the control and influence of every one of us that we absolutely *must* do. Rather, we need to redirect the guilt we feel around these subjects.

We've been born into a culture that ingrains hierarchies, prejudices and judgement from the get-go; we live in a society built on the backs of colonised countries, one swollen and bloated by capitalism's insatiable consumption of resources, and we still carry all of the inequity, racism, exploitation and environmental harm caused by that. We can't control what's come before, nor do we have the power of large corporations or mountains of money – but we can control the things we do. We can choose to absorb our own mistakes and errors of judgement so that they become a part of us. We can carry them with us so that we learn from them and operate in a softer way. And we can identify who the real 'we' are and hold them to account, standing up to corporations, systems and individuals who are actually causing the harm and damage we detest so much.

I think again about that little white butterfly. That accident was a fleeting moment, a tiny event, but it will never not be a part of me. Yes, I felt bad for taking their life. But did it not teach me to be gentler? To value even the tiniest of lives? These are lessons I now carry, and it feels pertinent to the way we must learn and adapt and act going forward if we are to address these crises.

We were ambling along a path through tall pines and Birch, heading towards the river. A plinking-plonking call radiated from the top of one tree and we paused to locate the songster. Perched upon the very tip of a Scots Pine, a Crossbill sang languidly, his body the colour of sun-baked bricks and his wonkily arranged beak silhouetted beautifully against the sky. I rarely see Crossbills but when I do, it's always lovely. To see a pair drinking together from a puddle, the red male joined by his mate in warm yellow, is just blissful. Their colour combination always reminds me of the 'red lorry, yellow lorry' tongue twister; perhaps that's another reason their beaks came to be so curled.

LOVE IS A TOAD

Before long, the rumbling gurgle of the Lui reached our ears and we peeled off from the path down towards the water's edge. A weather-and-time-bleached tree skeleton lay half submerged in the glass-clear water, its trunk smoother than if it had been sanded. The spot was busy and serene. The thick air telling you there was water nearby mixed with the mulchy smell of autumn into a rich and delicious concoction. We rested upon the tree's pale, smooth trunk, watching all of the water from the nearby mountains surge by in a dark, peaceful swell.

I asked Charlie how she was managing her own sense of grief and guilt. She described how her work in the conservation sector had helped her, especially a recent project managing a group of volunteers. Over 700 pairs of hands had come together to plunge tree whips into soil until collectively they'd planted over five kilometres of new hedgerow. It was these small examples of tangible action that she now hung on to. Whilst she still felt sadness and guilt, she said that she'd come to notice it didn't haunt her in the same way. She now finds it easier to ignore the voice that tells her she should have tried just a little harder.

I pictured some of that planted hedgerow in a few years' time. I imagine peering into it in spring, spying the brown and buff feathered form of a Linnet, hunkered down firmly upon her clutch of tiny speckled eggs. I bet, if you could ask her, she'd certainly tell Charlie it helped.

Charlie looked over my shoulder and waved to her partner Dave who'd caught up with us and was wandering down from the track with a wetsuit under each arm. Oh yes, a river swim. We hopped down from the tree skeleton and I started

THE GRANNY PINE

undressing, accepting my fate of a knicker-clad plunge. They were prepared; I was not.

'I'm still sad every day at what's happening to the natural world, but I feel less guilt and less shame.' Charlie seemed calm and at peace as she wrenched her wetsuit on. 'I'm more accepting that I'm doing my bit, and that's as much as I can give whilst remaining physically and mentally healthy.'

The river was bloody freezing, the sort of cold that makes your chest ache and shoulders tingle. I trod water, my fingers outstretched into the gentle current, drawing the smell of clean, clear water into my nostrils. It felt revitalising, the water's sucks and gurgles gently drawing us along in the flow as we bobbed under the trees. The Rowans shone coral orange in the grey October light. The Birch oozed honey-gold from their leaves, warm and fluttering against their silver bark. And the Scots Pines! Their copper trunks, their molten bark. I swear they actually glowed.

CHAPTER 7

Sluginess

Beauty | Ugliness

CHRIS PACKHAM
New Forest, Hampshire – 17 November

Eyeball to Eyestalk

Can you make eye contact with a slug? I couldn't be sure, but it definitely felt like their betentacled and beady eyes locked with mine for a moment. I gazed at the two inky-black pinpricks, the stalks they sat upon waving in slow motion. Yes, I know they're very simple eyes. Yes, I know it's likely they only detect changing light levels and can't form proper images. But eye to eye, organism to organism, it felt like we were looking at each other.

They were an ever-so-handsome slug. Their back was wrinkled and puckered. Folds of skin – at least, I think it's skin – formed minuscule slimy ruffles along the length of their sausagey body. They were the grey of winter sleet and the brown of milky coffee, and they were almost translucent, a bit like a well-sucked gummy sweet. They were adorned with markings. Mottles and blotches and spots, and two dark go-slower racing stripes around their dimpled shoulders. Do slugs have shoulders? Hmm.

They sludged their way along, leaving a wake of ooze-coated moss and goop-strewn bark behind them. It kind of looked like someone had wiped their fingers on the tree after gobbling a load of colourless treacle. Or something else even more gross, like snot.

I retracted my face from the proximity of the little mollusc and turned it skywards, taking in the towering woody form the slug was scaling. A colossal Beech, thick and stout, erupting into the canopy with confidence. It spread in the pattern of splattered paint, its limbs spraying upwards and outwards as if chucked with momentum when wet, twigs like thin dribbles and leaves like spattered flecks. The canopy shimmered with all of the colours of a hungry and fizzing fire: hot yellows and molten oranges illuminated in autumn sunshine.

I zoomed back into the slug on the tree. It seemed it was a Tree Slug. How very apt. They oozed their way up the trunk in super slo-mo, living their sluggy, mucus-filled life. Travel by self-lubrication, how wonderful. Eyeball to eyestalk, the tip of my nose to a singular slimy foot, I admired them for the many things they were. Lumpy and grey, oozing and gelatinous. Ordinary. Weird. Gross. Bizarre. Completely, undeniably ugly and, yet, exquisitely beautiful.

'Christ alive, Nancy! I've got my hearing aids in!'

The Roe Deer lolloped away, softly crunching through the undergrowth with no huge sense of urgency or fear. Chris looked down at the pretty little poodle – woolly black curls, floppy ears and the daintiest little paws – and sighed.

SLUGLINESS

She yapped eagerly and, along with the slightly larger poodle beside her, stared hungrily at the venison-on-legs as it faded into the trees.

We'd set off that morning into the woods behind Chris's old house. A month earlier, I'd joined Charlie on a walk around a place she didn't know too well. Chris, however, knew this spot like the back of his dogs' heads. We'd not been there long before Sid and Nancy had spotted the Roe and the barking erupted. I smiled at the audacity and confidence of such little hounds thinking they could tackle a beast of such heft and laughed when I noticed the Grey Squirrel inching up a tree only a few metres away from the two oblivious poodles.

The leaves at their feet rustled slightly with each body-shaking woof; it'd been a dry week and the forest floor was crispy and light. The sort of conditions that allow you to kick up a cloud of papery mulch as you walk, like wading through fresh, powdery snow. It was dazzlingly sunny, and my eyes hungrily slurped up the juxtaposition of the blue sky and fiery orange leaf litter. We wandered down a spacious ride, bordered by smooth Beech and gnarled Oaks that formed a hugging archway, the ground strewn with fallen logs in varying states of decay. Walking in those woods, you felt enveloped. You couldn't see very far in any direction: the view was obscured by thickness and texture, an understory of Hazel, young Birch and Bramble. Stands of tufted, coppery Bracken filled gaps too, showing the first hints of shrinking back as winter loomed.

I pointed out how difficult it was to get a clear line of sight – something I wasn't used to in a lot of woodlands – and Chris told me about the history of the place. Just as Charlie had described in the Cairngorms, the numbers of deer in the woods here used to be much higher. Chris explained how he'd look out into the fields in the evening and see a hundred Fallow Deer – any woodland regrowth was no match for so many chombling lips. Recently, the deer numbers had been reduced, and that had transformed how the woods look and sound. Chris bent down to gently touch the browning leaves of an Oak sapling, pointing out dozens more sprouting from the mulch around us. The understory around us, a bushy and deep layer of vegetation, clearly acted as a sound sponge. I could see it would also act as a place of shelter and source of food for other species. I imagined a Chiffchaff deftly weaving a tiny dome of grass, building her nest at ankle height in spring. I pictured Bramble flowers humming with insect life and Blackbirds gobbling juicy blackberries in late summer.

We carried on along the ride, the leaf litter under our boots deep and undisturbed. Autumn was poking its face out from every nook and cranny. At my feet, I spied a small protrusion of purple. Amethyst Deceivers! Quintessential little mushroom caps perched upon slightly wiggly stalks, all in various shades of violet, indigo and lilac. Amethyst Deceivers are one of my favourite fungi – I mean, even their name is brilliant. They're quite common but despite their lurid purpleness, they're surprisingly camouflaged against the oranges and browns of Beech leaf litter. It's a bit like one of those hidden picture tests: stare for a little bit and they suddenly start making themselves known. We crouched to admire a couple of them, soaking up their garish colour and greeting them like old friends.

Chris is someone I can be unashamedly nerdy around.

SLUGLINESS

I grew up watching him on telly in the 1990s and it's still weird to see the bloke from *The Really Wild Show* squatting in front of me, tickling the chin of a tiny purple toadstool. I'd always known him as a fanatical naturalist and admired his unquenchable thirst for the juiciest, nerdiest nature facts. But recently I'd got to know other parts of him too – his affinity for swearing (exquisite delivery of the C word), his wonderfully weird sense of humour and his intensely strong dislike of losing personal possessions (note: for someone who insists they *don't lose things*, I've seen him misplace plenty).

I was chuffed he'd taken the time to show me his patch, and a place that means so much to him. And on that sunny November morning, I could see why. The woods were busy. Nuthatches scaled trees, ascending and abseiling like a rock-climber without ropes. They were noisy as they scuttled, their *boing-boing-boing* calls ricocheting amongst boughs and branches. The sunshine seemed to be coaxing other birds into song too – a Robin's song trinkled like honey from lower limbs and I could hear more than one Song Thrush belting out their clunky mixtapes from the treetops. I took deep, lung-filling sniffs as we ambled along paths and rides, the busy scampering patters of two poodles following our slower pace.

'I'm just going to show you this tree . . .' Chris veered slightly off the track and we wandered into an open amphitheatre of trees. The Oaks and Beeches around the edge were quite uniform – straight-trunked and tall. But in the middle stood a beast of a different form. 'This is my favourite tree.' He gestured at the towering giant in front of us. 'It's a Beech pollard, obviously.'

It was obvious. Rather than a single trunk, the act of

pollarding had created this splayed, expanded creature. A goliath made entirely of limbs, its arrangement of muscular arms and tentacles reached powerfully for the sky.

'It's such a fine tree, the way it rises into this great crown. That pillar of deadwood in the middle. The way that branch there's fusing into the other one.' Chris gestured at different elements of the tree, pointing out all sorts of its features and forms.

I rested my hand upon one of its divided trunks, its bark smooth to the gaze but as rough as sandpaper to an outstretched finger. The twisting outer limbs surrounded a contrasting core of deadwood – an upright and sturdy pillar of rot encircled within the still-living tree. A gorgeous dance between life and decay in one organism.

As we stood in its presence, fluttering, dappled light trickled through the caramel canopy, sprinkling sunshine like flour through a sieve. My eyes were drawn to a particular spot on the trunk in front of me. Traversing a border between bark and velvety green moss, a slug – *the* slug – slimed its way slowly upwards.

I pointed the grey and sticky being out to Chris and we both leant in for an ogle, watching *Lehmannia marginata* going about their sluggy business. It was a moment of ordinary peacefulness: two nerds standing, slightly stooped, eyes fixed on the small creature in front of them. There was a comfortable silence; all these moments ask of you is to watch, to witness. And for a minute or so, that's exactly what we did.

Consider the slug. In all of its glorious slugliness. Think about every little thing that contributes to its magnificent, molluscian form. Their lumps, mucus, tentacles, slime and

SLUGLINESS

moistness (sorry). These are things we might consider unattractive or ugly, but isn't that quite funny? Slugs are objectively harmless, yet they're widely viewed as something foul.

I think slugs – and all molluscs, actually – are *gorgeous*. Leopard Slugs? Wearing a cardie of spots and speckles? Yes please. Brown-lipped Snails? With shells of candy stripes in vanilla and chocolate? *Double* yes please. There's something I find incredibly satisfying about their shape, their mode of transport, their oozalicious ways. The way their eye stalks unfurl, tentacles appearing from within themselves like some sort of greasy, eye-conjuring magic. Just why are slugs, and so many other species alongside them, considered ugly?

'I think it all comes down to an indoctrination of stereotypes.' Chris's gaze left the slowly snaking slug and wandered up the tree as he spoke. 'When we're kids, we're fascinated by everything. We pick up snails, we pick up slugs, we pick up worms and spiders. We don't have any preclusions when it comes to our intrinsic fascination for life.'

He's right. Kids adore these things. I was certainly always drawn to them: a three-year-old Lucy trying to eat worms like spaghetti (possibly because I'd seen it on *The Lion King*); a four-year-old Lucy playing with woodlice. I didn't have concerns about muck or slime, and if you'd have asked me, I would've considered a Garden Snail to be the most beautiful beast on the block.

'This perception of things being ugly, I think it's mostly conditioning. There are some studies suggesting people have an innate fear of some things, like snakes – and it makes sense that there's some genetical hard wiring – but other parts of it are learnt.'

LOVE IS A TOAD

'Think about it,' Chris continued. 'The first books we get that feature animals are kittens and puppies, often infantilised, with big cute eyes. And then the bad guys are things like the wolf, all of those creatures which history has demonised.' Chris pointed out that vilifying wolves was probably a useful thing to do when wolves were common and posed a genuine threat to people, who were regularly killed by them.

I smiled. It's funny in a sad way that something like the wolf is so widely recognised from storybooks, when most children have never seen a real one.

'We find ugliness in things that we perceive as harmful. You get stung by a wasp or a bee, or a fly lands on your cake and transfers some bacteria. Of course, many of these things aren't that harmful, or at least not any more, but our loathing of the animals persists. So I think it's complex; there are some biological things that are surpassed by irrational stereotyping from an early age.'

A lot of what Chris was saying made sense: quite a lot of our aversions to other living things are learnt and some of that has been useful in our evolutionary past. Some of these perceptions have been passed along down the generations, through folklore and stories, and have helped us learn what's poisonous, what's venomous or what hurts. But it feels as though in many ways, we've strayed from this rational, useful type of aversion and into something more about an aesthetic ugliness, one perhaps born out of an unfamiliarity. In modern Britain, we have little tolerance for aspects of nature that might cause us any inconvenience – things that infringe on our lives and give us any discomfort or irritation.

There are the species that dare to overstep our perceived

SLUGLINESS

boundaries, that encroach into our 'human world' where we can think wild things don't belong. Things that bite, things that sting – think wasps, horseflies, bees. There are also the things that are deemed unclean, dirty or outright gross: the cake-licking flies Chris was talking about or the munching molluscs inconsiderately leaving their slime trails everywhere. Then there are other species we deem 'messy'. Things that upset our ideas of tidiness and neatness, things like . . . *takes a deep breath* . . . *weeds* (say it with me: there's no such thing as a weed). And there are things we find it hard to relate to – creatures with physical forms and behaviours very different to our own that send shudders down the spine and elicit dramatic 'ughs' and 'ews'. Scuttling spiders, pincer-bummed earwigs, fluttering moths – all tend to freak us out a bit.

I enjoy testing my own perceptions and preconceptions of these things, letting the immediate impression of any ugliness pass by and taking a moment to really see whatever it is I'm looking at. There was a time in my life, as a teenager, when things like spiders unsettled me. If I sat in the grass in summer and something buzzed by my ear, I'd flinch. And if a hungry horsefly came near me, I'd run away squealing. However, I know now that this was just that state of unfamiliarity fuelling an inherent dislike or cautiousness of some aspects of nature. When you're unfamiliar with the flight style of a hoverfly or the silhouette of a shieldbug, then every little thing that flutters past you becomes a potential threat.

This is further compounded when you take into account the way we're taught about things as we grow up. Studies have shown that if we're told something is ugly, we're more likely to rate it as such than if our perception had been untainted. A good example of this is to take a look at the widespread acceptance of the beauty of butterflies. Type 'beautiful nature' into Google and it's not long before you come across a picture of a butterfly. But isn't it funny that there isn't the same shared appreciation of moths? Butterflies are delicate, dainty and colourful. Moths are annoying, brown and boring. Yet there are brown butterflies: Speckled Woods, Meadow Browns, Dingy Skippers (all gorgeous, of course). And there are some quite frankly ridiculously colourful moths: Elephant Hawk-moths, Scarlet Tigers, Rosy Footmen. Ultimately, their behaviour and anatomy is very similar; look at them closely and each will have beady eyes, scaled wings, six legs. They're also all related, part of the same group of lepidoptera. It's our own beauty standards that decide who's prettiest and so we prefer the Brimstone Butterfly over the Brimstone Moth.

Chris and I slowly encircled the tree (and its slug) as we chatted. Looking closely, I spied other residents of the Beech: a woodlouse trundling slowly up one crevice, a tiny spider suspended from an appropriately tiny web inside a damp hole. There was still a sense of bustle about – much quieter and less urgent than the fizz of spring, but busy nonetheless. Sid and Nancy busied themselves too, sniffing and circling us, their trotting making light crunching sounds in the fallen Beech leaves. Chris was contemplative.

'For me, it's less the physical ugliness; it's more attitudes I see as being the ugliest thing. All of these fears, or all of the physical things we see damaging nature, are only manifestation of an attitude. Attitudes of apathy or aggression. I think that's the ugliness,' he sighed. 'You know, people put shit lawns in their garden because they don't know better. But you've got people making and selling the shit lawns.'

I smiled. Chris's dislike for plastic lawns is well-known.

'You get businesses who profit from our fear of things, who seek to perpetuate the demonisation of pigeons, rats, cockroaches, mice and wasps, and all those sorts of things.' He paused, thinking for a moment, before continuing. 'There are people who don't know, that's fine. There are people who don't care, that's not fine. And then there are people who just want to keep bad business as usual, and that's very bad. And I think that's the sort of greater ugliness. That's uglier than the shit lawn, really.'

Bad business as usual. I liked that phrase. It summarised what feels like a very pervasive mindset in the West, where we believe we're entitled to keep doing something that causes damage – to people, to nature – just because it benefits us and because we want to do it. To extract what we want, use what we want, simply because it makes us money – like manufacturing plastic lawns, as Chris had explained. I could see now that ugliness does lie elsewhere. Ugly attitudes and belief systems manifest as ugliness in landscapes: fields plastered in slurry, rivers flowing with crap, vegetation burnt and razed, straight lines and emptiness. Have you ever seen a freshly flailed hedgerow? Bruised and battered and raw? Now *that's* ugly.

When I think about these things, I still need to steer myself away from misanthropy, from that person-to-person blame I talked about with Amy. The ugliness lies in the principles of a system that fuels the attitudes that cause the damage. So I see the flailed hedge, and I feel pain and revulsion towards the person who caused it. I even feel angry in the moment.

LOVE IS A TOAD

But I also know that it's a deeper, overarching culture that allows the battering of the hedgerow to happen. If we think nature's there to exploit, we see it reduced to a 'resource', like fish stocks or our soils. If we believe nature is 'other' – is separate to us – then we want to banish it with sprays, poisons and traps. And if we think nature needs controlling, if we feel like we can do what we want with it, it results in those poor flailed hedges. So it pains me to know there are those who believe the toad, the spider, the slug to be ugly. But it pains me more to see the ugliness that sits above it, the pervasive beliefs that allow our relationship with nature to exist in its current form.

We crunched away from Chris's favourite Beech and carried on into the woods. The warmth of the sun seemed to be encouraging all sorts of scents into the air – the earthy smell of leaf litter tinged with the sweet, autumnal whiff of rot. It was the season of decay, the time of year when fungi starts unravelling and dismantling all of the evidence of a fruitful summer. My eyes were drawn to fungal treasures in every direction, growing in crusts the colour and texture of peach fuzz across branches or protruding from stumps in clumps of mouse-grey mushrooms.

At one point, right in front of us, I spied a very familiar fungal form protruding from the leaf litter. Highlighted in a splodge of sunshine they resembled tiny powdery-white fingers, somewhat ghostly and eerie. I recognised them as Candlesnuff Fungus, a familiar rot-scoffer fond of old logs and stumps. There was loads of it about and each little form seemed frozen in a different gesture – some waving, some pointing and one almost perfectly resembling the hand sign for rock 'n' roll. I crouched down for a gander whilst Chris looked over my shoulder.

'It's funny. You might think decay is ugly—' he pointed at the Candlesnuff '—or you might think parasitism, or slugs, or, I don't know . . . volcanoes blasting down into forests are ugly things, but they're all part of a system. And that system is beautiful.'

As he spoke, Chris gently touched a fingertip to a poking end of the Candlesnuff. Admiring its tiny, perfectly proportioned place in the scene around us, he explained how recognising the interconnectedness of that system felt almost like a moment of epiphany.

The poodles had started to bound off ahead of us and Chris wandered after them. I stood up, giving the Candlesnuff a gentle prod goodbye, and jogged to catch up with him.

'Up until that point, I'd always taken things out, put them on a pedestal and worshipped them as individuals. So I would say, you know, the Sparrowhawk's beautiful. But I then realised it is only beautiful because it's eating the Blue Tit that ate the caterpillar, that ate the leaf, that grew from the Oak that was spread by the Jay, and . . .' Chris paused and took a deep breath. 'Do you know what I mean? When you get right into it, it's then that all of a sudden, your perception of nature's beauty expands exponentially. That, for me, is the greater beauty.'

The crunching underfoot slowly transitioned into a squelch as we entered an altogether soggier part of the woods. Squeezing through a screen of young Beech, we came across an area of the forest floor that had flooded. Shallow pools sat in subtle dips in the ground, the big Beeches around them

LOVE IS A TOAD

isolated on little islands. It was completely still. I walked up to the edge of one broad puddle and peered into it, like I was looking through a chasm in the floor of a cave. The water was totally clear and held a medley of Beech and Oak leaves so gently and calmly it looked as though they were suspended in glass. Some leaves floated near the surface, their fiery yellows and oranges amplified by wetness, in the same way a pebble always looks brighter if you lick it. A couple of inches lower, I could make out the subtle silhouettes of more leaf litter, plastered together in darker browns like a patterned wallpaper. As I peered over the edge of this chasm that wasn't a chasm, it appeared unfathomably deep and I felt as though I'd tumble into another realm if I was to tip my face forwards and roly-poly into the water. The reflections! There were so many. Reflections upon reflections, a pool of mirrors. I could see the forest floor, the mottled canopy and the sky beyond it simultaneously. A flitter of movement caught my eye and I watched as the silhouette of a bird flew through the treetops somehow both above and below me.

It was incomprehensibly beautiful and in the moment, I felt the gravity of that beauty acutely. Juxtaposed with the previous conversation around ugliness, it felt as though the scene in front of us shone even brighter, as if all of its gorgeousness had been concentrated and distilled. Aren't we lucky to be able to see beauty? And especially to be able to find it so much in other life, in nature. Seeing and feeling beauty is to experience joy. It's to feel gratitude, respect and admiration, simply for what something is and nothing more. It can be as simple as appreciating the aesthetic – a Foxglove looks gorgeous, after all. But for me, it's something greater

SLUGLINESS

than that. It's not just what something looks like but what it is, what it does, and how it links to that thing, and that thing, just as Chris had described.

Beauty reveals itself in so many ways; we can detect and appreciate it with every sense we own. Beauty lies in birdsong, the way a Curlew burbles its way into your chest so that you feel it in your soul. It lies in the comforting coolness of mud felt by probing fingertips. It lies in the scent of Honeysuckle, winding its way up your nostrils, and in the acrid oiliness of a seabird's feather, catching in the back of your throat as you sniff it. Beauty lies on the tongue, in a moment of sweetness, sucked from the plucked flowers of White Deadnettle.

This isn't to place nature upon a pedestal or to imply that it's all butterflies, rainbows and bunny rabbits. You see, I've realised that our personal interpretations of beauty can be challenged. Our usual definitions of what makes something beautiful are limited by lots of invisible rules and notions, all of which can be questioned and expanded. The more I've explored nature, the more I've realised that beauty isn't just the voice of the Nightingale, the splendour of the Peacock Butterfly or the sweet scent of Bluebells in spring. Beauty exists in nature's wholeness – and that means it exists in everything we don't like about it too.

Whilst nature is a thing of energy and life force, of grace and elegance, it's also harsh; it guarantees discomfort and suffering. We exist in a cycle of fertility and flourishing and lushness, but also of predation and parasitism, of death and decay. In the past, when I first entered the 'nature world', I tended to shy away from this. That was, until things got a bit weird.

*

LOVE IS A TOAD

The lump on my throat was itchy at first. It nestled against my collarbone, about the size of a Malteser. It felt a bit like a horsefly bite, except it was November, so Mum made me go to the doctor. By the time Christmas came around, the lump resembled a small boiled egg embedded under my skin. A medley of jabs and pokes, biopsies and scans later, and I had a diagnosis. Mum and Dad sat with me in the oncology department as the doctor laid out a six-month treatment plan for Hodgkin's lymphoma. He laughed when I asked if I'd be allowed to have a glass of wine – I was 23 and still thinking about the weekends.

Shortly after New Year, the contract on my first job came to an end. Only a week later I started chemotherapy. I was about to head into the year balding and jobless. *Fab.* In the months that followed, I felt pretty rotten as nausea, lethargy, bloating and brain fog became my constant companions. I learnt how to tie headscarves, developed an attachment to mango sorbet, and accidentally waxed my chemo-weakened eyebrows off one night after a fancy dress party – apparently using liquid latex to achieve a convincing Voldemort has its risks. Skint and getting by on benefits, I tried to keep busy on the days I felt good. I walked and walked and walked, exploring every green nook and cranny I could find on my doorstep. And I felt a shift. Without a purpose or a time limit, a walk became about curiosity and exploration.

As spring sprang, I found myself noticing life I'd never noticed before. Plants and critters, birds and fungi. I'd find a thing and take a pic of it on my phone. Then I'd find another thing and do the same. Later on, curled up on the sofa with my sorbet, I'd take to Google. Page after page I'd scroll, trawling through images, trying to find something similar to the millipede or flower or spider I'd spotted earlier. A proper millennial naturalist, my camera roll slowly became infiltrated with life, almost as though the bugs had scuttled under the clean glass screen and the mosses had germinated amongst the wires and circuit boards. I began posting my finds on Instagram. It soon became a digital diary of the things I'd learnt and seen and experienced. The fascination flowed naturally, and I found myself craving these interactions more and more. When I felt well, I'd pull on my wellies and head out to find things. When I felt rubbish, I'd scroll through my bird apps, comparing finch flight patterns and warbler songs.

Spring melted into summer and the lump in my neck melted away too. I sat in the doctor's room in August, bloated, bald and beaming as I absorbed the words 'in remission'. My parents were buzzing too. What a weird old time. Two completely different types of experience juxtaposed. On one hand, it was rubbish. I was facing mortality in my early twenties and had spent half a year feeling like a sack of shit. I was scared. My veins ached from the six-hour infusions I took every fortnight. My tongue and mouth felt sore and tasted like the smell of damp clothes, and I'd shaved my head to a buzz cut after I'd grown tired of hoovering up clumps of hair. On the other hand, I'd experienced something strangely precious – having permission to take things slowly and to learn at my own pace. And so, in spite of the fear I felt when I was ill, I have fond memories of this time too. Throughout a pretty crap period, nature had been all of the clichés: my solace, an escape, a distraction, a soother. I'd found joy – thick, pure and undiluted. It's cheesy as heck

LOVE IS A TOAD

but I was utterly besotted. As though I'd been looking at something pretty but blurry, and someone had finally given me glasses and I could see it clearly.

My relationship with the natural world had shifted. Up until that point, it'd always been about the beautiful stuff – watching and identifying birds, insects and wildflowers. But I'd come to realise that my first impressions of nature weren't complete. I hadn't finished. Spending more time observing meant I was seeing more – seeing things properly. My eyes were opened to gore, death and drama. I watched predators tear prey to shreds and parasites devour their hosts from within. And I found I was just as enthralled by it all as I was the pretty things. As time went on, I could see I was also learning the same lesson about myself. As my body ached and bloated, I came to understand my own vulnerability and mortality. I began to see that I'm as subject to the rules of the ecological world we live in as any other organism. Cancer taught me that I'm as soft and squidgy, vulnerable and temporary as any caterpillar, mushroom or fluffy baby Blue Tit. And that brought a whole lot of perspective.

I used to deny nature's true nature, close my eyes to the mundanity, the gore and the grossness. But not now. Now, I find prettiness tucked away in a pile of Otter poo. Grace lives in the eye socket of a Hare's skull and wonder pulsates through the maggots that writhe in it. In the very moment a Sparrowhawk clasps a beating breast of feathers in its talons, pins it to the earth and unlocks a chest of scarlet treasure with a life-force-stained beak – that's where beauty exists.

This type of appreciation – of nature's wholeness, its warts 'n' all (quite literally, in the case of toads) – is my version of

SLUGLINESS

spirituality. A sense of connecting with something bigger and more wonderful than I could possibly ever comprehend. To be able to see beauty is a gift, but it's also a muscle you can exercise. It's a grounding and valuable way of relating to the world, and one that can grow and expand if you let it. That means accepting our own vulnerabilities as a species in an ecosystem, knowing that we'll experience pain, discomfort and hardship, as well as love, pleasure and joy. It means accepting the incessant itch of a Mosquito bite, whilst appreciating the Mosquito's anatomy that allows it to draw energy from my blood.

I'd totally lost any sense of direction. Together, we'd wound through the forest, hopping over the ripple-less puddles and cutting across open rides bathed in warm November sun.

We slowed to an amble, coming to the edge of a grassy clearing with a fallen log in the middle. At my feet, still under the shade of the canopy, I spied a smattering of small pale dots clinging to an especially twiggy twig. They were a dull white, the colour of scuffed trainers, and would have been easy to overlook, except I had an inkling of what might be underneath. I crouched and teased the twig gently from beneath the leaf litter, being careful not to knock or snap it. Holding it up, I twirled it around to look at the underbellies of the little white mushrooms. Each one was a tiny protrusion of perfection, an impossibly small and delicate fanning of paper-thin gills. The gills radiated from the centre of each mushroom where it erupted from the twig outwards towards the subtly fluffy rim. They looked like little vortexes and sat in incredibly eye-pleasing clusters along the length of the peeling stick. I held it up against the twinkling sunlight and the little mushrooms lit up with a warm and gentle translucence. They looked a little bit like when you hold a torch behind your ear. Variable Oysterlings, I think.

We approached the fallen log in the glade. It had a level of moistness and smoothness that told me it'd been there for a good while. The bark had cracked and fallen away from much of it, leaving a seat of hard, paler wood, slightly tinged with the green of slime and algae. The main trunk of it forked, and so Chris took a seat on one branch and I slumped on to the other.

In that little clearing in the woods, the peacefulness sang. It wasn't silent; I could still hear the Song Thrush repeating his phrases of the day and the content chattering of something like Goldfinches a little further away. At this height, the sun highlighted the embroidery work of a thousand spiders, their lace-like webs hanging in the most delicate patterns from the old brown seed heads of Docks, coated in a fine dew. Bigger drops hung from the tips of Beech and Birch leaves around the edge of the clearing, twinkling in the stillness and sunshine. We paused in a moment of brief admiration.

'See, look here.' Chris gestured at the scene around us. 'You've got the gold in those leaves and you've got the silver on the grass. And all that corroding Bracken. There's the feel of it all, the wet on my knee, the wet on the leaves and the light they reflect. The Nuthatch!' Chris stopped to listen to the call of the little grey scuttler ricocheting around the treetops behind us. 'Just the smell of it all – the smell changes so rapidly at the moment. And look at all those drips, suspended.' He paused once more. 'I mean, if that doesn't turn you on, what will?'

CHAPTER 8

Whatever It Was, It Wiggled

Awe | Hopelessness

TOM ASPINALL

Eastern Moors, Derbyshire – 18 December

'This, Lucy, is what we call *wasted land*!' Tom flung his hand out, gesturing exuberantly at the landscape in front of us. It was a cluttered jumble of standing trees, fallen logs and mosses – lots and *lots* of mosses. Most of the trees were Willows. Some stood high – young and strong and reaching skywards. Others were cracked and splitting, tousled and woven together from when old limbs had crashed on top of each other. Some of the Willows were entirely horizontal, their main trunk toppled but their branches at right angles, still lunging determinedly for the canopy above. They all grew from a carpet of sog, the ground below them a mix of sucking mud, pools of water and voluptuous mounds of vibrant moss.

'It's good for nothin', it's producin' nothin', and it's *disgustin*' and untidy!' Tom's dry sarcasm, delivered in an exquisite Yorkshire accent, was impeccable. His sense of humour is one of my favourite things about him; it feels as though he's taking the piss in every other sentence.

'You know what it is?' He turned to me, deadpan serious, face close to mine, and paused for dramatic effect. 'It's UNKEMPT!' He cracked a smile and I couldn't help but laugh.

We cast our eyes over the wet woodland – there was an unusual amount of tree cover for this part of the Peak District. The expanse of woodiness stuck out like a sore thumb; you could see how it might be perceived 'mess' in comparison to much of the landscape we had passed on the way. There was no neatness, nor any straight lines, just bushiness and texture and depth.

Tom pushed his glasses up his nose and ambled onwards into the trees, wobbling slightly on the sodden and soft ground. He's always made me laugh like this – his rants and gushes and observations always parcelled up in silliness and wit. One of his favourite subjects is his garden. It's a small patch, only a few metres square, but it's a place he worships and cares for tenderly. In the height of summer, it's an eruption of vegetation, tufted and lustrous. It wasn't long before it came up in conversation and I asked him how his little patch had fared over summer.

'I know I go on about this a lot, Lucy, and I'm going to blow my own trumpet, but my little garden is bloody *awe-inspiring*.'

I laughed at his unashamed lack of humility, but he's right – it is. Tom's been working hard to build his own vegetative congregation. He's gathered over 30 species of wildflowers so far. If you were to reach into one of Tom's

WHATEVER IT WAS, IT WIGGLED

pockets in summer (and I'm not for a second suggesting you do), your fingers might feel some bitty, granular mulch in the bottom of it. Pinch a bit of that mulch and pull it out, and you'd be faced with an assortment of seeds of all shapes and sizes – grasses and wildflowers he's snarfled on his walks around his home.

I asked him how his Pocket Mulch™ project was going and if he had gained any new planty residents this year. He laughed, telling me his method was generally to shove some seeds in the soil and hope for the best. That year, his Musk Mallow had germinated in an instant but his Meadow Cranesbill seeds had taken over six months.

'And the Goat's Beard! I got that from a field on a walk near me. You know those huge seed clocks?'

I *do* know those huge seed clocks. If you've not seen the seed head of a Goat's Beard, you need to picture a colossal Dandelion clock, as big as an apple. A cluster of fluff-headed seeds, clumped around one focal point, looking like a freeze-frame of a firework at the peak of its BANG. And their flowers are gorgeous. Their petals are perfectly spaced rays of sunshine yellow, adorned with freckle-like black specks. Between and behind the petals are sepals – dagger-like green spikes impaling the air around the flower dramatically. It's like someone took a Dandelion and dressed it up in its gladrags – all pizzazz and glitz and glam.

'I just chucked some seeds from it into my garden. And one day, I was sitting and I was like . . . *wait*. Oh my god, it's here! I've got one!' The joy and enthusiasm radiated from Tom and I could tell he felt honoured that the Goat's Beard felt at home enough to germinate in his back garden.

LOVE IS A TOAD

Tom has lived in the same house for a decade and for six years of that he's been developing his miniature meadow. What was initially a patch of lawn has become a place that hosts an abundance of life. He relishes how much the 'mess' he cares for ruffles the neighbours' feathers. Compared with those of the rest of his street, his garden is positively jungle-like, and there's been more than one comment hinting about the need for mowers and strimmers to make a visit to his house.

Standing in front of this other patch of mess – an expanse of wet willow carr in a corner of the Peak District – Tom knows that some people would perceive it similarly, as an untidiness that needs managing and reining in.

The patch of 'mess' can be found on the Eastern Moors, a nature reserve sitting in the 'Dark Peak' area of the Peak District, which stretches over 14 square miles and is made up of expanses of bog, meadows, grassland and woodland. The reserve contrasts with much of the neighbouring land, which is largely uniform, rather bleak, grouse moors, intensively managed for the shooting of Red Grouse. Shooting on a driven grouse moor involves the flushing of large numbers of birds into the firing line of shooters. In order to get those large numbers of grouse, heather is burned to encourage the younger growth that grouse prefer and any predators that might eat Red Grouse are controlled. This includes those we can legally kill (whether you agree with it or not), like Foxes or Stoats, and those which shouldn't be killed (but frequently still are), like Hen Harriers and Goshawks. Walking on one of these moors is a bit like walking on a moonscape: the heather is burned in a patchwork, leaving the hillsides looking like

WHATEVER IT WAS, IT WIGGLED

some sort of crazy quilt made of scraps of scorched earth, sizzled vegetation and bushy, knee-high older growth. Then there's the towering hags of peat – large areas of erosion that resemble crashing waves made up of the blackest soil. Trees are a rarity and you can walk for hours without seeing very much life at all; it's not unusual to spend a whole day up there and only see five species of bird. Despite this, they're areas of great potential and if the pressure of management were to be lifted, many of these places would support a bustling wealth of upland wildlife. The Eastern Moors are a grand example of this; here land management is carried out with wildlife in mind. Bogs have been rewetted (drains and eroded gullies blocked up, so that the landscape can hold more water), the pressure of nibbling, grazing lips has been lightened, burning has stopped, trees have been planted and others simply allowed to grow. And it's still early days. It's quite exciting to think about what this place will become over time.

I've wandered around this patch a few times with Tom; it was the first place we ever went nerding together. In spring, we have watched snoozing Adders and Common Toads on the move. In summer, we saw Whinchats – slick and dapper little birds with bold white eyeliner – feeding their fledged chicks. We've admired flourishing verges of wildflowers in the sunshine and blotchy white Mountain Hares nestled in the frost, and, one time, a pair of zooming Merlins hunting a Meadow Pipit – falcons in miniature, working together to secure a feathery meal.

Now it was *very* December. Grey and grizzly, the low sky hung in a mood as far as the hills stretched. Tom had heard reports that a Great Grey Shrike was knocking about and so our eyes followed every birdy silhouette that flitted past, both repeatedly twitching for our binoculars, like cowboys holding nervous hands over their holsters.

No shrike to be seen, but a scattering of Redwings zoomed into view, alighting in the tops of the nearest Birch trees. Redwings are just *gorgeous* birds. Warmish brown and speckle-bellied with a neat flick of cream eyeshadow. When you see one lift its wings in flight, you're treated to a splash of rich, rusty orange, nestled deep in their armpits (if birds have armpits). It's the same colour as sun-soaked Beech leaves in autumn. I remember learning how to identify their call and feeling like I'd acquired a new superpower. If you've not heard it yourself, there's a magic way to experience it. The next still night you get in December, step outside, tilt your face to the stars and cup your ears (don't be afraid to look like a weirdo). Hold still and listen – you might just hear groups of Redwings overhead. Often travelling in the safety of darkness, they make contact with each other in the inky black with a high-pitched and almost whispered *t-seeeep*! It's delicate and beautiful and entirely fitting for such a lovely bird.

The Redwings' calls punctuated our chatting as we walked, their silhouettes speckling the bare winter branches of the Birch trees like feathered leaves. I relish them whilst they're here, knowing they'll depart in spring to go and breed in northern Europe.

Tom wanted to show me a particular little patch of wet woodland. He set off determinedly along a rather path-free route, taking a 'shortcut' across the bog. We traversed the lumpy, hummocky terrain, a mix of squelchy bog patches

WHATEVER IT WAS, IT WIGGLED

my wellies sunk into and rounded tussocks of Purple Moor Grass – a surface that leaves you walking like you're five pints in, staggering your way forwards with shaky knees. I watched Tom wobble ahead of me, making a beeline for a stand of trees in the distance. He paused and bent down to prod something at his feet. As I drew closer, I could see it was a verdant and bright pillow of Sphagnum moss.

'*Sphagnum capillifolium*!' Tom gushed. He fondled the surface of the clump, which was protruding from the base of a young Birch tree. *Sphagnum capillifolium* is an exquisite creature. Sphagnums are bog mosses which grow in soggy and acidic places, forming mats and mounds, quite often looking as though they've bubbled up from below the surface of the earth. A patch of Sphagnum is made up of lots of individual little plants – each one rootless and straggly, topped with a little gumdrop button head. They're lovely to look at in the singular but clump a load together and that's when things get *really* sexy.

The mound of moss in front of us was tightly packed, creating a satisfyingly even pattern, bobbly like a head of cauliflower. Some of the plants forming the clump were a vibrant green, the colour of limes, and others were the deep red of strawberry jam. The two colour forms blended into each other in some places – a greenish background splashed with red wine.

'I don't think I'll *ever* get sick of Sphagnum mosses.' Tom smiled.

I knew Tom loved his Sphagnums; he'd spent some of his lockdown evenings teaching me how to ID them over Zoom and a beer. We had met for the first time in early 2020, before we knew what the year ahead had in store. Shortly after our first face-to-face chat, everything switched to a 2D world of Zoom and phone calls. As lockdown eased a little, we made plans for a walk and so began a tradition. Once a week (when we were allowed), we'd pick a place, I'd bring something tasty to eat and Tom would bring a brew or a beer, and we'd wander about and nerd together. We climbed trees, ogled flowers, watched birds and wandered for miles. We ranted, we laughed, we cried. On one walk, we raised a toast to a wonderful colleague we lost during the pandemic. Colin Wilkinson was a warm, gentle and friendly naturalist, who would always take the time to teach you things. We remembered him as we sat overlooking a wooded valley that was a favourite spot of his. Our walks became a much-needed point of peace and serenity in a rather unsettling year, and the pinnacle of joy within them was the moments we spent looking at little things. The following spring, during one walk on the Eastern Moors, on a little stretch of sandy path bathed in spring sunshine, Tom and I watched something magical unfold.

The thing that caught my eye was the fuzzy, marmalade-orange bum. It zipped from side to side in the air in a swinging, fluid motion. It was quite entrancing. Bums of that colour, at that time of year, could mean only one thing: Tawny Mining Bees. Unbelievably cute, it's always worth keeping an eye out for the ginger shoulder pads and behinds of the female bees on warm days in spring. This particular one landed on the path ahead of us, on a disturbed and scuffed patch of sandy earth. There was a scraped ridge at the side of the patch,

WHATEVER IT WAS, IT WIGGLED

which she made a beeline for (sorry) and proceeded to dig, as mining bees tend to do. I held a hand up to stop Tom, and we crouched slowly and awkwardly to watch. The little bee excavated a little soil, creating a volcano-like mound, then took off in a buzz, zipping away in the sunshine. I suspected she'd soon return, perhaps laden with pollen to provision her nest with, so we decided to hunker down and wait. Five minutes . . . ten minutes . . . twenty . . . Nothing. No sign of her. I stared fuzzily at the path in front of us, my eyes slightly crossing as they drifted out of focus, mid-daydream. In the warmth of early spring sunshine, I could've happily had a little snooze.

Ping. There. A tiny, almost indiscernible movement amongst the grit and the gravel. Only a foot or so away from the Tawny's digging spot. I wasn't actually *sure* I saw anything. Maybe it was a light gust disturbing the ground. Maybe it was a fly. Hmm.

There. This time my eyes reacted faster, pinning down the micro-motion to a precise location. Squinting, I could make out an infinitesimally small projection – thinner than a whisker – protruding from the earth. It must've been two millimetres long, max. Whatever it was, it wiggled. It quivered and twitched, in the way something that's *definitely alive* tends to do. What on earth?!

Ping. Another one. *Two* infinitesimally small projections, side by side, sticking up in the sand. They wiggled in symmetrical unison and, suddenly, I understood. Antennae. A pair of antennae, belonging to someone. I nudged Tom in a tense, vibrating state of excitement and gently pointed out the little feelers. Together, we shuffled forwards on our

LOVE IS A TOAD

bellies. We must've looked quite weird – face down, side by side, our noses only inches from the footpath in front of us. We arranged ourselves so that we could look down upon the mystery antennae.

The wiggling continued for a few minutes more and it seemed as though the feelers had grown a little longer, perhaps reaching a whopping three millimetres. Amidst the movement, the surface of the soil itself started to rumble (if grains of sand can rumble) and it became clear that whoever this was, they were on their way out. Smack bang in the middle of the two antennae lay a tiny pebble. It was smaller than a grape pip, but proportionately it was the size of a boulder compared to the little antennae-owner sitting beneath it. Taking a blade of dried grass between my fingers, I ever so gently prised the pebble away. A minuscule face appeared. Two beady eyes, the colour of hot cocoa, stared up at us from the dirt. The face seemed buoyed by the sudden influx of sunshine and ramped up its activity. After a few more minutes of wiggling, an entire head had freed itself from the compacted earth and had started turning left and right, taking in the world around them. More wiggling, more shuffling, and there soon followed a pair of legs, then another, and another.

The dinky bee rested for a little while after they'd emerged. They were coated in a fine, powdery dust and spent a good few minutes preening and washing themselves, wiping their body and head with their forelegs before drawing them through their mouth. They reminded me of a tiny cat, grooming themselves peacefully and absent-mindedly. Their body was slim and shiny, and marked with yellow stripes and

WHATEVER IT WAS, IT WIGGLED

rusty splodges. They looked sharp and streamlined, distinctly lacking in the fuzziness department. For a bee, they didn't look very bee-like at all.

Whilst we'd started this belly-dive watching the antics of a mining bee, the owner of the wiggling antennae was something different. A wanderer, a roamer – this was a nomad bee. We have a whole bunch of nomad bees in the UK. I think this particular one was an Early Nomad Bee, *Nomada leucophthalma*. All of the nomads look a bit more like wasps than bees; they're skinny and hairless and don't collect pollen. What they do do, however, is fascinating. Nomad bees are cuckoos – not in feather or flight, but in their behaviour. In the same way the infamous bird lays its eggs in the nest of another, nomad bees will cuckoo mining bees. Females sniff out a nest, wait until it's unoccupied and sneak in to deposit her own egg in an unsealed chamber. The nomad egg will then hatch, scoff the mining bee's larvae and have a lovely old time feeding on the pollen provisions provided by its host until it's ready to pupate.

What Tom and I had witnessed, in that tiny patch of earth on an early spring morning, was the emergence of a new nomad. The very moment a freshly pupated bee burrowed their way up from a submerged chamber, shifted sand and grit and stone, and clapped their eyes on the outside world for the very first time. We'd seen a bee's first steps, its first taste of fresh air. Tom and I had witnessed the first time a little nomad bee had ever seen the sun! And to know that did wonderful things to my brain.

In many ways, what we saw was a very ordinary thing – something that happens on a daily, hourly, minutely basis during spring. But it was also incredibly special, something utterly wondrous and captivating. I wonder how many nomad bees emerged that warm day in late March? And how many came out to a welcoming committee of waiting fans, practically cheering them on? It was such a special thing to share with a friend too – our pooled joy seemed to hang in the air afterwards. Here was that Type 2 joy again, the sort Nadia had described on our walk together; something transcendental, something that takes you out of yourself.

These moments of magnificent mundaneness are the things Tom and I thrive on; they're our bread and butter.

Our boots squelched up the same path where we'd watched the nomad magic happen. I reminisced as we stepped over the spot, now damp with all of the sog of December, and I wondered who lay beneath the surface, preparing themselves to emerge in just a few short months. We headed down into a grassy dip where a stream lay peacefully burbling. A fallen tree sat in the middle and our rumbling bellies told us it was the perfect spot for some butties. Vegan cheese and pickle, mmm. Shortly after tucking in, I noticed something equal parts shiny and tiny plop on to Tom's shoulder. It was an absolutely – and I cannot stress this enough – *minute* little beetle. Its wing cases were a sort of bronzy-brown, its head and shoulders black. It rumbled over the creases of Tom's coat as though marching up and down hills. I pushed my finger into the softness of the jacket, providing my fingernail for a platform for the beetle to wander upon. It paused for a moment, and Tom and I hunched over to get a closer look.

'Fascination is the thing that's probably been static my

WHATEVER IT WAS, IT WIGGLED

entire life. Nature's just endlessly fascinating. And you'll never get to the bottom of everything,' Tom observed, whilst the little beetle appeared oblivious to our presence. It kept waving its little blob-ended antennae about and we both smiled. 'I think everybody can be fascinated by our place amongst millions of other organisms and species,' he continued. 'I reckon everyone starts with it, and then some people lose it, so it's not about getting into it, it's about what maintains your interest in it beyond childhood.'

When I think about it, an innate interest in other living things seems to exist in every kid I have ever met, so maybe Tom is right. Maybe we are all born with a natural fascination that isn't always nourished or is even snuffed out in later life.

The beetle by now had scuttled up my knuckle, traversing a whole finger to reach the peak point of my hand. It paused, shuffled its bum a little bit, opened its wing cases as if with the press of a button and took off into the woods.

'Other living things just being. I don't know why that gives me such a good feeling, but it does.'

Exactly. It gives me such a good feeling too. Like the little nomad, here was something tiny, but in that moment, it felt immense. It brings me comfort and peace to know there are things like that going on all the time, everywhere. And these moments often take you out of yourself, to the point you can totally forget what's going on around you.

The first time I saw a Redstart properly, I was in the midst of a colossal nosebleed. I was halfway through my chemo and had gone for a walk in Dovedale, in the Peak District, with a few mates.

LOVE IS A TOAD

At this point, I was still a nature newbie, just dipping a toe into birding. On the days I felt better, in between bouts of chemotherapy, I'd pore over books, apps and web pages, slurping up information like you would a slushy on a hot day. Like most of us, I was initially drawn to the sexier species – the big, dramatic and colourful. Turning the pages of my *Handbook of British Birds* a couple of weeks earlier, I'd ogled the illustration of a male Redstart, drawn in a somewhat proud and chest-jutting pose that made him pop off the page. He seemed exotic and ethereal. I'd never known he was something you might see in the UK.

And yet, here he was. Right in front of me. He sat upon a gnarled old Hawthorn nestled at the foot of Lover's Leap, those gorgeous descending notes tumbling from his perfect little beak, his whole form shaking with the effort. Matt, my partner at the time, was trying to clamp tissues over the red ocean pouring from my nostrils, bless him. But I was determined to see this bird in the flesh and feather. The neatness of his slate grey back, the white and black of his face, and the belly – the little belly! Fire and molten lava, or as orange as the jelly in a Jaffa Cake. I was smitten. In that moment, nothing else mattered. I couldn't tear my eyes away. I felt awe.

Lunch finished, Tom and I resumed our walk. More Redwings peppered the sky in front of us; at times, we were totally surrounded. They skipped from Birch to Birch as they called to one another. Enveloped by a chorus of their '*t'seeps*', Tom and I continued to talk about this feeling of fascination that's both intangible and yet very specific. He explained

WHATEVER IT WAS, IT WIGGLED

how, in those moments, he finds himself becoming totally immersed in another living being just being itself.

'Those moments seem so simple and yet they're not. They're incredibly complex and they're a part of everything else. And that blows my mind.'

I loved the way Tom explained these emotions, putting emphasis on all of the right words, so that I couldn't help but be drawn into the feeling with him. And he was right – he'd described my experience with the Redstart perfectly.

Tom leant slowly towards me and smiled. 'Do you know what one of my favourite things is?' he asked. His excitement almost crackled as he described the anticipation of a wonderful thing, an oncoming flock of Long-tailed Tits. 'You hear it, you almost feel it! And as soon as you do, it's like, *Where are they? Where are they?!* And then, one by one, they trickle through – it's heaven!'

I knew exactly what Tom was referring to: the moment a gregarious flock of Long-tailed Tits (aka Bumbarrels) weave their way past you. You hear them well before you see them, their soft, rattling call sounding like a tiny purr as they chitter and chat to one another. Shortly after the first purr, they'll arrive. One, then another, then another! Bird after bird, they weave like a thread through the undergrowth, almost as if tied together; each bird's long, skinny tail seems to point to the one behind them as they embroider the treetops in black, white and rosy pink. These little birds are soft and unassuming, and to be in their presence is to be surrounded by a beautiful, gentle energy. Surprisingly carefree and unafraid, they'll often come right past you, their beady, pink-lidded eyes observing you curiously.

LOVE IS A TOAD

'You know those magic encounters, when for some reason a wild creature just isn't that terrified of you? You get that moment to properly observe something and look it in the eye. Like that Dipper we saw in the White Peak, wasn't that amazing?! Things like that take you to the point where your brain can't comprehend something, you're just totally engrossed, lost in the awe of it all.'

The Dipper encounter in the White Peak was another memory Tom and I regularly revisited. Wandering alongside a rocky river on a muggy summer's evening, the sunlight had already faded from the gorge when we spotted it. Perched upon a square ledge of stone, what looked like an old weir, the Dipper emitted a short burst of its burbling, scratchy song. Then, only a handful of metres away from us, it simply sat. For 20 minutes or more, Tom and I were graced with the presence of a bird who couldn't have been less arsed that we were around. We watched with glee as it bobbed rhythmically on the spot for ages. It seemed so involuntary and unthinking, like the way you catch your toe tapping along to music automatically. Every few seconds or so, it blinked and the whole world seemed to light up in its eyes in a shock-white flash.

Dippers are utterly mint. Firstly, they are adorable. Here is a pot-bellied bird, rounded and portly looking, who bobs up and down on the spot like they're excited about something or really need a wee. Secondly, Dippers are dapper. Their black, white and chocolate-bellied plumage is gorgeous. Stare at a Dipper's back and you'll see the slate-black feathers are bordered in a way that makes them look like the scales of a fish, or some sort of emo mermaid. Third, and perhaps best of all, Dippers fly underwater. As if using some sort of sorcery, they disappear into the most frantically flowing parts of a river without a second thought, zooming through the current with unexpected grace as they search for some tasty invertebrate to scoff. That's where those gorgeously weird white eyelids come in; all birds have a 'nictating membrane' – a third eyelid – it's just the Dipper's is white, so it stands out more. Apparently, they can use these flashes as communication, effectively winking at each other to flirt or intimidate, which is obviously brilliant. They're categorically one of my favourite birds and this close encounter was incredibly special. In those minutes spent in the presence of the Dipper, I felt as though every sense I possessed was heightened.

The concept of awe is interesting. It seems as though the meaning of the word has changed over time. At one point, it was used to refer to great fear or dread, and in the past it's had strong religious or power-based connotations. Generally, though, the accepted definition of awe today is a sense of utter wonder, respect, reverence and amazement. It can be felt when confronted with beauty, music or art or poetry. It can appear between people, in moments of great emotion and collective solidarity. And we can very often experience it when we encounter nature – be it a sunset over the sea or a Daisy in a crack in the pavement.

Nobody's really sure why we feel it. There are theories – one suggests it could have evolved to help us absorb new, big information. When we experience awe, we often reflect upon it, and that might mean we adapt and shift our mindset in useful ways. Other theories suggest it helped us socially, encouraging cohesion, connection and generosity. And some suppose it might have a practical use – looking out over big views and vistas may have helped us find shelter or food sources.

But, a bit like when it comes to love, I don't really know if we need to know what awe is for; the magic lies in the fact we're able to experience it at all. This wonderful, slippery thing appears suddenly, like a gift. You can't force it, you can't predict it. It can come in the magnificent moments or the mundane ones, arising from the wondrous or the everyday humdrum. It's under the rocks where the millipedes scuttle and woodlice huddle. It's in the air, thick with the sweetness of Honeysuckle and rippling in the wake of a zooming Swift. Awe lies in the barbs of a feather, the eye of an owl and the glint of a Dor Beetle's belly. And by leaning into all of those ingredients with gusto and unashamed joy, fully unleash it and feel it buzzing around our skulls.

So no, I've no idea what awe is, and I don't think I want to. To know might take some of its magic away. To be lost in amazement, mysteriousness and wow feels like a fundamental experience. If we can no longer wonder, where's the joy in that?

We had now rumbled up and out of the dip, reaching a high point on the moors that gave us a view over the wider landscape. The gentle arcs of the hills in front of us resembled the curving contours of a body, and they also bore scars – the oddly square and singed patches left behind by the burning of heather. It looked as though a toddler had been given free rein with some electric hair clippers, chaotically shaving bald

WHATEVER IT WAS, IT WIGGLED

patches into some poor soul's scalp. Except it wasn't a scalp; it was a whole hillside. It looked raw, ugly and empty.

Tom looked out at the distant moor, a pensive look on his face. 'You know, growing up, I had this idea in my head that other places in the world were more "nature-y" than Britain. And that is true – but I thought there were justified reasons for that. And as I've got older, I've realised that it's not justified at all.'

It's weird, isn't it, how many of us in Britain are brought up with this concept of nature being 'elsewhere'. When we think of wildlife, we tend to picture big sexy animals – the Giraffes and Polar Bears, whales and Orangutans we see in picture books or in slo-mo, orchestral documentary scenes voiced by Dave Atters. This interaction with wildlife media induces an awe with several steps removed, experienced from the comfort of our sofas, where we can see but not smell, listen or touch. These sorts of shows are brilliant, of course – they're entertaining and educational, giving us an insight into the lives of species we'd otherwise never know about. But they do put an emphasis on the extraordinary: the biggest, the most colourful, the most dangerous. And they also teach us that nature is elsewhere, in some remote, otherworldly wilderness and not on our doorstep.

Tom said that when we think about the natural world like this, it takes us further away from the life at our fingertips, the rather more ordinary living beings that should be a part of our daily lives. When we don't consider our own home as a place to see nature, then we don't expect it to be there and we don't know to look for it. It also means we can't look at our own landscapes with a fair, critical eye; we can't see the damage, the sickness or the emptiness, nor can we start to try to heal it. When we're this detached, when we don't know what the alternative could be, could look like, it's no wonder we can't ask for even the simplest changes in the places we live.

'Like road verges!' he exclaimed. 'How about we don't cut them all the time? We could make positive progress by just *stopping* – but we won't even do that. For the sake of tidiness!'

I could feel the exasperation radiating him and I wondered if, amidst all of these frustrations, he feels any hope.

'Are you even asking that question?!' he laughed. But then he became more serious.

He explained that it's the absence of hope he notices more; how his feelings of loss and grief combine into a sense of despair. Like Chantelle and Charlie had described, these worries had started to affect Tom's mental health over time, to the point where he'd begun to have nightmares.

'I dream about my garden in the height of summer when everything's buzzing and I find out someone's mown it all. Or I dream I've cut my Birch tree down. And as soon as it's happened, I think, *What have I done?!*'

I must admit, I laughed a bit when he told me this. Knowing how much Tom worships his little garden – of course it was the subject of his anxious dreams, bless him. But that driving sensation behind them, one of hopelessness, is very real. And it can feel especially strong when we see acute examples of loss in front of us. When you encounter something representative of a wider problem – a Hedgehog slumped lifeless at the side of the road, an entire field yellowed and shrivelled with the herbicide glyphosate.

WHATEVER IT WAS, IT WIGGLED

A few years ago, I was walking along a path by the River Severn and a female Goosander bobbed up from beneath the surface. I smiled for a second before noticing the small lead weight dangling from her beak. Coiled around her bill, face and neck, the fishing wire had firmly taken hold of this beautiful bird. Seeing her swim in the middle of the current, knowing there was nothing I could do to help her escape her fate, shattered a piece of my heart. I thought about it for weeks afterwards. I still think about it now.

Combine these personal moments of witness with our now relentless exposure to statistics and headlines, and it's no wonder the outlook appears as bleak as a singed grouse moor. We have our own eyes and guts telling us something isn't right, and then it's reinforced by the information we hear all around us. It can be easy to slip into a state of apathy and indifference. What's the point, right?

Hopelessness isn't pleasant; it's scary and it's uncomfortable. But is that all right? Do we actually have to have hope?

If I'm talking about my worries or sorrow when it comes to nature I am almost always asked, 'Yes, Lucy, but tell us, what gives you hope?' It's like a knee-jerk reaction – we can't be all doom and gloom; everything needs to finish on a positive note. But are we really helping anyone if we're not being honest? I've stewed on this and I'm beginning to wonder if hopelessness itself – or at least a lack of hope – could actually be a useful thing, in the same way that guilt can be. Tom had thought something similar.

'I think my hopelessness rouses anger. Getting to that point of hopelessness can really light a fire in the belly.' We paused mid-step, our conversation briefly interrupted by a moment of

LOVE IS A TOAD

beauty. A Kestrel sliced through the grey December sky and paused in focused hunt, quaking with the effort of holding her spot in the air. She hovered right above our heads. We watched her, first suspended in a quiver and then diving like a feathered arrow to secure her rodentish lunch.

Tom continued his line of thought as the Kestrel carried her catch to a nearby tree for devouring. 'I think, for me, teetering on the edge of hopelessness probably is valuable. Sometimes it kind of rekindles a fire, in a weird way.'

Rekindling a fire. When we're at that point of hopelessness, we've not really got anything to lose. That discomfort can drive change, it can help form ideas, it can instil a *f*ck it* attitude that sees people take risks for the greater good. We've seen from oppressed people across the world, and throughout history, that action, movements and transformation can emerge during times of great despair. In times of conflict, occupation, genocide, war – hopelessness is a daily fact of life for many. But I could see Tom was right, that hopelessness brings other things with it; things that bind us together. It's in the moments where everything seems lost that collective support and kindness appear. It's then that a spark can ignite.

It's quite likely that we're at the beginning, if not in the midst of, a colossal shift in culture – a big change in how things are done. The system we're currently living in – one that's bad for people (save for the privileged minority) and bad for nature – has been centuries in the making. Change is desperately needed. Big changes, ones that might feel impossible or scary or unsettling. But that doesn't mean we can't still act. One thing I've come to realise is that I don't need to believe that my actions will make a difference.

WHATEVER IT WAS, IT WIGGLED

That is to say, I don't need to have hope in order to do the things I believe to be right, to be best for others and for nature. Hope, by its very nature, lies in a place we can't see, way beyond the horizon. We might never see the results of our work – we'll never know if we're successful – but that doesn't mean we should give up. We can choose to do the work despite the insecurity of it all. Despite hopelessness.

We don't have control of the outcome for the whole landscape, but we do over the way we operate within the little metaphorical meadow around each of us. Here, amongst the Buttercups and Clovers, we can cultivate joy, we can grow little parcels of awe to gift to others, and we can open new eyes to the wonders of hoverflies, and Harebells and Minnows.

One evening, when I was feeling particularly grumpy and hopeless, I stumbled across a piece of writing by author Margaret J Baker: 'If I cannot hope, and I do not wish to embrace despair, what am I left with? The work. I have the work.'

The wall in front of us was delightfully mossy – that eye-pleasing combination of grey stone and moss so green it almost glows. We slipped and stumbled over it, clambering into the soggy woodland beyond. As I jumped down on to the boggy floor, I held out a hand to steady myself, leaning upon the soft and mossy branch of one of those cracked and leaning Willows. Looking down, I noticed a clump of sunshine yellow under my fingertips and lifted them to reveal a small explosion of feathers. The yellows were accompanied by greys and blues, and I realised I was looking at an ex-Blue Tit, the remains of a Sparrowhawk's plucking session. I snaffled a couple and tucked them into my empty lunchbox; feathers make great gifts to tuck inside birthday cards, even if they are a little bloodstained.

The woods were deliciously wet. Here again, the forest floor was formed of boggy pools and moisture seemed to cling to every surface. Wintry fungi seemed to be protruding from every angle – the weirdly gelatinous tufts of Jelly Ear and neon yellow orbs of Lemon Disco. The Willows in here felt old; half of them seemed to be mid-collapse or in the process of being devoured by the bog. Tom and I wandered around in a peaceful sort of silence, finding our own little scenes of wonder and fascination to poke at. At one point, he found a particularly handsome clump of *Sphagnum fallax* and I busied myself by ogling some nice lichens. After a while, Tom piped up again.

'You know, I am kind of hopeless, but I'll always keep trying. I can't face not trying because I think it matters too much. It might be you're having a horrible day, but then a crack in the pavement has got a beautiful little flower in it. And suddenly that's everything. It lifts you, even when everything else is awful. Those little nature moments are the things that keep you going; they're the stuff I live for.'

Tom had barely got the last word out when it happened. The first purr, I wasn't so sure about. But the second. Oh my. They were here. *They were here*!

Just as Tom had described, after we first heard them, the Long-tailed Tits appeared, pouring through the bare Birch canopy in the same way water trickles down a gradual slope, darting at random in different directions. The leader reached us and, in a moment of nosiness, dropped down on

WHATEVER IT WAS, IT WIGGLED

to a lower branch of Birch, dangling upside down like a fluffy trapeze artist.

I looked at them, they looked at me. And in that very second, everything twinkled. I felt as though their call purred in the deepest folds of my soul. I felt their softness without touching them, their lightness without holding them.

Bumbarrels. Bumbarrels! We live in a world with Bumbarrels!

CHAPTER 9

For the Love of Oil Beetles

Empathy | Othering

MEL PARKER

Studland Bay, Dorset – 21 January

'Naturists,' the sign exclaimed, 'may be seen beyond this point!'

The sign was big – so big you couldn't miss it – and it was wedged into the sand on thick wooden posts, smoothed by salt and wind and sand so that it almost resembled driftwood. More sand whipped at its base as we approached it, carried by the 50-something-mile-an-hour winds of Storm Isha. It was January. It was nine degrees Celsius. I wondered if any naturists would brave the beach today.

Isn't nakedness a funny thing? Or rather, isn't our attitude towards it funny? Our most natural form is expected to be swaddled and covered. But to be naked is bloody brilliant. To be naked is to feel free. Have you ever legged it into the sea, nothing but salt and skin and the tickle in your tummy as the waves lift and drop you? It's the stuff life's made of, I swear.

LOVE IS A TOAD

Mel and I mused about nudity as we stumbled forwards, pushed by hefty gusts, our hands stuffed into our coat pockets against the nibbling cold. We'd checked the forecast in the days before but decided to *screw it* and go for a wander regardless. On the south coast of Dorset, we'd headed to the sandy stretches of Studland Bay for adventure. We'd both spent a while here the previous summer, working on BBC's *Springwatch* during a heatwave. It'd barely dipped below 29 degrees over the three weeks and so early morning sea dips became a daily ritual before work.

Today was a little bit different. The lolloping dunes and stretching sands of Studland weren't doused in sunshine; the day had an altogether greyer quality to it. That said, I think beaches in winter are just delicious places to be. When you walk on a beach in the gloom of December or January, you feel exposed in the best way. Cheeks tingling, hair whipped – even the salt seems to taste better on the tongue in winter. And the smell! There's a very distinct wintry scent to beaches, a savoury dankness of seaweeds and spray saturating the cold air. It feels as though you can draw it deeper into your lungs than at any other time of year. I love it.

The sky over the sea was a boiling pot, rumbling with every shade of grey – the colours of storms and smoke and the whiskers on a grizzly old dog's chin. We giggled nervously at the absurdity of our mission before turning towards the rolling dunes behind us. Mel lolloped up the first dune ahead of me, her feet sinking in the soft sand so that she walked with a slow wobble.

Mel is an exquisite human. She's warm and gentle, and one of the funniest folks I know. Her excitement and joy for

FOR THE LOVE OF OIL BEETLES

wildlife fizzes and bubbles over in a way you can't help but be drawn in by. We'd met working on *Springwatch* a couple of years earlier and bonded over the surreal task of measuring out the equivalent weight of all of Britain's mustelids (the group of mammals that includes Otters, Weasels and Pine Martens) in potatoes, using only a tiny set of kitchen scales. A friendship was formed as we attempted to pile a Badger's worth of spuds into a small bowl under extreme time pressure before a live TV show. After our root vegetable-based ordeal, we discovered a shared love for small things, each of us equally smitten by parasitic wasps, moths and Cockchafers.

Mel's mum grew up in Kenya, living between the city and a farm near Kitale. It was a normal part of her mum's upbringing to be outside with other kids, getting dirty, watching plants grow and getting to know the animals – so Mel was raised like that too. She told me fondly about planting some Bluebells at the bottom of the garden with her dad and how she would watch with excitement each spring when they popped up.

'Where I was in nature, I was happiest.' She smiled. 'I guess the thing that brings me the most joy is learning about stuff. When I was younger, it did not occur to me that I could just be delighted by things. And now, it's sort of my job to be delighted by things.'

Mel's a researcher for wildlife telly, working on productions about wildlife in the UK and across the world. She spends her time researching the species being filmed, trawling through academic papers and other accounts to find what other people know about any given beetle, bird or fish.

'I do work that involves looking into a lot of detail about

nature. I think the reason I have this affinity for the weird and wonderful is that it's mind-blowing to me how things have absolutely incredible life strategies hard-wired into their DNA. Like Oil Beetles . . .' Mel paused, vibrancy and enthusiasm oozing from her words. I knew what was coming. This girl's affinity for Oil Beetles is on another level.

Mel learnt about these invertebrates when she was making a short film about them – before that, she'd never seen one or known anything about them. But it turns out Oil Beetles are both wonderful and ridiculous-looking little creatures. They're chunky, hefty beetles, which seem to be made up of about 50 per cent backside. They're slow and bumbling, dragging their massive, rotund bums behind them. The five species we find in the UK are either all black or have a gorgeous purple or blue iridescent sheen to them.

Mel took a deep, anticipatory breath, launching into an excitement-filled description of her new favourite critters. Female Oil Beetles will lay hundreds and hundreds of eggs – up to 40,000 in her lifetime – because they have such a small chance of becoming an adult. The eggs are laid in a burrow dug by the female and hatch into tiny yellow larvae known as triangulins. The larvae have six legs (like all insects) adorned with specialised, hook-like feet. Once they've hatched, they leave the burrow and scurry up to the top of the nearest flower they can find. And then, they wait.

Mel explained how the triangulins must get four things right to succeed in becoming an adult Oil Beetle, and how all four of these things are totally dependent upon luck. First up, it must be a flower that they scurry up; it can't be any other sort of plant or structure. It also has to be a flower that attracts pollinators. You see, those three little hooks (hence the name 'triangulin') on the end of each foot enable the beetle larva to latch on to unsuspecting flower visitors. This is where the second stroke of luck comes in: the triangulins don't want to grab hold of any old flower-feeding insect – they specifically need to latch on to bees. And thirdly, it can't just be any old bee. It has to be a solitary mining bee, a species whose life cycles involve digging (or mining) burrows in soil or sand.

'But not just that!' Mel continued, her excitement ramping up even more. 'It's got to be a *female* mining bee because she has a lovely well-stocked pantry for her little baby bee egg.'

Mel told me that if a triangulin can check off these four strokes of luck (a flower, tick. A bee, tick. A mining bee, tick. A female mining bee – BINGO!) whilst remaining undetected (perhaps a fifth element of luck), then it will be carried to precisely the place it wants to be. This sneaky little hitch-hiker will find itself inside a mining bee's burrow, complete with tasty pollen provisions they can consume. Then all that's left to do is to pupate into an adult Oil Beetle, starting the cycle again.

'Just thinking about how improbable that is blows my mind. They're not deciding these things, they're not making these decisions. It's just hard-coded into their DNA. Isn't that completely mind-boggling?!'

Mel was in her element, gushing about the intricacies and complexity of the living things she adores. We'd shared a moment with an Oil Beetle when we were in Dorset the previous spring. On a particularly hot and sticky day off, we'd walked miles along the cliffs of the coastline, hoiking up and down hills and finding wonderful things to be excited about. Halfway up a thigh-achingly steep slope, I was a short distance ahead of Mel when I spied an Oil Beetle on the path at my feet.

Mel began to reminisce fondly. 'It suddenly turned into a very chaotic nature encounter because I sprinted down that hill – I probably could have died – and then sprinted halfway up the other side of it, just to see this Oil Beetle. Oh, my god! It wasn't even like meeting a celebrity. It was like meeting God! Here was this thing, so tiny and so improbable, and it was in my hand. And it exists through billions of years of random chance, kind of like me, but also much cooler. If you don't know what an Oil Beetle is, then it's just a black beetle. But when you do know, it becomes this improbable, beautiful and bright little spark in your life. When that Oil Beetle was in my hand, it was my friend. It was the best. I genuinely loved that beetle with all my heart.'

I told you this girl liked Oil Beetles. Mel's joy for such a small, bizarre critter simply shone. I still smile regularly at the memory, the image of her gently cupping the clumsy creature in her hands, beaming with admiration as she did. She meant every word too.

'It feels like a ridiculous thing to say because we're taught that it's ridiculous – but it isn't! I believe that's what we're built for – for loving things. Someone in the past observed Oil Beetles, they learnt about them and then taught me about them, and so I was able to find the same baffling joy in them. And I did! That's the thing about researching in detail – there are so many things that become your kin, your friends, your family, that you love just because they exist.'

I knew how Mel felt. I too feel that love for things just for

FOR THE LOVE OF OIL BEETLES

being so perfectly, wonderfully them. Even on a stormy day in January, we were surrounded by other lives being busy.

A small gaggle of Brent Geese, buffeted and ruffled by the wind, flew determinedly past us. It looked as though they only just had control of the situation, and kept emitting their soft, babbling honks as if to reassure one another. Out on the water, just past the point where the waves were breaking, a rather nonchalant-looking Great Crested Grebe bobbed up and down with the roll and swell of the sea, seeming as calm as if they were bobbing in a millpond. And on the shore, just ahead of us, a young and grey-speckled Herring Gull appeared to be attempting some sort of aerial acrobatics, soaring up into the wind with focus before giving in and dropping to the ground again. As we drew closer, we could see what was actually happening. The gull had acquired a mussel and was carrying it up into the air so that it could drop it, trying to smash the clamped black shell open and gobble the gooey goodness inside.

We'd covered a good bit of ground, with a mile or so of sandy beach stretching behind us. We were well past the bold-lettered naturists sign – firmly in the naked zone. Alas, the only other people on the beach were a few well-wrapped dog walkers, hunkered in their coats and bracing against the relentless wind. At the very end of the beach, just as the coast curved into the shelter of Poole Harbour, we came across a little cluster of rocks protruding from the otherwise uniform stretch of sand. They were small and inconspicuous, not big or weathered enough to support proper rock pools, but they presented an opportunity for nosiness nonetheless. The two of us crouched in naturalist's squats, hunching over our knees and exposing our fingers to the cold to have a poke and nosey.

Twinkling amongst the neutral browns and greys of the rocks were little dots of bright yellow. A closer look at one revealed the tiny whorled shell of a Flat Periwinkle. Now, I want you to imagine the cutest snail you possibly can. Something so adorable it makes your lip quiver. That's what Flat Periwinkles look like – dinky marine snails with shells the exact colour of Buttercups. They rumble around rocks and seaweed, chombling on algae with their scraping, rasping little mouths. Their eyes resemble pinpricks of ink and they have a pair of gooey-looking tentacles, which they flail around in slow motion as they move. Looking around me, I could see others – plenty of yellow ones but other variations too. Some were the colour of marmalade and others were patterned with orderly, chequered speckles of rusts and browns.

Mel and I gawped at the adorable marine mollusc in front of us. I imagine the two of us, hunched over and cooing, looked quite bizarre. Just like the Oil Beetles, I utterly loved these snails.

'I think that humans have this incredible hard-wired capacity for loving things,' Mel said, watching another periwinkle plod their way over some seaweed. 'Humans are empathetic creatures at their core. We extend empathy to other humans and to the fluffy animals that we live alongside, but I think that sense of empathy can include everything.'

Yep, even periwinkles. Especially periwinkles. My fingers were already freezing but I didn't care. I placed them gently under the lip of the chunky, barnacle-encrusted rock nearest to me and gently flipped it over, exposing its underbelly. We both leant in for an ogle and I asked Mel what she meant about extending that empathy.

'You know, I think empathy is a core part of our evolution. Being able to have an experience and accurately relay it to another animal of the same species – to say something like "don't eat that berry" – you can see that at the core of human communication is empathy. It's the reason why so much of the hominid fossil record is people being kind!'

Mel explained to me that you can literally see human empathy and kindness in the fossils of early human species. She told me of examples of fossils showing healed bone breaks and fractures, which couldn't have happened without the care and nurturing of other individuals. Injured and disabled individuals were in some cases physically carried by their tribe or family, showing how our distant relatives cared for and empathised with each other. We continued to nosey at the underside of encrusted rocks, admiring a particularly alien-looking Sea Spider as it scuttled across barnacles and sea sponges.

'But I think our empathy was never meant to just be for humans,' Mel continued. 'It's why we're able to form these bonds with creatures and places and environments. Like, people name their cars! And I love that.' She laughed.

It's funny, isn't it? Whilst I can't relate to naming a car, I'm sure many of us have named less-than-animate objects in our lives – a habit that's born out of affection. For me, this way of relating to other life feels pretty natural. To connect with the experiences of other beings, be they a person or a Robin or a little clump of moss, seems to me to be one of the most human things to do. To do it is to

LOVE IS A TOAD

witness, to have compassion and to understand things from another's perspective.

If we put ourselves in the shoes – or the paws, or feathers, or leaves or even pedal mucus – of other living things, it can broaden our perspective and help pluck us from our tendency to look at things with a human-centric view. You might think it's a bit anthropomorphistic, that we're projecting our own feelings and perspectives on to life forms that think and behave nothing like us. You might think we should be more objective, more scientific and less emotional when it comes to the way we relate to other living things. But humans are *not* inherently objective, scientific creatures. Our tendency to empathise and relate to other species (and each other) is part of our very make-up; it's all linked to our ability to connect, to communicate and to tell stories. For me, opening my mind up to at least *try* to imagine the life experiences of other beings is where a lot of the joy in my exploration of nature lies.

When we watch a Blue Tit feed her nestlings, aren't we rooting for them to survive? When we see a hoverfly become entangled in a spider's web, don't we find ourselves hoping they'll manage to wriggle free? When we watch a Mallard bathe in the pond he bobs upon, splashing water up and over his back in peaceful, rhythmic motions, backlit by soft sunlight – isn't there a small part of us that relates to that sensation? The invigorating power of cleansing ourselves on a hot summer's day? I certainly found myself empathising with both the solitary bee *and* the little triangulin clinging to her leg as Mel told me about Oil Beetles. When we watch other life – be they hunting, fleeing, fighting, mating or playing – we can't help but relate.

FOR THE LOVE OF OIL BEETLES

Our fingers, thoroughly salted, wrinkled and wet, had started to ache in the biting wind. After one more lingering gaze at the underside of another rock (this time admiring the scrawled calligraphy cast by Keel Worms and their calcareous little tubes), we placed it back and headed towards the shelter of the dunes, hands stuffed back into warm and dry pockets.

Tottering over the first smooth and sandy humps, we soon came across some areas of more mature dune cloaked in clumps of heather as well as Marram Grass. Beyond them, we found ourselves within a patch of wet, soggy woodland. Here, a messy jumble of Willows and Alders had found a moist refuge behind the shelter of the dunes, growing around and within shallow pools and bigger ponds.

Once amongst the trees, we could finally lower our hoods. Storm Isha was being kerbed by the hummocks of dunes behind us, and so our eyes and lips were freed from the sting of the cold and salty air. I was still thinking about the things Mel had said earlier, about how we tend to lose that unashamed and excitable empathy with other life as we grow older. I wanted to poke at this more and understand what was holding us back from regarding nature as something that we're both part of and equal to.

'Being able to categorise and name species is important because you need to be able to name something so you can talk about how to protect it specifically,' Mel began. 'But equally, that labelling shouldn't make you feel as if something is any "less". The labelling that a lot of science is based on doesn't actually have to dictate the closeness with which you relate to things.'

There are species that we deem attractive, interesting or

useful, like Hedgehogs, and others that we tend to think of as the opposite of these things, like blowflies. But I like this idea that despite those ingrained teachings, and despite things like labels and categories, we can choose to form our own relationships with the living world, however we like. After all, we're dependent on a whole ecosystem in which every living element is interconnected – one which both sustains us and limits us. So perhaps we need to extend our affection and broaden the focus of our empathy.

The trees around us were flickering with birdlife; it seemed we weren't the only ones relishing a bit of shelter from the wind. Above us, the husky voices of Greenfinches wheezed away, contrasting with the tinkling chatterings of Linnets.

Out of the reach of the gusts and flurries, the overlapping branches of the Willows were motionless. Most of them were encrusted with the tufted forms of lichens in the same pale greenish-blue as the shallows of white sandy beaches. This was a familiar habitat and, as we walked, I felt my subconscious listening for the telltale sound of Willow Tits.

Eight years earlier, during the spring I was undergoing my chemotherapy, I signed up as a volunteer to do some bird surveys with the RSPB. It seemed like a useful and interesting activity I could crack on with on my good days, and it would help me learn about birds too. So, when I had the energy, I'd head to various patches of wet, willowy woods armed with my clipboard, binoculars and a small portable speaker. Ramping up the volume to max, I'd use it to play the scratchy, indignant calls of Willow Tits – always for two minutes at a time – and then wait.

FOR THE LOVE OF OIL BEETLES

As April became May and then June, I trundled along footpaths in the streaks of wet woods you tend to find along canals and rivers playing calls at regular intervals. Before I started the surveys, I'd never seen a Willow Tit. During my training, they were described to me: tiny greyish-cream birds with neat black caps and a fiery, territorial nature. I learnt they'd declined rapidly and that these widespread surveys were attempting to map where Willow Tits might still be clinging on.

I still remember the first responder to my canned tit vividly: a single individual, perched only feet above my head as they scratched and screeched their fury at the invisible intruder.

Over a few weeks, I watched these characterful little birds go about the busy business of survival, provisioning their nests built in hollowed, rotting stumps. Feeling sick and lethargic, I found myself relating to their fragility and vulnerability as I observed the tiny population clinging on in the wet woods. I'd discovered a new thread of empathy with nature, having in common a drive for survival in the face of pressure, be it habitat loss or cancer.

Mel and I squelched along, glancing around at the wooded tangle around us. *Willow Tits would love it here*, I thought. But I knew you don't get them in this part of Dorset any more – only their incredibly similar relatives, the Marsh Tit.

More silhouettes flickered above and around us as we walked, the colour and detail sucked from their forms by the greyness of the day. I enjoyed their company regardless, relishing the sense of interaction and company you get when you're escorted by a chattering flock of birds.

LOVE IS A TOAD

Mel was still thinking about our conversation and continued chatting as we ducked under the lichen-clad branches above us. 'There are so many layers of abstraction between us and the nature that's sustaining us that it becomes impossible to truly understand. Our connections are hidden behind a layer of Tesco's plastic, and when you've got a layer of plastic over your vegetables, and you don't see it in the ground, you don't think, *I need to protect the Earth, and the places and the environments that allow the things that sustain me to grow.*' Mel sighed, her fingers reaching to stroke a particularly bushy clump of Usnea lichen above her head. 'We look at what we need as if it's not part of nature, and that nature is over there, that nature is something "other".'

Mel was right. How can we have true gratitude, reverence or empathy for nature when most of us don't get to be close to it? That in-depth, slow intimacy with nature, and the way it provides and sustains, has been taken away. Most of us no longer get to revel in the wonder of a beanstalk growing, forage blackberries in early autumn, plunge our fingers into the soil. Mel's use of the word 'other' feels like a key point here.

The word 'other' might be most familiar as an adjective (or perhaps a noun or pronoun) – but it can also be a verb too. To 'other' is to view or treat someone as intrinsically different to ourselves, to consider that we are one thing and they (whoever they are) are quite literally something else – something other.

We do it with people. In Western human society, hierarchies exist in all sorts of ways, including within institutions of power, social class, race, differing abilities, gender and sexuality. It is in these ways that we tend to 'other' people, to negate others' humanity and so see them as less worthy of our respect or empathy. There is a hierarchy of people (generally, the whiter, wealthier and healthier you are, the higher up that hierarchy you sit) and below that, there is a hierarchy of other life. Encapsulating that hierarchy is an overarching view that frames the whole of nature as 'other' – looking at it as something separate to us, different from us. Nature is something other and therefore it's also something lesser. Aren't we the most intelligent species on the planet, after all?

So often, nature is described in a way that makes it seem *over there*. We talk about 'going into' nature; we describe it as something you can connect, or indeed disconnect, with. Nature is something of a leisure activity or a pastime. You go into nature with your binoculars, you look at birds for a bit and then you come home, back out of nature and into your safe little box.

This is so deeply ingrained that it's quite hard to pinpoint where it begins and where it ends. I'm responsible for using othering language myself, probably subconsciously within the very pages of this book. Many times I've caught myself in a moment of admiration for another life form, wondering at the instincts of the earwig, amazed by the adaptations of the Gannet. But in doing that, I'm forgetting that we're made of these things too: we're as much a big bundle of instincts, adaptations and drive as any other living thing. I think this belief – even though it is largely subconscious – is a significant element of the ecological grief we're processing.

Nature is often seen as our dominion too, a pool of inanimate resources from which we can take what we like –

LOVE IS A TOAD

just as Mel had described. This mindset stretches back into history; it's something we've been handed down and which persists in modern culture and ideas. If we look at the legacy of colonialism, a mindset of superiority was the driving force behind the coloniser's actions: to see themselves as superior to other people and to nature allowed them to feel entitled to take land, to exploit resources, to extract and to dominate. We can see how this mindset still exists today in the entitlement of big businesses and corporations – in the fact they're allowed to continue to pollute, exploit people, deforest, emit carbon and produce plastic, even though we know it's bad. In a capitalist world, nature is still regarded as a resource and not as a living, breathing, animate entity. It's seen as a thing that we humans sit outside of. And if nature is not a thing we feel part of, then we don't have to feel as though we owe it anything, be that our gratitude or custodianship.

We wove our way through the trees, beautiful in that grey, wintry sort of way. After a short while, the Willows and Alders gave way to Birch trees, dotted amongst tussocks and bushes of Common Heather and Gorse. We decided to veer off track and attempt to traverse a soggier patch of ground between us and the beach. Here the Birch seemed small and stunted, rising from boggy pools and speckled with more witches' broom. Mel and I slipped and stumbled along, attempting to hop from hummock to hummock and avoid an accidental paddle in the bog below.

We continued to chat and, between slips and bouts of giggling, Mel pointed out that there is another side to all this too. When people talk about rewilding, nature restoration or pristine wilderness, they tend to have a peopleless environment in mind, and that only adds to that othering mindset.

I've seen this viewpoint shared widely and I've probably even held it myself at some point. Because we see the damage inflicted by human activity, we think that nature is better off without us. But that's not necessarily true.

'Because humans *are* nature!' Mel agreed. 'There are entire tribes that move through the land and look after it. They're aware that the resources they need to survive are part of that land; they might be looking after the Buffalo or they're looking after their food plants. Our fundamental ability to survive is based in nature and that nature still exists.'

Humans *are* nature. How on earth could we get this far without being part of it? I think this feeling links back to that misanthropy I spoke to Amy about and includes a good dollop of that collective guilt that I discussed with Charlie. In talking all of this through with them, I could now join the dots a little easier. When we feel culpable in a world where horrid things are happening, it makes sense that we might feel the world would be better off without us. But, in giving in to these beliefs, we're forgetting our roots. A closeness with nature isn't just in our species' past; you can still see it happening in the present. As Mel pointed out, plenty of communities, cultures and indigenous groups across the world do live in harmony with nature. The model that lots of us live in – of capitalism, consumption and a fractured relationship with the natural world – isn't in our nature. We're not doomed to follow that path; we can choose to live differently.

'We are taught individualism in Western society; it's drilled into our heads that being self-reliant is the only and best way to live,' Mel continued. 'But actually, with the challenges we're facing and that nature is facing, being part of a collective is far more powerful.'

At that moment, a streamlined grey streak cut through the air above us, emanating focus and ferocity from its sleek body. A Peregrine, only a shade darker than the heavy storm clouds above, soared above the treeline ahead of us. The air was immediately filled with a sense of panic and scattering – lots of little birds making themselves scarce. A second later, another streak appeared: two Peregrines now, rocketing and wheeling through the air as if the gale-force winds were nothing but the tickle of a light breeze on a summer's day. We whooped and jumped with excitement at seeing such badass birds defy the bluster of Isha and continue about their birdy business as usual. I imagined their muscular and merciless talons wrapping around the still-warm body of their feathered prey, one life in exchange for another. All part of the same interconnected, tangled community of life and death that we belong to too.

'There's no use in us looking at ourselves as individuals. And I mean that in the literal sense: you are not an isolated being as much as society tells you you are!'

Mel was right. We have thousands of species of bacteria living inside us: by some estimates, less than half 'our' cells are human cells – the rest belong to our microbiomes. This comes back to nature's interconnectedness and the blurred lines between species, and even individuals. Perhaps the antidote to seeing nature as 'other' is to work on accepting it is, in fact, just one big soup of which each of us is a tiny drop.

FOR THE LOVE OF OIL BEETLES

Mel nodded at this. 'You know, there's no shame in requiring other people, in needing community and to work as a collective. We are much more powerful if we operate as a super organism. If you look at anything in nature, nothing exists in isolation.'

I think community is the right answer here. We can push back against the idea that we're outside of nature by accepting our place in the wonderfully diverse and ecologically complex community that nature is. When we accept the mindset of othering, we learn that we're special, that we're the most intelligent species on the planet, that we're top of the food chain. But we humans are not special. We are different; we can do things *differently* to other species, to other life forms, but this does not make us better (or worse) than them. Humans are gifted with amazing things. We have the ability to feel joy and grief, and all sorts of other emotions (though, for all we know, slugs could be the biggest joy-feelers and, as Nadia said, butterflies could be the biggest grievers). But other life forms are gifted with other things. The Oak with a quality that lets them support hundreds of other life forms. The Garden Cross Spider with her spinnerets that allow her to form intricate silk structures stronger than steel. The Yellowhammer can scribble and scrawl her signature upon her eggs as she lays them, and blowflies can take the soupy rot of death and convert it into bodily energy. These are all gifts. None better, none worse, just different.

Our shortcut back to the beach had brought us to an almost entirely flooded path. The two of us hopped and tiptoed along the edge of it, clinging to branches and the trunks of trees to steady ourselves. The whole of the woods either side of the track were flooded, the water hugging the bases of trees in every direction.

'Shared joy and shared grief – they're not opposites, they're part of the same thing. We can categorise and name these emotions but they all come from the same place,' Mel said. 'It all comes from this thing that we're hard-wired to do, which is to empathise, and love, and want to protect the things that we empathise with and that we love.'

Oh, Mel. I could see how empathy could be one of the most effective tools for shifting us away from a mindset of self-interest and of the individual. Instead, nature needs us to adopt a common-interest perspective – a mindset that considers life collectively.

After a little more slogging, we spied the first soft hump of the dunes in the distance. Finally – dry land and sand. As we wandered back through the towering hummocks, we came across another board, plastered with large, bold letters.

'NATURISTS!' it promised. 'MAY BE SEEN BEYOND THIS POINT!' it speculated.

As we reached the beach again, we paused for another breath. Shoulder to shoulder, we looked out over the wind-whipped sand and rolling, undulating waves beyond.

The wind had really picked up now, salty spray mixing with airborne sand. The few walkers we saw earlier had scarpered and we pretty much had the beach to ourselves.

And so there was only one thing for it. Tops off, knickers cast into the dunes, we stripped and legged it across the beach, our bare bums pelted with sandy prickles and icy stings. Before I knew it, we were in, rolling with the swell, slapped by the waves and laughing hysterically.

CHAPTER 10

The Pink People
Belonging | Detachment

NICK ACHESON
Cley Marshes, Norfolk – 3 February

'Ooh – the pink people are flying over!'

I craned my neck, squinting into the sunlight. A smattering of soft, slightly squeaky honks rained down from the azure blue sky and I made out a group of gently flapping silhouettes heading for the horizon. Nick raised a hand to his eyes, forming a visor so he could watch the geese too. We smiled as they hooted into the distance, tightly knitted together and wings beating rhythmically.

I absolutely *adore* the sound of Pink-footed Geese – or 'the pink people', as Nick fondly calls them. It's an undeniably goosey sound – that trumpety and rather honkalicious noise we associate with these long-necked waddlers – but it has its own unique qualities too. It's softer and more high-pitched than a Canada Goose's, a little less shouty. When a flock of them flies overhead, it sounds like they're discussing something inane and frivolous, like what they had for tea

LOVE IS A TOAD

or who's got the pinkest legs. It's a sound I find deeply comforting, the sound of home in autumn, when tens of thousands of the gentle little honkers arrive in their neat 'V' formations, filling the air with their goose song.

Pink-footed Geese feel like old friends; they've always been a presence in my life, even before I knew who they were or where they'd come from. Sitting in the back of my nana's car as she'd nipped to the shops – perhaps only five or six years old – I remember watching a seemingly never-ending stream of them pour overhead. They were there as I grew up too. I spent a few years slogging away in a shoe shop, stacking boxes, sticking sale tags on boots and holding wriggling children as I measured their feet. I remember escaping to the shop roof in the autumn – swinging the hefty fire door open with arms full of empty boxes for sizes four and five. I'd stand on the flat roof, flattening the cardboard and jamming as much as possible into the recycling bins. Over my head flooded thousands of Pinkies arriving for the winter. Their formations looked like scrawled handwriting; their plaintive voices familiar and entrancing.

Geese are a topic of mutual gushing between Nick and me. We're both from flat, veg-growing places on opposite sides of the country; the wide, expanding scenery of Norfolk reminds me of Lancashire in many ways – and one of those ways is geese.

Pinkies in particular tie these two spudlands together. They're tough and compact little birds. I always imagine they land with a thump and waddle with heavy splats on their rosy, webbed feet. In spring and summer, they raise clutches of Pinkie goslings in colder places like Greenland, Iceland

THE PINK PEOPLE

and remote archipelagos off Norway and Russia. Then, when the icy front of winter looms, they'll take off and head south to spend the coldest months in comparatively warmer climes. The geese first arrive in Scotland in September, flying over the mountains of the Highlands and stopping in spots along the east coast. Some continue on to Lancashire, on the northwest coast of England. A whole heap more will take off again and carry on, joining more birds from Iceland on the east coast in Norfolk. Travel around the countryside in winter in any of these places and you're likely to see hundreds of them peppering the fields, whispering honks and waddling as they nibble and graze the stubbly remains of crops like wheat, spuds and sugar beet. At dawn and dusk, they'll head off to roosting spots, and that's when you're treated to a spectacle of the *pink people* – their arrow-headed arrangements (called skeins) cutting across the sky, thousands of them on the move.

The geese have become a significant beat in the rhythm of Nick's annual calendar, ebbing and flowing with the seasons with a comforting predictability. It's the same for me too – their voice is the sound of home and of place, the sight of them a thing that conjures colours, smells and a sense of reassurance.

On this sunny, blustery morning, the two of us stood looking out across the wide expanse of Cley Marshes, a nature reserve in north Norfolk. Like at home, the sky was big and flat and vast. Bright, late-winter sun illuminated bubbly, frothy clouds in the whitest white, making them sort of hard to look at. The wind pulled and whipped them along at speed, so that it became a day of intermittent sun and shade, changing between the two every couple of minutes.

LOVE IS A TOAD

Following Nick from the road on to the reserve, it felt like we were plunging into a maze of reed beds. Lofty and floppy-topped, they rustled in the breeze so that we were surrounded by an audible wall of gold.

'I walk here all the time.' Nick gestured at the path in front of us where a bridge crossed a deep blue pool of water cut into the fluttering reeds. 'I think about it as a sort of rosary, where you're constantly telling the same beads. You walk a path, you walk it again and again, and it just becomes deeply embedded in your soul.'

I'd never used rosary beads, but coming from an Irish Catholic family I was familiar with the concept. I likened it to the familiarity I feel with a much-rubbed pocket pebble, knowing the lumps, bumps and outline of the form I've thumbed countless times. It was clear Nick knew this place well; as we walked, he pointed out the spots he'd seen different wildlife over the years and seasons. An Otter in that ditch last week. A Kingfisher on this post on early mornings. The spot where Wild Celery grows in spring.

The flatness of the marshes gave us a wide-reaching view, and over the whispering crests of the reed beds, to the south-west, we could see the outline of the nearby village and its little steeple. It was sweet and picturesque, like a little doodle on the horizon. I asked Nick what it was about this place he loved, why he'd decided to meet me here for a walk.

'My father's family is from Blakeney; generations of them are from there. And so this place has a deep hold on me. My grandfather was the doctor in these villages and my parents got married in that church over there.' He gestured at Blakeney village behind us. 'I went to school in Holt and fell in with this group of friends, and we all got into birds and . . . *Dee-DEE, dee-DEE, dee-DEE!*'

Nick suddenly broke off, looking skywards and making this weird noise. 'Look, goldies! *Dee-DEE!*' he shouted and pointed at a little flock of Golden Plover, enthusiastically imitating their high-pitched call. Their silhouettes were sharp-winged and sleek, and the small bunch of birds moved in tight, urgent unison.

Nick carried on after the birdy interruption as though nothing had happened. 'We used to come here every week throughout school. And so it was just the place where all of these things were, where I learnt all of these sounds. It's the place where I was given knowledge and a sense of belonging.'

It was such a nice spot to visit; I felt grateful to Nick for showing me a patch that means so much to him. We were surrounded by a bustling February soundscape – the aforementioned honks mixed in with the babbling of ducks, chiming of Redshank and *peee-wits* of Lapwings, all playing over a backing track of rustling reeds. Walking through the maze, a faint pinging sound tinkled through the solid wall of vegetation, starting off behind us and getting closer. It whizzed past in a hurry, the hint of shadows flickering amongst straight stems – something not quite visible. I recognised the pings as the weirdly metallic sound of Bearded Tits; it seemed a huddle of them had passed us very closely. I love these little weirdos. Their bodies look like chubby little spuds, with splayed, skinny legs like cocktail sticks which grip the reeds in some kind of avian version of the splits. As if this wasn't enough of a reason to like them, the males have frankly ridiculous facial markings – bold black triangles that,

LOVE IS A TOAD

depending on your perspective, either look like an impressive handlebar moustache or an amount of eyeliner reminiscent of my own MySpace era. (You can google 'emo eyeliner' if you have no idea what I'm talking about.)

The reed beds opened up a little and we followed a path cushioned either side by stretches of grass. Small brown birds skipped and bounced upwards from the vegetation, tussling with each other in the air and descending back into the cover with a flamboyant flutter.

'We're surrounded by mipits!' Nick cried, his words mirroring the flamboyance of the Meadow Pipits that danced all around us.

I love the way Nick talks about wildlife; he gushes naturally, his words always fabulous and full of flair. He's constantly in tune with his surroundings and makes evocative and colourful observations of the things he sees, hears and smells. Every walk with him is guaranteed to spark a bit of wonder and joy. He says hello to every passer-by, taking the time to point things out to them. Nick *adores* nature but it's obvious that he loves sharing it with other people above everything else.

'I was the child whose bookshelf was full of nature books – I was just obsessed with animals. And then when I was nearly 13, I was adopted by a teacher, Dave, who is still a great friend of mine. He took a group of us out each week and showed us wildlife. He opened up this world of magic.' I could picture the young Nick in my head, a scrawny lad, wide-eyed and enthusiastic, seeing his first Bitterns and learning the names of dragonflies.

'Our teacher put names to things – to insects, flowers,

THE PINK PEOPLE

birds, processes in nature. And it gave us a vocabulary; it gave us a map with which to navigate the natural world around us. It was a gift!'

How lucky. There's this wonderful window in childhood where – if the right conditions of luck, opportunity and circumstance collide – you might encounter a mentor like this. And if you do, an inextinguishable flame of fascination can be lit for life. I didn't discover the wildlife on my doorstep until I was an adult, yet I still count myself as one of the lucky ones. I was privileged enough to grow up with green space on my doorstep. There wasn't a naturalist I knew to teach me the names of things, but the love for other life still seeped in, like heavy rain soaking through a not-so-waterproof raincoat.

Can you imagine what it would be like if all kids had a love-filled, curiosity-soaked positive force as they grew up? Nick says it himself – he's nothing special; he's just a kid who got a chance. How many more Nicks are there who don't?

It's clear that Nick deeply values his teacher's influence and the door it opened for him, allowing him to dive headfirst into a lifelong love affair with wild things. In the school holidays, he'd sneak across the local airfield to go and watch wildlife on a farm. There, he taught himself about wildflowers, picking pieces of things he didn't know and taking them back home to identify until his head was full of flora.

Now, Nick is dead good at names. It's like he carries around a thick address book in his head, packed with the scrawled personal details of the living beings he loves and knows so well. As we walked, he spoke their names out loud, greeting them as we passed.

The gravelly path had started to slope gently upwards,

LOVE IS A TOAD

lifting us out of the reed beds so that we were above the great flatness. We could see a good distance in all directions. It was beautiful; the sunshine illuminated the reed beds so that they contrasted with the blue of the sky and the reflections of splodged clouds sat in the pools of the marshes.

'This is my soul place.' Nick smiled as he looked out over the land. I could feel the affection oozing from him. Nick grew up here but he lived in South America for over a decade, where he was welcomed and made to feel as though he belonged in someone else's landscape. He'd come home a while ago, despite thinking he'd never return to the UK again.

'It was exactly this time of year when I got home. It was a day like this, a bright, clear day full of Wigeon and Brent Geese. That was 16 years ago now. *Do do do do.* Hello, Redshank.' He greeted the little red-legged wader who'd trotted into view in the pool we walked alongside. Nick told me that once he'd returned, he decided to give up flying and stay put in Norfolk. And so he began to rebuild a closeness with the place he grew up in.

'Since being back, I've learnt to slow down and not have the nature-chasing mindset I used to have. I try to just let nature show itself to you, and that way you see so much more. *So* much more! I now make pilgrimages – I have certain things every year that I have to do just to honour the passing of the months. And I now feel so close to this place. I have a great sense of belonging here.' He looked around the marshes below us, vibrating with the busy bustle of wetlands in winter.

'That on the bank just up there, 50 yards in that direction, is the one place I've ever seen Corn Parsley.' Nick gestured up the path ahead. 'And that's special for me. Whenever I

THE PINK PEOPLE

go past in early summer, I will always stop to look for it. I know that when I walk out to the Point in May and June, I'll see the whole spectrum of beautiful coastal shingle flowers and salt marsh flowers. I will see *Frankenia* . . .' He paused, concentrating hard. 'How do you say *Frankenia*? Sea Heath! I'll see Sea Heath and Matted Sea Lavender and Rock Sea Lavender. They're friends and I now make a pilgrimage to see them. Every year, I honour the flowering of these flowers, or the booming of the Bittern, or the arrival of the Hobbies and their bashing after dragonflies, or the flying of the Swallowtails – ah, Swallowtails!'

Nick's wonderful, energetic gushing was interrupted by his own memory, placing an excited hand on my shoulder as he mentioned Swallowtail Butterflies. A year earlier, we'd had a magical encounter with them – my first time seeing a Swallowtail. Nick had taken me to Hickling Broad in June and we'd stumbled across a pair of Swallowtails dancing and swirling in flirtation. One had landed to feed on a Bramble flower and Nick had snapped a photo of me looking at it, my nose only inches from its blue, red and black-splodged tails. Once again, his wonderful words described them perfectly.

'They're like scraps of scribbled tissue paper, the way they flutter over the reed in that apparently fragile way. But they're so strong and so vibrant and sexual. They're just alive! Ooh, look!'

Nick was distracted from his own distraction by a small plant at his feet. Before I could blink, he was crouched, looking fondly at the narrow stems of some Wild Celery growing at the side of the path. I love how equally excited he gets about every living thing – geese, butterflies, plants.

LOVE IS A TOAD

It was so clear that Nick is of this place and he knew every inch of the spot he'd brought me for our walk. He has a deep familiarity with the land and the life in it; he's truly a part of it, and it obviously brings him solace, peace and joy.

The outdoors brings these things for me too. When I walk around the woods, the park, the hills, I feel like I'm a part of them and them of me. But I didn't always have this feeling. As a kid, I could tell you all about the treefrogs I'd read about in books but didn't know what an Orange Tip Butterfly was. I only came to know – really *know* – the life on my doorstep as an adult. That relationship blossomed, cultivated and watered by the people around me who took the time to share joy and teach me things, plus of course a good dollop of curiosity and childlike wonder.

And whilst I was lucky enough to be able to play outside, it was always with a subconscious belief that what I was doing was wrong, naughty, against the rules. I've realised that I've been carrying a strange spectre with me, one I've not noticed until relatively recently. It had been there for as long as I can remember, clinging to my shoulders like an invisible little goblin, whispering into my ear and telling me I shouldn't be here, that this wasn't my space. As a kid, I didn't feel as though the fields were really ours to explore; it somehow always felt as though we were trespassing and intruding (and often we quite literally were). Piggybacking that goblin instilled a sense of cautiousness, a fear of stepping out of line, breaking rules, of going where I didn't belong.

Isn't it strange how so many of us feel this way? Certainly in England, where we're given strict rules about where we can and can't go. But to want to explore and roam, isn't that the

THE PINK PEOPLE

most natural desire in the world? To hanker for the woods on top of the hill? To slip into the river and rinse the salty sweat from our skin on a hot summer's day? To scale the wiggly limbed Oak – the one that looks like it's stretching out a gnarled hand and saying, 'Climb me'? Yet there are invisible, intangible rules that stop us doing so, ones that tell us 'no' and send us packing.

As nature's played a bigger part in my life, I find I can shed that spectre increasingly often. Don't get me wrong – it's still there. This sense of unwelcomeness is deeply ingrained after all. But I do feel differently about it. I can't even entirely explain what's changed; over time I've become more familiar with nature, I've experienced the right to roam living in Scotland, and I've started giving less of a shit. What I know for sure is that the feeling of belonging was absent, and now it's not.

For me, to belong in nature is to feel an intimacy. It's a deep sense of interconnectedness – I am not *in* nature but *with* it. It's feeling that I know and recognise nature, and that it recognises us right back. Eyeball to eyeball, nose to snout. To feel belonging in a place is to feel embraced, to feel held. I no longer feel I am playing the role of a spectator. I'm not peering through glass at a specimen or exhibit. Now I am in the exhibit, I *am* the exhibit, with my kith and kin, my fellow forms of life force. I now feel like part of the picture, rather than just looking at it. In this way, I know that my interaction with a Robin is as valid and natural as the Robin's interactions with the Blackbird, the Fox and the Oak. To feel that I belong, and that nature belongs with me in return, is one of the deepest elements of nature joy I have.

LOVE IS A TOAD

We rumbled along above the reed beds, my hands tucked in my pockets against the nippy February wind. Turning a corner, I heard a strange noise, a guttural, bubbly cronking rippling across the wet meadow to our right. The meadow was strewn with the charcoal-and-ash forms of hundreds of Brent Geese, grazing and waddling their way across the grass. As we watched, more birds flew down to join them. Nick pointed out a family group – an adult pair joined by two grown goslings, their backs adorned with neat white stripes that their parents lack.

'You know, these are the many times great-grand offspring of geese that I knew in 1987. And the same with the Wigeon and the Pintail and the Teal. To know that I knew their great-great-great-great-great-great-grandparents is extraordinary! And to know that the people who've guided me and taught me must have known their great-great-great-great-great-great-grandparents . . .' Nick paused, I assume to catch his breath. That was a lot of 'greats'. 'I feel such a debt to those people who've handed on this love, and I feel like one link in a chain of people who've loved this place and the life in it.'

I loved that idea. It feels like a bit of magic, to know you're in the presence of an individual organism whose ancestors you met generations ago. Again, it emphasised that sense of fitting in Nick has with his home; his connection with other people links in with his connection with geese and their connections to each other.

By now, we were close to the sea. After a few minutes more walking, we ambled up on to a shingle embankment. The beach stretched from left to right, the shingle an uncountable accumulation of pebbles of different textures, colours and

THE PINK PEOPLE

sizes. There was a delicious cackle ahead of us, the sound of soft waves cracking through the stones on the shore. We watched as two women stripped down to their cozzies and legged it into the sea, complete with bobble hats. They shrieked and laughed with glee, and I thought about Mel and I going for our stormy dip a month earlier. I knew the tingle they must have been feeling and felt joy watching them jump in the waves.

We wandered along the shingle for a while, the pebbles grumbling and gossiping beneath our boots. In the distance, we could see the silhouette of a largeish bird. It had the hunched and tugging shoulders of a gull that was mid-scoff, and, getting closer, we could see it was a Great Black-backed Gull, tucking into something rather big. The rather big something was also rather smelly; the stink of rot hung on the breeze well before we reached the carcass. Smooth in silhouette and draped belly up across the stones, it was the body of a massive Grey Seal, its dense fur lying flat as though it was still wet. Its side was folded open in a large, blubbery gash; this was the spot the gull had been feasting upon. It was morbidly beautiful, peaceful and gross in tandem. I bent down to look at the five perfect claws of its front flippers, making sure to hold my breath. Stiff, wiry whiskers protruded from its snout; they felt tough and sturdy against my probing finger. The lower half of the seal's face had been eaten away, and I spied the jawbone lying on the shingle next to its body. Some of the teeth appeared to be loose, a bit wobbly. Hmm. My treasure radar started tingling. Before I could talk myself out of it, I'd donned a glove (from my rucksack's 'death kit'), wiggled a couple out of their sockets, and popped them in a specimen tube to clean up later at home. Don't judge me.

I wondered what had happened to the seal; was it a natural death? A case of old and weary seal bones coming to the end of their life? Or was it something else? Pollution or entanglement in discarding fishnets? We pondered this and Nick elaborated on the changes he'd seen in his patch over the years, and how he felt about them.

He started off with Willow Warblers, explaining how he'd sobbed when he heard his first one after his return to the UK. Now they're nearly extinct in Suffolk, and declining in Norfolk. These little birds seem to sing sunshine; I regularly get their song stuck in my head in spring and summer – a proper earworm. It's heartbreaking to think about them disappearing.

'All these things are winking out. Spotted Flycatchers were common; they bred in my childhood garden. Turtle Doves – they were never common in my life or my birding life, but they were still regular. And they're now down to a tiny number.' He shook his head and I felt the sadness emanating from him. 'Nightingales! We're within a mile of where Nightingales have lived my entire life, and now they don't. They're retreating; it's like they're falling off the face of the planet,' Nick sighed.

Nightingales feel like a particularly pointed and clear example of loss. I only heard my first this year, standing on a moonless night in mid-April, not able to see the hedgerow in front of my face. The bird sat in his den of thorns and Bramble, pulsating his song into the dark. I felt every note ripple in my throat. I felt the weight of his song in my soul – quite literally: I could physically detect the weight of it, like a dense and smooth pebble vibrating somewhere in my ribcage.

THE PINK PEOPLE

It was as if he was being held under an auditory spotlight, with no other song or sound to be heard, pure, undiluted, distilled.

Nightingale song is something people should know, a voice that should sound as familiar as a good mate's as it resonates from bushes and shrubs in our towns and cities. But how many people have never heard of a Nightingale, let alone listened to their music? This songbird should be part and parcel of what it means to be a human living in this part of the world. But for most of us, it's not any more. The Nightingale has gone; it's been removed from our landscape. And in turn, we've been detached from it, in the way we've detached from so much of our relationship with nature. Nick nodded as I expressed this thought.

'You're right. More and more of our daily ways of making a living, of surviving, are taking us away from nature. Whereas for the entire span of human existence, we've had to understand nature in order to survive the day, to feed our children, to keep them safe from danger.'

Reaching the end of the beach, we wobbled back down the embankment and on to another path snaking through the marsh. After a short while, we came across a hide and sat on a seat outside, turning to feel the warmth of the sun on our faces. Nick sighed, closing his eyes.

'People should be free to experience nature on their own terms, but there's also the fact that the landscape is simply not peopled any more. A distant, distant uncle of mine, who farms near Burnham Market, told me that when he took on the farm in the fifties, there were 60 people working on the farm and one in the pub. Now there are 60 people working in the pub and one on the farm.'

LOVE IS A TOAD

Nick described how so much land no longer has people working on it in the way they did before, their labour having been replaced by machines and chemicals. 'It means people are not knowing nature on a daily basis. And because they don't have that daily *knowing*, they're not daily *seeing*. They're not thinking, *Oh that cock Grey Partridge has got his female in the hedge there. And that Yellowhammer must have her nest down in the scrub at the bottom of the hedge, and this place always floods, and is where the Snipes sit in winter, and, if we head to this field, we'll always see a Barn Owl at three o'clock*. People just don't have that rhythmic relationship that comes with constant exposure to nature.'

Our bench overlooked a still and stretching pool. Shortly after we parked our bums, a Marsh Harrier appeared, slinking lazily over the reeds and tilting this way and that, as if it could only just be bothered flying.

The state of detachment Nick was describing feels to me to be a key element of nature grief. And it feels like the right word to use: we find ourselves removed, separated, *detached*. Or rather, we've been removed, we've had something taken away, and we've been taken away from something in return. The word 'disconnect' is bandied around a lot within the conservation sector – and I have used it too, possibly even in this book. But I don't think that's quite the right word for the state we find ourselves in. To describe us as being disconnected from nature implies that the onus is on individuals; it's somehow our fault. But we know that our 'disconnect' from nature is widespread and pervasive. People don't feel as if they don't belong in nature because they're uninterested or oblivious; they're uninterested or oblivious

THE PINK PEOPLE

because they have been detached. These things are the symptoms, not the cause. But how did we get to be here? How did the detachment happen?

'You know, this is our habitat. And for the millions of years that we have existed, it has been our habitat. That is, until the Industrial Revolution. We've seen this move away from an agrarian society and it means that for a few hundred years, people have been divorced from that daily relationship with their place.'

Nick held his binoculars up as he talked, watching a Curlew as it paddled around the edge of the pool closest to us. 'There's been this erosion of people on the land, of people growing their own food in some way, of living alongside the land. Now our livelihoods are taken away from the outdoors and put into offices and into clouds and cyberspace. Ooh, hello, Shoveler.'

The spade-faced duck swam out from behind some reeds, shortly followed by her iridescent-headed mate. I love the way Shovelers feed, spinning in circles as they kick up food from below, filtering it with their rather ridiculous bills.

'In the past, we would have had to understand the seasons, the soils, where fresh water comes from, what things are dangerous, what things we can eat. And it's still the way that billions of people on earth have to live.'

We looked out at the farmed landscape beyond the nature reserve. This sunny December day it was empty and I tried to imagine how it would've looked in the past. Nick was right. Only a few centuries ago, the countryside would've been much more populated, with rural peasants, cottagers and small-scale farmers, working closely together with shared responsibility for land. Over the course of just a few hundred years – such a tiny blip of time – much of Britain's land has been taken into private ownership. Where it was previously collectively managed (in one way or another), it now lies in the hands of a relatively few individuals. This idea of land being 'owned' by someone is a very modern one – yet it's the reason our lives look like they do today.

Beginning around the thirteenth century, right through to the 1800s, land in England was taken from the hands of the many in a series of events and laws referred to as the enclosures. Previously collectively owned, collectively managed or publicly accessed land was abruptly and aggressively closed off. Communal pastures for grazing livestock, woodlands used for firewood, timber and pig grazing, fenlands and marshlands used for fishing and fowling – much was fenced off or drained or otherwise altered. Displaced rural folk ended up in towns and cities, where their labour was channelled into factories and mills and other products of the Industrial Revolution. Similar patterns of rural depopulation happened in Scotland with the Highland Clearances, with huge numbers of people forcibly removed from land, often to make way for sheep farming.

This history – very much shortened and simplified here – can explain why we live the way we do today. Our survival is no longer intimately connected to the land, at least not obviously, and most of us work in ways that involves spending much of our time inside. As Nick says, our livelihoods no longer depend on knowing nature on a daily basis. And if we aren't living next to the Corn Bunting or the Cuckooflower, then how would we know who they are? Why would we care about them? For most people, a working

THE PINK PEOPLE

relationship with the land is out of reach. Farming is difficult to get into if you've no family history of it, and it's very hard and often isolating work. Nature conservation isn't much better – a poorly paid sector propped up on the free labour of volunteering, its exclusivity means it's financially out of reach for lots of folk.

Today, nature and the outdoors isn't considered a place to live and work; it's often seen as a space of leisure, somewhere to go hiking, birdwatching, mountain biking. Again, access to nature in a leisurely respect still isn't equal or equitable. Financial barriers, hostility, snobbery and prejudice all play a part here, resulting in more of those mindsets around 'the right people' being seen to be in the countryside. And then there's the infrastructure of the countryside itself which seeks to exclude us too: Keep Out signs (like Amy's in the woods), fences and walls, sometimes accompanied by angry men who own guns. If you're made to feel like you're not that 'right' sort of person, of course you'll feel as though you don't belong. If we wander into the countryside and get shouted at, threatened, even, the result is that we feel like we shouldn't be there.

Whilst I feel a deep love for nature, and I've grown my own sense of belonging within that, I also know I'm detached from nature in many ways. I'm sure I'm not alone in yearning for a hands-in-the-soil relationship with the land, a reciprocal relationship with the earth that feeds us. To feel so reliant upon a system of supermarkets and prepackaged food is to feel helpless, severed, detached. Not everybody needs that Natural History™ relationship with nature – but if we rework that daily intimacy back into our lives, it would have the side

LOVE IS A TOAD

effect of cultivating a closeness with, and therefore knowledge of, other living things, just as Nick described.

By now, the Shovelers had company – dabbling ducks seemed to fill the whole pool in front of us. That's something I love about this time of year: the combination of winter and water, an eyeball feast of ducks and waders simply being busy. Gadwall flirting, Teal preening, Shoveler spinning – heaven.

But our duck ogling was suddenly and explosively interrupted. A gravel island in another pool seemed to erupt with glob-winged silhouettes – hundreds of Lapwings taking to the sky in a noisy, flappy panic. They climbed towards the clouds, spreading out in fearful, fluttering confusion. Higher still, a faster flock of Golden Plover zipped away, all speedy and streamlined. Nick knew exactly what was going on.

'Oh, the Peregrine's chucked all the Lapwings in the air! That's got to be a Peregrine reaction, all those Lapwings going loopy like that. I don't see it but we know it's about . . .'

Zoom. There it was! A rocket of a bird of prey surged through the air only metres above our bench. We watched the sharp silhouette of the Peregrine cutting through the flock like a hot knife through butter. 'Wow, he's on a mission. He's just put up a load of Dunlin here. Ahhh. They're just death on wings!'

God, I love Nick's narrations. The Peregrine hurtled out of sight, the sense of excitement and awe hanging between us afterwards. My heart thumped in my chest as though I'd been hunted by the Peregrine myself.

After a short while, the cloud of panic seemed to subdue itself as the Lapwings and plover floated back down to earth. Everything felt calm again, and Nick and I smiled as a Little

THE PINK PEOPLE

Egret swooped into view in front of us, landing in a flourish of ruffling white plumes. We watched it fishing, placing one yellow rubber-gloved foot sneakily down in front of the other and focusing furiously on little fish below the surface. The sun shone from behind it, illuminating the bird in a brilliant brightness that seemed to make it glow.

'So beautiful, that scene with the light and the dappling. Oh, Little Egret, you're a fabulous thing. I hope you get the fish! But I hope you leave enough fish for everyone else. Not too full, that would be gluttony.'

I think it'd be a brilliant thing if more folks talked to wildlife like Nick does. The scene in front of us radiated a peacefulness and loveliness. We watched in silence for a few moments, and Nick seemed deep in thought.

'You know what I think we need? We need to see a revolution in attachment to place, in belonging. And we urgently, desperately need a revolution in humility.'

The Egret struck, fast as a blink and sharp as a dagger, snatching a sliver of a fish from the water at its feet.

'To belong in nature we have to be humble to nature and all that nature gives us. We also have to accept that others belong too. Other organisms, and other humans, belong equally. This isn't our landscape to determine and control. We've already taken so much; we've boxed nature in. Yes, nature's got these nature reserves, but a few hundred years ago, a few thousand years ago, it had so, so much more. And it gave us so much more as a result.'

We left our bench, the cold starting to worm its way into our bodies despite the February sunshine. Winding back through the marsh, we heard the giggling of a Little Grebe and shortly after spied it swimming along a watery ditch, cut into the swaying reed beds.

'In order to switch people on, you need them to have access. People need to belong; they need to have that deep, intimate, personal relationship with nature.'

The Little Grebe disappeared in a blink, its tiny bum dipping under the surface as it dived for food. Nick smiled.

'It doesn't have to be about naming or knowledge, no. It's about giving everyone that feeling: *This is my place. This is my habitat. This is where I have a relationship with nature. This is where I belong.*'

We reached the last pool of the marsh before getting back to the visitor centre. A faint honking filled the sky and another skein of pink people soon drifted into view, forming a wobbly 'W' in italics. On the edge of the water closest to us sat a single male Teal, a duck of perfectly neat proportions and exquisitely pretty plumage. He sat, preening his wings and tail with his bill, the cream stripes and emerald markings on his head shining in the bright light. At one point, the sunshine seemed to focus like a laser beam upon his speculum – the patch of iridescent teal green on his wing. Nick was enthralled, as he is with so many living things.

'Look at that little Teal. Oh, in the sun! Thank you for showing us your wing, that was very kind.' With these words, the Teal stood up and lazily entered the water, spinning around so that we were faced with his rump bordered by pale yellow patches of plumage.

'Ah! And his buttery chump, just fabulous!' We both laughed. The Teal remained oblivious.

'Buttery chump: maybe that'll be my new Twitter handle.'

CHAPTER 11

The Antlebump-tumps
Familiarity | Outrage

NICOLA CHESTER
Gallows Down, Berkshire – 23 March

THE SOUNDTRACK OF SUMMER

We make contact for a still, lingering moment. One single eye staring unblinkingly into mine. A perfectly circular ring of molten gold, a pinprick of the inkiest black. A ruffling of charcoal plumage, a stiffening of a spine much smaller than my own. A twitch of a stiffening tail, arranging it just right. And then, you begin.

Tumbling, gushing, pouring from a gold-rimmed gape, a waterfall of everything that is good. Beauty in sound form. Pulses and ripples in air, interpreted by the inner workings of my skull. One of the most delicious noises in nature, I reckon.

I see you, Blackbird. I see you singing and I feel your song. Reverberations in my ribcage, tremors in my throat. A melody so rich I can almost taste it, guzzled like thick honey, sweet and nourishing and yum.

Your song is something everyday, something quite

LOVE IS A TOAD

ordinary. But it's infinitely special too. You are part of me and I am of you. I hear your words and know who you are. I recognise your voice like a best mate's. I feel cosy and cuddled by your music. Eyes closed, listening, absorbing every note. So comforting, so familiar. The soundtrack of summer, of humid evenings in July. You sound like home.

You know those days in early spring, when everything's just '*mmm*!'? The sort of day when you relish the first ticklings of sun on the back of your neck, like the warm palm of a loved one. Those bright and vibrant days when everything looks a bit more colourful, like the saturation on a photograph's been turned up. The 23rd of March was one of those. Compared with my wander with Nick in early February, everything felt different. The air had a thick whiff of springiness on it – Dandelions sautéed in sunshine, the scent of life just getting on with it. The sky, a tummy-tingling blue, was splodged with clouds, whiter than sunlight on top and grey-bellied below.

Strolling through a rickety wooden gate, Nicola greeted me with a beam as warm as the sunlight on my skin. She approached me with a hug from a distance, arms wide before she was anywhere near close. I'd found my way to her little terraced cottage, tucked away down a meandering rural lane; it was cute and homely, somewhere you'd immediately want to go into for a brew. Nicola had invited me to join her on a wander right from her doorstep, so we set off, be-wellied, making our way down a winding road as we chattered away.

Only a few minutes in, rounding a quiet corner, Nicola paused and tilted a single finger towards the sky. She smiled at me with wide, excited eyes. 'There! Can you hear?'

THE ANTLEBUMP-TUMPS

We'd stopped by a rather industrial-looking water station – all squares and fences and tarmac. Behind it stretched empty fields and behind them, a small patch of trees and some cleared forestry. From the sky of white splodges, a sound was belting downwards. A *lu-lulu-lulu-lulu-lulooooo* descended like a waterfall running with thick fluid. I recognised the notes carried on the wind as the syrupy voice of the Woodlark, just delicious. It's a song I'd listened to many times before hearing it in the flesh and feather a couple of years back. I'd tap the little 'play' button on my bird app, eyeballing the motionless sketch of the punk-crested, speckled brown bird as I listened to its blissful music. The first time I heard it in real life, trickling down from a cold spring sky on Budby Heath, it took my breath away.

We stood basking in the gorgeous sound. Such an unexpected treat and such lovely company to share it with. Nic's another nature nerd I first bumped into online. Books are her thing; she's a brilliant nature writer and works as a librarian in her local school. Meeting in real life a couple of years earlier, I experienced her gentleness and loveliness in person; she's the type of person you just want to *smoosh*.

The Woodlark's babbling faded as we walked on, cutting through a little gap in the hedge lining the road. We followed a skinny path, compacted by many wandering feet and paws, across fields of stubble and freshly planted rows of crops. Ahead of us, rising from the flat fields, a sizeable hill sloped upwards, towering like a grassy tidal wave on the point of breaking. At the top, silhouetted against the blue, was a wooden structure in the shape of a 'T' – an old gibbet that gives the hill its ominous name of Gallows Down. Standing

LOVE IS A TOAD

at the base of the slope, I gazed at the summit. No mountain by any means, but enough of an incline to generate some huff and puff and to make you aware of your calf muscles. We started to hoik our way up the grassy rise, chatting through our breathlessness.

I knew Nicola was familiar with every path and hill and wood in the local area, and she told me about her upbringing here in rural Berkshire. Her grandad had regularly taken her out on walks, playing in chalk streams with her and picking things to eat, like Hawthorn leaves. When she was young, she was very shy and anxious; moving house a lot meant she'd gone to five different primary schools and so she didn't find it easy to make friends. During this time, the outdoors provided her a great source of comfort and she discovered her own way of rooting herself through learning birdsong and the names of plants and trees.

'It gave me that sense of security that I associated with Grandad and my love for him, and just being safe,' she explained.

Young Nic had looked to the natural world for a sense of consistency and had found comfort in getting to know the wild characters around wherever she lived. It made sense: the rhythm of the seasons is predictable and dependable; you feel like you know what to expect next. And associating this with her grandad made sense too. Nature can be the setting in which connections with our most loved ones form and grow. This doesn't have to be in a formal sense, through birdwatching or organised learning, but something softer and more informal. When I think of my fondest childhood moments with my parents, I can see the vast majority of

THE ANTLEBUMP-TUMPS

them took place outdoors. Whether it was my mum squirting washing-up liquid over sheets of my dad's work tarpaulin to make an improvised slip-n-slide in the garden, or my dad cutting springy whips of Willow to make us bows and arrows to play with – here nature was not the focus but the backdrop. Nature as the middleman.

We took a narrow, diagonal path, me trundling along behind Nic, and cut across a stretch of open access chalk grassland. Later in the year, this would be a bustling bounty of chalk-loving wildflowers. On this sunny Sunday in March, there were whispers of plant life already poking through, coaxed out by the spring sunshine. Dotted everywhere were the nodding heads of Cowslips, not quite ready to show their buttery faces yet.

At the top of Gallows Down, the land fell away beneath our feet, the landscape below resembling a map, complete with tiny model villages and buildings. The wind whipped at us, held back by nothing in the surrounding flatness. Here, on a plateau of chalk grassland, we encountered our second lark of the morning. The Skylark burst from the ground, as if conjured from the grass itself, and rose into the sky in a stiff and determined flutter. I could hear his voice, unending and seemingly without pauses for breath, a liquid concoction of trills and whistles and scratches and pulses. He continued in his relentless melody, rising and rising until barely a pinprick in the sky. *What a bird.*

Further along, a couple of feathered silhouettes soared ahead of us. Red Kites – a pair of them – gambolling on gusts with their paper aeroplane tails. They seemed almost to be having fun in the bluster; they could've been fighting or flirting, parading or playing – only they knew. Underneath them, the early spring worshippers were in bloom – spires on Gorse bushes throwing sprays of yellow into the air and smatters of Blackthorn blossom, the white flowers contrasting vividly with nearly black branches.

Reaching the iconic gibbet, we paused for the view, our jackets flapping in the bluster. The wood of the structure was smoothed by the hands of countless visitors who'd stood gazing up at the ominous crossbar towering above them. It was quite spooky, to think about the silhouettes of people hanging there in the past. Nic looked out fondly over the landscape she knew so well, pointing out the borders between shires: Berkshire to one side of us, Hampshire to the other. She picked out other features too: the water tower where her kids had played (against the rules), their little cottage, the local castle and its expansive grounds. There were the woods where she used to see Woodcock, the chalk meadows she'd traversed despite the 'private' signs, the farm where she'd encouraged the farmer to protect nesting Lapwings. It was clear the whole lie of the land around us was extremely familiar to her. A place she loved deeply, for both its beauty and its blemishes.

'You know what I would love?' Nic held her hand to her eyes, squinting in the sunshine as she looked down upon her home. 'I would love to be able to stand here without looking at those plantations, and that felled wood over there, and the Cherry Laurel – grr. That really annoys me.' She gestured to a hedge of planted Cherry Laurel – an invasive species – only just visible and lining a distant lane, and sighed.

From this perspective, it was easy to see the landscape in

THE ANTLEBUMP-TUMPS

its current state – rigidly organised with lots of straight lines denoting field margins and plantation boundaries. It was also easy to see the potential, the places where a bit of bushiness and complexity could be let back in, the places where those boundaries and straight lines could be blurred.

A shivering seemed to take a hold of both of us at once; the wind still carried the cool grip of March despite the teasings of spring sunshine. We ambled over the rounded summit of the hill, winding our way down a wiggly, sun-soaked path and out of the wind. The track cut through several chalk meadows, the short vegetation still in its shrunken winter form, but braced and ready to spring and swell into a bushy mix of grasses and wildflowers. A couple of meadows along, I noticed a sudden change in the terrain under our feet. Where the path was previously wide and flat, it now narrowed, squeezing its way through a lumpy field of hummocks and tussocks. There were hundreds of them; it looked as though somebody had attempted to lay some turf over a field full of bowling balls. I had an inkling about what was going on. Nicola clocked the expression on my face.

'Yes, they're anthills!' she confirmed, pointing to the ocean of little mounds erupting all around us. 'They're from Yellow Meadow Ants. I call them antlebump-tumps!' Nic beamed and I couldn't help but smile back; it was an apt and adorable name for them. 'I believe this whole patch has never been ploughed and it's just *full* of plants: Wild Thyme, bedstraws, mixtures of all sorts of wildflowers. Come up here in June and they're just beautiful. They're all different; you'll get one that's covered in Calamint and Wild Basil, another that's Wild Thyme and Squinancywort. And of course you get the Hares nestled between them. I love them. They're like pillows, aren't they?'

By this point, we'd both dropped to our knees and were ogling the anthills with arses aloft. Even before the growing season had got under way, you could see the huge variety of plant life carpeting the anthills, like a colossal green shawl knitted and draped over the soil beneath. Crawling around like giddy kids, we admired them from all angles, pinching off a bit of Wild Thyme and nibbling the comforting flavour of homemade stews. Nic pointed out the whorled leaves of the Squinancywort she'd mentioned, yet to erupt into its tiny delicate pink flowers. I'd not knowingly seen this plant before and I loved its name – it felt great to say. I looked it up in my battered flower guide when I got home and found out it was once used to treat a type of tonsil infection called Squinancy (now known as Quinsy). A pretty flower with a satisfying name and medicinal history to boot – how brill.

We both mooched around on our hands and knees for a bit, admiring the mounds in a peaceful silence. It felt calm and cosy nestled amongst the antlebump-tumps, so we wedged our bums between the little mounds and sat in the sunshine for a natter. Nic pointed out more Red Kites soaring lazily, their *weee-awee-wee-wee* calls ringing out over the hillsides. From a clump of trees to our left, we heard the tick-tock rhythm of a Chiffchaff belting out his predictable beat. It was *so* nice to have them back – a sound totally lacking only five days earlier was now being sung and flung from every other treetop. As spring flourished, it would become part of the background, an everyday sound, but for now we basked in it greedily. Nic smiled at me.

THE ANTLEBUMP-TUMPS

'I think, for me, it's that everyday relationship with nature that's so important. Obviously, at times it can't be literally every day, but what I mean is that it's the normal things, the everyday bits of nature – that's what I love. It's the Chiffchaff . . .' She gestured to the little two-note singer nearby, who was still going at it relentlessly. 'One day it's not there, the next it is, and then, before you know it, it's a daily presence. It's the tree outside work that I know so well and I just watch it go through the seasons. It's a big Maple, with a little bench around it, and every day I say, "Hello, friend." It's the drive to work, where there's that certain bend in the road where you quite often see the Dunnocks doing their wing shuffles on top of the hedges. Naughty birds.' Nic laughed, her face lighting up in a cheeky, twinkling smile.

Ah, Dunnocks. Small, greyish-brown, always scuttling on the ground – they're quite innocuous and innocent-looking little birds. But, as I've witnessed with my own eyes, they have a frankly brilliant sex life. Dunnocks' mating strategies are complicated and fluid; they'll change according to the conditions in any given year. Sometimes they're monogamous, a standard male-female pair raising a brood together. Other times, a male will mate with a couple of females, acquiring parental duties for two different nests – phew. And sometimes, the females are in charge. A female might take on two male partners, allowing each one to mate with her multiple times. Each 'session' lasts only a matter of seconds, but if you're doing that a hundred times a day between multiple partners, it's . . . a lot. And it gets weirder. If you're a male Dunnock and you suspect the female you'd like to mate with has already copulated with another male –

LOVE IS A TOAD

that's not ideal in terms of passing along your genes to the next generation. This is where cloacal pecking comes in. Oh yes. To try to ensure his competitor doesn't achieve daddy status, the second male will peck at the female's cloaca (an all-purpose orifice, used for mating and defecation) until it becomes pink and swollen. Eventually, after much pecking, she'll eject his rival's sperm and proceed to mate with her new suitor. This is presumably not exactly comfortable, but it is ultimately to her benefit: not only is she able to fertilise her eggs, but she'll have two enthusiastic and invested male partners, each believing they're the brood's father and so contributing to their upbringing.

Still basking in the sunshine amongst the antlebump-tumps, Nicola was talking more about experiencing the soothing cycle of the year. 'There are a particular couple of weeks in early March when the Fieldfares will go up into the trees and chatter. They'll be threaded through the treetops and it sounds just like a river. When you hear that, you know they're just about to leave. It's like the opposite of the Swallows, who are on their way back. When you hear it, you know that, although it still feels very much like winter, spring is coming. And that'll happen next year, and the year after, and the year after. It's just those familiar markers; it's reassurance.'

Nic's words seemed to exude the reassurance she described. I'd never noticed this about Fieldfares before. Indeed, only a few days later, when the sun had gone and it felt cold and wintry again, I walked past a clump of trees that chattered like the babbled muttering of a river from their tops. And I knew exactly who it was.

THE ANTLEBUMP-TUMPS

For me, the familiarity that Nic talked about is such a deeply ingrained component of nature joy. It feels comforting, like the warmth of seeing a loved one, of being greeted by a friend or pet, or taking the first satisfying sip of a long-awaited brew. Familiarity with nature is a closeness I know in my whole body; it's in the recognition of sounds, the distinguishing of smells, tastes and textures. It's one of the most treasured aspects of my relationship with nature – to know what's around the corner, whose faces I'll see next.

But familiarity is more than that too. I like to think of it as a sort of potion of different forms of intimacy, a feeling that embodies some elements of other aspects of nature joy I've delved into this year. Mixed into that potion is the comprehension of nature I talked about with Charlie – the experience of learning, understanding and observing other life around you. Then there's the sense of belonging I discussed with Nick, to feel that one belongs to a specific place, as part of nature. For me, familiarity is something that's developed and distilled, that's come from getting to know nature over time. It's now so deeply ingrained, in fact, that at first, I found it hard to put words to it; it felt as plain and obvious as saying 'snails are beautiful' (don't argue with me on this, they are).

To be familiar with other living beings around me feels like one of the greatest gifts there is; I don't know how it could be beaten. It is there in April and the joy of spying the first twirling Swallow of the season, all tendril-tailed and swooping through the air like the blissful flick of a paintbrush. It's in October, when the first soft and reassuring honks of the Pinkies trickle downwards as they fill the skies

LOVE IS A TOAD

with their wobbly 'V's. Familiarity is waking up on that one day in August when it just smells *different*. Summer's still here, it's still warm and lush and green, but suddenly and inexplicably, you find yourself thinking about autumn. All down to a teasing hint, the sweet whiff of the season of rot and the smell of blackberries. It's found in February in the subtle shift in the Great Tit's voice – a picking up of the pace, a song suddenly sung with more gusto and pizzazz. You hear that energy and you know we're teetering on the brink, about to tip into spring. Then, when it does tip, you know who's going to be singing next, and who after them, and who after them, as the season plunges into a delicious flow of birdsong.

The best thing about a closeness with nature is that it's undeniably, unchangeably *yours*. Your relationship with the living world is unique, an intimacy that's simply between you and the beings you know. It can be as formal or as silly as you like; it can be a secret you keep to yourself or a love that you shout about from the treetops. We each have our own familiar faces, our own comforts, our own well-trodden paths. And best of all, it's something that grows and swells over a lifetime, accumulating like a House Martin plastering mud into her nest, beakful by beakful.

Nic and I were being repeatedly visited by insects coaxed out of hibernation or pupation by the warmth of the day. Or perhaps it was our clothes – between Nic's yellow coat and my pink jumper, it seemed we resembled giant sources of delicious nectar, drawing thirsty critters from all around. In a furry-bummed blur, a creature with a comedically long facial appendage landed on my sleeve and attempted to slurp something sweet and pollen-like from me. Their wings were almost invisible, like a cartoon character's whirring legs, and they hovered and probed over me repeatedly, attempting to find the centre of this colossal Fuchsia flower. I apologised to the Bee Fly for the confusion and took a moment to admire their wonderful and absolutely ridiculous appearance. If you've never seen a Bee Fly, try to imagine a picture of a bumblebee drawn by a five-year-old. They have two wings (not four, like true bees), a frankly scrumptious fuzzball of a bum and a long, pointed proboscis, giving a hummingbird a run for their money. When they hover, they stick their skinny little legs out awkwardly, as if they're beginner pilots and haven't quite got the hang of flying yet.

Like Mel's Black Oil Beetles, Bee Flies are kleptoparasites of mining bees. Attracted to the hole of a bee's nest, female Bee Flies swoop down in mid-flight, dipping their bums in the dirt to coat their eggs, before flicking one down the bee's burrow like they're chucking a ball in a game of rounders. To me, Bee Flies are a niche and nerdy harbinger of spring; seeing my first Bee Fly each March generates that excitable and comforting peak of familiarity Nic had described.

After a few failed probes, the Bee Fly appeared to give up, pausing for a quick hover at eye height before zooming away across the anthills.

We continued chatting, watching hoverflies and tiny flower beetles land momentarily on our sleeves. Nic told me how she has her own markers of the seasons, like my Bee Fly. In her teens and early twenties, she worked looking after horses.

'Not owning them, but borrowing. I'm a great borrower of things. You know . . . librarian,' she laughed. She explained that when she worked outside during the winter months, she'd always be listening to the birds in the background. The Fieldfares and Redwings were always there – but then there'd come a point early in the year when she would hear the Mistle Thrushes join in. She described how their beautiful, bone-cold song has a certain weariness to it, and at a time of year that seems never-endingly wet and muddy, it feels like they're going through it with you. 'Then all the other birds start to join in and you think, *We've made it!* And that's what I mean – all of these memories and points throughout the year become touchstones, don't they?'

Touchstones – that was such a nice way to put it. It nods to the tactile and intimate relationship we have with those markers, the ones you look for throughout the seasons and every year, touching them again and again until they're smoothed by familiar fingers. I also like to think of them as stepping stones: we hop from one, to the next, to the next. I'd hopped on to the Chiffchaff stone around St Paddy's Day, hearing their name sung from the top of an Ash tree. Next, in an enthusiastic flurry of scratches and whistles, I'd hopped on to the Blackcap stone, and, shortly afterwards, the Willow Warbler's, with their fluty waterfall of a song. The reliability and familiarity of those stones, and the rhythm of leaping from one to the next, is indeed a very joyful thing.

Interrupting our natter in a bounding, bouncing flight, a small blob of buttercup yellow soared over our heads towards a stand of Hawthorns behind us.

'Oh, hello! A little light bulb!' Nic greeted the Yellowhammer and I couldn't help but smile at another one of her lovely descriptions. 'You know, when the children were growing up, we had all sorts of names for things. We weren't able to do a lot with the kids, but we did have lots of picnics. And so we used to call the Yellowhammer the picnic bird! They'd be singing all the time when we were eating, you know, *a-little-bit-of-bread-and-no-cheese?*' Her voice went all high-pitched as she impersonated the little yellow songster. It's such a good way to remember their song, a catchphrase that matches up with the syllables of their repetitive call. 'The kids made up their own words for it. When they wanted some cake, they'd say, "Pretty-pretty-pretty-pretty-pleaaaaaase!" So it quickly became the picnic bird.' Nicola laughed.

I loved this! A backing track of birdsong feeding into the tasty, formative memories of little ones.

It's wonderful that we can make up our own names for things, that we *do* make up our own names for things, in a way that encapsulates our own personal relationships with them. You can really see it when you start delving into our history of common names for the plants and animals around us. In the past, before the development of modern taxonomy and the standardisation of our language for nature, we had countless local variants of names. These names are fascinating – and sometimes a bit weird – as they speak of an intimacy with nature that's since faded, that everyday closeness that many of us don't have any more.

Take woodlice. There's something scrumptiously satisfying about woodlice, isn't there? The way their segments link together. The way they scuttle, flattened to the earth like dinky armoured tanks. Their kinked and wiggling

LOVE IS A TOAD

antennae. Their tiny babies, tucked away under mum's belly like joeys in a kangaroo's pouch. Woodlice capture imaginations everywhere because they *are* everywhere. And this is reflected in the almost ridiculously rich history of their local names. By some estimates, they have more common names than any other animal in the UK. Some of them are adorable: names like Roly-polies and Pea-bugs obviously refer to how some species (we have around 30 in the UK) roll up into a ball. Others, like the name woodlouse itself, tell us of their association with rotting, woody places: Carpenter's Fleas, Woodywigs and Wood-bugs. There's Billy-bakers, Billy-buttons, Nutbugs (in north-west England), Pishamares (in Norfolk) and Slaters (in Scotland). Across the south-east of England, several common names refer to grandparents. Gramfer Gravy, Granny-greys, Grandfather Dicks – could these be a sign of affinity or endearment for the little scuttlers? I hope so. Some of my favourite local names for woodlice are the pig-themed ones. For some reason, these crustaceans of dank and dark places had porcine associations, with local names like Chiggy-pigs, Chookie-pigs, God's Little Pigs and – one I particularly love – Tiddlyboars. Nic had yet another local name for them. 'I don't know what species they are, but we get big ones up here on the chalk grassland so they must be a speciality. We call them Chalky Cheeselogs!'

I love knowing that these tiny creatures have been a significant presence in so many people's lives over centuries. They were certainly a main character of my own childhood. For some reason, I called all of the biggest ones I could find Edward. Turning over stones and old bricks, searching for their huddled grey forms, I'd poke fingerfuls of them into a little plastic bucket. Then I'd build them a woodlouse village. An isopod utopia! A crustacean civilisation thriving at the bottom of the garden. I'd erect a perimeter fence out of pebbles and craft tiny houses out of a section of loo roll tube, topped off with a paper cone roof. Next, the 14-legged inhabitants would be added to their gated community. I'd watch in peaceful bliss as Edwards and their families would rumble about the settlement I'd built for them, my brain sparking with stories and character plots for them all.

It can be easy to scoff at informal names for things, but these common names are important for different reasons. They tell us stories – names inevitably soak up folklore, weaving myths and superstition into the titles of some of our most familiar creatures. There's Witchags, another name for Swallows, whose swooping, dark silhouettes could look like little witches. There's Witches' Eggs too – the name for the young stage of a Stinkhorn Fungus, when it resembles a goopy egg, nestled in the leaf litter (another common name comes in once the Stinkhorn has erupted into its fruiting body: Dead Man's Cock. Sorry). Devil's Helmet is another name for Aconite, a highly poisonous plant, and Come-and-Cuddle-Me is a lovely common name for Pansies, which were thought to help cure heartbreak and lovesickness.

Other names tell us stories about a species' appearance or behaviours, which can often be seen in the wonderful old common names of lots of birds. Mistle Thrushes are also known as Stormcocks, due to their tendency to sing no matter the weather. In parts of Scotland, Bitterns were called Bull-of-the-bogs, presumably down to their moo-like booming echoing through wet places. Nuthatches were known as

LOVE IS A TOAD

Nut Jobbers, which is just brilliant. A Creepie is a Dunnock (the frisky little ground-scuttlers) and a Cutty is a Wren (with their stubby, 'cut-off' tails). My mum and dad both call Starlings Sheppies, apparently derived from the Starling's habit of snarfling ticks and insects from sheep's backs.

Names also give us clues not just about nature but about humans too, teaching us lessons about how our ancestors might have lived. This is perhaps most obvious in our naming of plants, lots of which still nod to the ways in which we used them and interacted with them. Take, for example, the link between cows and many species of plants. Humans have kept and tended to cattle for thousands of years in the UK, and have come to associate – and therefore name – a whole suite of plants with cows in one way or another.

First, we've literally placed the word 'cow' into lots of plant names. Cowbane – the bane of the cow – is a highly poisonous plant that you don't want your cows (or yourself) to munch on. Then there's Cowslip – these nodding, soft yellow flowers were said to grow where cows had 'slopped', meaning they might grow where cowpats have fallen. Then there's Cow-grass, or Cow-cloos, alternative names for the familiar face of Red Clover. Cows are said to relish grazing upon it and it can help produce good milk when they eat it alongside a mix of grasses and other plants.

Next up, there's 'milk' plants – species like Common Milkwort and Purple Milk Vetch are both linked to cows by their name. It was thought that cows grazing in places these plants grew would produce more milk; again, maybe a diet rich in a variety of palatable plant species makes a healthier cow? Then, perhaps most famously, there's the 'butter'

THE ANTLEBUMP-TUMPS

bunch of plants. Top of the list has to be Buttercups which – as well as being associated with the good old under-the-chin butter game – were also used in some places to rub on cows' udders. Despite being inedible to the cows themselves, it was thought that treating their udders with an ointment made from bright yellow flowers would help the cows produce a rich, golden-yellow butter. There's also Butterbur – a paddle-leaved plant we used to use to wrap up slabs of butter before the advent of fridges. And there's Butterwort. The presence of 'wort' in a plant's name usually means that at some point, we've found it healing or otherwise beneficial (as with Milkwort and Squinancywort). Butterwort is a carnivorous plant and has anti-bacterial properties that prevent its insect prey from rotting before they can be digested. In the past, we've taken advantage of this and have used the plant to treat sores on cows. Not only that, but some cultures in northern Europe used the plant to help curdle their milk to create a kind of traditional buttermilk.

I find it fascinating that such a variety of plant life has a connection and relationship to one of our most valued animals – connections that we've either detected or forged ourselves. I picture this as a web of associations, sprawling out in a dot-to-dot-to-dot between cows, humans and plants. It's a perfect example of both comprehension and of story-telling – our ability to understand the life around us and to weave that knowledge into names and stories.

These names show us that even in our relatively recent past, a certain level of familiarity with our wildlife was present and deeply ingrained. They allude to an intimacy, telling us that wildlife not only had a daily presence in our lives but also

LOVE IS A TOAD

a daily relevance. My own sense of familiarity with nature still feels young and new, a closeness I only started to develop properly as an adult. And this is the case for lots of us. Most people in the UK don't grow up with that daily familiarity with nature any more, a disparity that widens the poorer and more marginalised you might be.

The guttural, throaty *KRONK* was followed by a powerful and satisfying *swoosh-swoosh-swoosh*, that sounded like someone shaking their washed sheets before hanging them up. The duo of Ravens surged over our heads, two silhouettes of the jettest black, their powerful wings carving muffled hisses out of the air. Ravens always seem to eyeball you as they fly over; looking up, you see the glint of a knowing, beady eye and feel that tinge of an instinct telling you you're being watched.

The pair of kronkers glided away from us, their croaky and inane chattering hanging in the air long after we could see them. I sat hugging my knees and resting my chin upon them, gazing over the fiercely managed fields and small scraps of woodlands. Nic pointed one particular patch out to me – if you could call it woodland at all. It consisted of neat rows of trees, all of a uniform height and encased in some sort of tubing. Until recently, it had been a fantastic mix of Hawthorn scrub with a few bigger trees in there, until it was completely cut down.

Nic had a mix of exasperation and livid bewilderment on her face. 'These estates are being given public money to fell these woods, just to plant new ones.'

What would've been a little safe haven for scrub lovers,

THE ANTLEBUMP-TUMPS

things like Whitethroats and Yellowhammers, small mammals and shrubby plants, had been razed to the ground. Frustrating enough, but to know that the replanted whips, swathed in plastic tubes, likely counted towards some tree-planting climate targets was simply enraging.

'You know, I got that closeness with nature when I put down roots here. I wanted to know what birds were singing and what the trees were because it gave me a sense of security that I associated with Grandad and my love for him. And then, very quickly, I learnt that it could all be taken away from you, even in the place you feel you belong in.' Nic reached down and twiddled with a bit of Wild Thyme on the mound nearest to her, smiling a sort of sad smile.

She gestured into the distance, towards a cluster of buildings and houses that made up Greenham Common. Nic had lived there for a little while as a child and found her own wild playground near the stables. Here she'd listen to Nightingales and Nightjars, well before she even knew what they were. Then, one day, she turned up to find the whole patch had been fenced off by the RAF so that nearly a hundred ground-launched cruise missiles could be stored there. The effect of these changes stuck with her.

'You can fall in love with places on your doorstep, sure, but I learnt it'll be taken away at any moment.'

Nicola sighed and the two of us looked out over the landscape ahead of us, silent for a few moments. A deep humming drew my attention downwards and I looked at my pink sleeve to see a thirsty visitor, a Red-tailed Bumblebee. I suspected she was a queen – she was quite sizeable (with a chunky rouge backside to match) and out this early in the year. I hoped she'd find some nectar nearby and a safe hidey-hole in which to establish her reign as the queen of her nest.

Nic told me about the corner of a nearby field – a little patch of land that had been set aside for at least a decade – where until recently, six pairs of Lapwings would nest every year. That patch had recently been ploughed and those birds hadn't returned.

'Not only have the birds gone but the connection with them has gone – the people who would've heard them and listened to them. That kind of access to nature is such an important thing. It's so unequal and I'm very lucky – I'm very privileged – to be able to access nature. But so many can't. I'd love to see people up here and share that joy, and say, "Hello, isn't it a lovely day. Listen to that bird!" Lapwings aren't here any more and neither are people, because it's been made to be so. And that is sickening, isn't it? That's a feeling of grief but it's also bloody anger! It's outrage!'

I think it can hit harder when you see anger in someone otherwise gentle and soft. That's how it felt listening to Nic; I felt the dejection and outrage saturating every word as she spoke.

Outrage is a very tangible, bulky element of the bubbling grief soup I carry around. It feels like one of the hardest emotions to deal with, white-hot, spiky, fizzing and rumbling, always threatening to bubble over. It's not simply anger; I feel anger when I stub my toe but I don't feel *outrage*. Outrage comes when anger's born of a sense of injustice, of wrongdoing and unfairness. When it comes to the nature crisis (and the way people are treated within it), I feel it often. It shows up when

THE ANTLEBUMP-TUMPS

you hear about the bosses of water companies earning millions whilst daring to increase customers' water bills, as their companies pump our sea and rivers with liquid excrement. It shows up when you know that significantly fewer children (and adults) from poor and marginalised backgrounds get to access nature – that the people who need the restorative effects of nature most have the least access to it. The outrage comes when you turn the corner to walk down your street and see a raw, gaping hole in the familiar skyline. It's in the gut punch you feel having known and loved that tree so much, yet you were unable to defend it from the roar of the chainsaw. And these instances stick in your memories.

At the end of the street where I used to live was a grassy verge. A small patch of Cowslips used to grow there each spring – not many, only a handful. But every day I walked past them, they'd bring me a little bit of joy. Their butter-topped, droopy flowers would remind me that spring was about to go boom. Except one day, they were gone. I found them mown down for no reason other than neatness, and I cried as I draped their limp forms across my fingers.

Later that year, as winter began to nibble and gnaw, I walked along a stretch of canal towpath that had become familiar to me during lockdown. Bordering the path were three chunky, tall Oaks, standing side by side, all handsome and at least 300 years old. But this time, there was a gap. All three trees had been felled, cut brutally at waist height. I saw a strange line running across them. Looking closely, I realised that it was a thread of barbed wire. The old, rusted wire intersected the trunk where the Oaks had enveloped it over time, wrapping thick, woody lips around the sharp barbs.

LOVE IS A TOAD

Here were trees who'd eaten metal, who'd seen life pass them by, stood in one spot for centuries – but wouldn't any longer. I found out later they'd been cut down to allow access for yet another retail development. I was broken-hearted, and I was outraged.

Another Red Kite cast its angled silhouette over us, twirling without any real urgency or haste in the air above us. We both leant back in the sun, admiring the bird's lethargic flutters.

'It's hard because you have to go through the world behaving like a normal person when you feel like this. You can't be angry all the time. Because you have to be a good mum, or friend, or daughter . . . or librarian.' Nic laughed and I imagined her charging around her little school library in a flurry of fury. 'You know, I believe outrage can be gentle, in a way. You can do these things kindly and softly.' Nicola smiled again, still watching the slowly looping Kite as it continued to *weeee-awee-wee-wee* above us. 'I try very hard to see it from others' points of view, to reason and to learn. I write as furiously as I can; I try to move people so they can see how sad and wrong and unnecessary all this destruction is. I write as an act of resistance to the loss of nature and I think the ferocity in it is me baring my soul, being vulnerable and honest.'

I like to think of outrage – much like with hopelessness – as a fuel. I imagine that I'm carrying a little bundle of sparks, a cup of smouldering embers nestled somewhere in my chest. Sometimes, those embers might be softer and dimmer, like the gentle glow of a Glow Worm's bum. Other times, that little bundle ignites into something blazing and fiery and molten,

THE ANTLEBUMP-TUMPS

a flame that shines brightly with indignation and strength. If there's a thing I've learnt from Nicola, it's that outrage can be soft. It can be warm and gentle and understanding, but still shine brightly in resistance and focus. Nicola is a brilliant example of how you can be fired and motivated to challenge injustice, to confront the things that devastate, hurt and enrage us – but to do that with all of the warm and wonderful qualities that are the best bits of being human.

On our amble back through the woods, we were greeted by the smiling faces of every springtime flower going. It seems the sun hadn't just cheered us up. I crouched down to admire the tiny white petals of Barren Strawberries and the Primroses, as yellow as left-out butter. One bank held a whole constellation of bright yellow and vivid white stars – Lesser Celandines literally gleaming in the sunshine – and white Wood Anemones, dotted satisfyingly amongst them.

Later that evening, snuggled up in bed, I took myself back to that spot on the sloping hillside, sitting amongst the Calamint and Squinancywort (still brilliant), and surrounded by antlebump-tumps. Soaking in early spring sunshine, relishing those first touchstones of the season – the Chiffchaff singing, the buttery belly of the Yellowhammer, our skin tickled by hoverflies. It was as if the tap had been turned on and spring was gushing out with gusto. One of those days in early spring, when everything's just 'mmm!'.

CHAPTER 12

Face Down, Bum Up

Gratitude | Yearning

LEIF BERSWEDEN
Bentleigh Bank, Wiltshire – 29 April

There's something really quite special about Cowslip yellow. Each plant has a handful of flopsy, drooping yellow flower heads dangling from stalks of a soft, pale green. It's the same pale yellow as the marzipan of a Battenburg cake – quite subtle and lovely. On this April evening, there were hundreds of them splodged over the grassy, downward-sloping hill in front of us. They're unpretentious, Cowslips. Not too cocky, not too gaudy. Chill and mellow.

'I just love them,' Leif agreed, crouching down to admire the buttery splodge closest to him. 'Every year I'd come here and there'd just be this sea of yellow. And in August, there'd be Devil's Bit Scabious; those slopes in front of us go purple in the same way this bit goes yellow with the Cowslips. And the smell of it!' He was off now; there was no stopping him . . .

'Devil's Bit Scabious kind of smells like frying onion and it would just hit you in this oniony wave. It was just so good.

LOVE IS A TOAD

Ooh, and there are Autumn Gentians at the same time too. Little purple flowered plants. I was *well* pleased when I found them. And Carline Thistles! They're mad-cool thistles that flower at the end of summer. And actually, on top of all of that, there's the Horseshoe Vetch – which in June has a ring of golden yellow pea flowers, a bit like a horseshoe – but in late summer they turn into these wiggly seed pods that look like fancy pasta.'

I don't think I'd ever heard anyone describe a thistle as *mad-cool* before. Nor had I heard someone compare wildflowers to pasta, come to think of it. But this was a man who loves plants. Leif's admiration of one type of flower had cascaded into another, then another, and another in a fizzing and enthusiastic gush.

We were standing at the top of a small stretch of chalk downland, gazing down upon a mix of grasses and early spring wildflowers. Leif told me he called the small hillside in front of us 'Bentleigh Bank' (after the nearest farm he could find on the map), but that its real name was unknown to him. It was a tiny patch of open-access grassland, ('only about one sixteenth of a square kilometre, I once worked out'), and it had escaped the churning of the plough and sprays of fertilisers over the years. As a result, it had been Leif's nerd-dom as a teenager; the spot he used to head to on the search for wildflowers and butterflies – quite the contrast to my own teen years, spent drinking cheap knock-off vodka in a park in Preston.

Earlier that afternoon, I'd met Leif for the last in a year full of wild walks. He'd planned a wander of his old patch; a wiggling and looping route around his childhood playground, across a wooded and meadowed stretch of the Wiltshire countryside. Another old internet friend, I'd started following Leif on Instagram a long time ago. We'd promised to go for a nerdy walk together for years, but it wasn't until 2022 that we finally met in 3D. When I did, he greeted me with a big, squeezing bear hug and a smile that shone brighter than Buttercups. I came to know him as a gentle and soft soul; a man who whispers fond greetings to the first Wood Anemones of spring, who tears up at the sight of Bluebells and who rescues every bumblebee he finds stranded on the pavement. A big old softie with a penchant for Pansies.

Our walk began with a trundle along a short stretch of road before joining a footpath. Even on a shortish length of country lane, we had to repeatedly lunge into the verge in a test of our reflexes as we dodged oncoming 4X4s – all suspiciously white and shiny for vehicles that are supposed to be 'off road'. After one particularly aggressive driver revved passed us, I found myself almost lying on the verge, nose-to-nose with a little purple flower with dark green leaves. Leif was sprawled in a patch of the flowers too and, whilst waiting for a couple more cars to pass us, he plucked a scallop-edged leaf from one and handed it to me. 'Ground Ivy,' he told me, pointing out the way it crept along the ground a bit like regular Ivy crawls up trees. He snapped a leaf off himself and popped it into his mouth, motioning for me to do the same. I held it up, admiring the leaf's kidney-shaped silhouette with a cartoon cloud outline, and took a tentative nibble. A strong, herby and almost minty flavour exploded in my mouth – something bitter but not at all unpleasant. Leif laughed as my eyes popped. 'Good, isn't it?' He explained how many plants that grow in ordinary places are edible, species that are related to well-known herbs, things that we would've used in herbal medicine and staple foods that most of us no longer remember we can actually eat. Inspiration flashed across Leif's face and he declared a challenge for our walk – to spot (and taste) as many edible spring plants as possible. This I liked the sound of. Lunch was already a fading memory, and an afternoon of munching wild plants and flowers sounded both fun and tasty.

Heaving ourselves out of the verge and scurrying along the last stretch of road before we reached the footpath, I asked Leif about his childhood here. He explained his dad had encouraged his love for nature, taking him birdwatching or looking for insects. But young Leif got frustrated with things that could run or fly away from him; he just wanted to get close to the wildlife around him.

This I could also relate to. More than once, as a young kid, I'd stood outside, arms outstretched, hands cupping a sad cluster of breadcrumbs, hoping that if I stood still for long enough, the birds might come and land on my 'branches' to eat.

'I remember saying to birds and insects, "I'm not going to hurt you, I just want to look at you!" But it never worked. And so, I was left with the plants at my feet, which obviously couldn't run away . . .'

Leif sort of trailed off and it was my turn to laugh. You couldn't fault his logic. At this point, he bent down to pick the noodley seed pods of a plant growing from the base of the wall. I recognised the little white flowers and serrated arrowhead leaves of Garlic Mustard – the same plant I'd nibbled almost a year earlier on my wander with Nadia. It did pretty much what it said on the tin too; as I nibbled the pods, I tasted the familiar burst of bitter mustard, accompanied by an after-tang of garlicky-ness.

With this new friendship, he could spend as much time as he wanted staring at plants and learning the differences between them. And, he explained, a big part of this growing friendship was realising that plants are actually alive. He popped the seed pod in his mouth and stooped over to pet the leaves of the little Hedge Garlic fondly. 'And not just that they're alive but that they're living creatures that do all the same things animals do. They just have to do them in a different way because they're rooted to the spot. Getting into plants opened up this whole world of organisms that face all the same challenges on a day-to-day basis as animals; they've got to put food on the table, they've got to reproduce and they've got to make sure they don't get eaten. But they have to do all that without being able to move. And, to this day, I just find that brilliant!'

I love hearing people talk about the things they utterly adore, and it was becoming clear that Leif loves plants as much as Mel loves Oil Beetles.

The track took us down a ginnel bordered by tall bushy hedges of Hawthorn with a thick margin of Cow Parsley in front of them. We ran our hands over the white, fluffy heads of the Cow Parsley as we walked; they felt cool and slightly damp to the touch, perhaps from a shower earlier in the day.

'The more I learn about them, the more I realise that plants are the ones in charge,' Leif continued. 'They're the ones running the show. They're the ones who are enticing insects to come and pollinate them. They're the ones who build ecosystems. They turn light into life! I think we always kind of think of it as the animals taking advantage of the plants, but actually, it's the other way around.'

Plants *turn light into life*. I loved that. And he's right – plants are absolutely mint. They can be so easily overlooked, seen as the habitat where *actual* wildlife is seen, not as wildlife itself. But if you look closely enough, the hidden worlds of plants reveal themselves. One of my favourite things about wild plants is their shapes and forms. Just looking at them chills me out; I find peace, satisfaction and eye-pleasing beauty in the mightiness of trees and the delicacy of wildflowers. I look at Rowan and Ash, their pinnate leaves arranged either side of a stem like chunky green feathers. I gaze at curled fern fronds paused mid-unfurl, made up of the same spirals as sea snails' shells or the coil of a snoozing millipede. Have you ever lay on your back in a bushy field on a summer's evening, staring up at the silhouettes of the grasses? Cock's-foot, Foxtail and False Oat-grass peppering the sky with their seed heads, looking like splatters of paint thrown at a canvas. Plants have *so much* to give us, if we can just slow down to their pace and accept the gifts they're offering.

Cow Parsley was the next edible offering from the plants on our walk. I'd been too nervous to try it before – the one thing I'd learnt about the Carrot family (that Cow Parsley belongs to) is that its members are either very delicious or very deadly. Plants with umbellifer flowers (flowers with spokes that look a little bit like brollies) include yummy things like Cow Parsley and Pignuts (the little roots taste like woody spuds), but they also include species like Hemlock Water Dropwort – something you *really* don't want to eat. Being in the hands of a botanist reassured me though, and I nibbled at the Cow Parsley leaves with only an inkling of nervousness. It tasted like its namesake, parsley, but perhaps just a little 'grassier' than the kitchen herb. As I was still chewing it, Leif reached further into the hedgerow and plucked a couple of young and still bright green leaves from a Hawthorn bush. He told me that one of its common names is 'bread and cheese'.

I thrust a small tuft of Hawthorn leaves into my mouth, chewing them and trying to find any resemblance to a slab of cheddar on a white crusty loaf. The leaves were kind of bitter with an almost thick, fatty quality to them that's hard to describe. Apparently, kids used to call them 'bread and cheese' because they're quite filling, not particularly because of the flavour. I didn't dislike the taste, however, and went back for more as Leif carried on.

He described a teenage Leif, when his relationship with nature was all about finding new things, ticking species off lists with a collecting sort of mindset.

Leif smiled, reminiscing about this younger botanical self. 'My relationship with nature now is not like that at all!' he laughed. Gone was his desire to see as many species as possible, or search for rare plants in far-flung corners of the country. Now, his outlook had shifted, he explained. Today, his joy comes from the familiar and ordinary, the bread and butter of the plant world. Species that show their faces every year, the ones he grew up with, like Bluebells and Hawthorn blossom.

LOVE IS A TOAD

'It's kind of in the same way that you get to a point in your life where it's no longer about getting as many friends as possible. Like, when we were kids, it was all about how many Facebook friends you had, wasn't it?' Leif laughed.

Ahh, Facebook. I am a couple of years older than Leif, though, and can also remember the politics of the MySpace Top 8. *Eesh.*

'But then when you get older, you start to focus on those relationships that mean the most to you,' Leif continued. 'And that's what you give your time and your love and your energy to. You nurture those relationships and give to them because you know that what you get back is going to be the best form of friendship.' Leif had crouched down and was tilting a Dandelion's face towards him with an outstretched finger, as if tickling the chin of a much-loved pet.

Leif's old relationship with plants sounded a bit like parts of the birdy world – a competitive one where your status is determined by the length of your . . . *ahem* . . . list. I do get the value of listing; I like to keep an informal note of the things I've seen from my bedroom window (Peregrine Falcon, oh yes) and I used to keep a train station bird list, counting everything feathered I could spy whilst waiting to squeeze on to the 07:53 to Birmingham (a fly-by Green Woodpecker was a nice surprise one morning). That said, for me, it doesn't translate into a deeper intimacy with the lives I'm ticking off. When the objective of nature watching becomes about numbers, it leaves less wriggle room for the slow and pondering bumbles I enjoy so much. I related to what he'd said about the bread-and-butter plants. Just as

FACE DOWN, BUM UP

I'd discussed with Nic, there's endless joy in building that relationship with the day-to-day species we see regularly, where that fondness and familiarity lies.

Leif handed me some more edible greenery – a plant very familiar in its bristliness and clinginess. The little hooks on its leaves snagged at my tongue like Velcro as it went down; it felt a bit like a small cat was licking the inside of my mouth – though I imagine a tad less fishy.

'It makes water taste really nice if you soak it in it.' Leif laughed at my facial expression, telling me how Sticky Weed is full of vitamins and good for things like eczema. Once I chewed past its texture, I did enjoy the taste – quite cool and lightly grassy.

Then it was my time to shine, bringing the fifth course to our botanical menu. Nestled in the foot of the hedgerow I spied the deceiving leaves of White Dead Nettle, resembling its stinging namesake but lacking any of its punch. I crouched to pluck a couple of the white flowers, handing one to Leif. We 'cheersed!' them together like tiny pints before each sucking the little drop of sweetness from their tube-like bases, something my mum had taught me when I was little.

We'd reached the opening in the hedgerow and so squeezed through it into an open field, peppered with Dandelions and White Clover. These were two very familiar flowers and I liked how Leif had referred to them as friends. I asked him if this was really how he regarded plants.

'Yes, my relationship with plants has a lot of parallels with my human friendships. In the same way that I'm grateful to my friends for their love and support and the joy they bring me, I'm massively grateful to the natural world

LOVE IS A TOAD

for all of those things as well. I mean, I know nature doesn't love me . . . but, does it?' Leif laughed.

I loved the idea of looking at other life through the lens of companionship. It made complete sense to me. With our human friendships, we know that no two are the same. There's your quiet-but-hilarious friend and your bright, soul-of-the-party friend. Then there's the one who always looks fabulous and lifts you up with compliments, and the one who gives the warmest hugs and best advice. Now I think about it, I can see that I get this variety of support and depth from nature too. When I'm hot, she cools me: a plunge in the river on a hot summer's day. When I'm anxious she soothes me: the song of the Blackbird as a long day draws to a close. The Oak holds and supports me with her strength as I climb her boughs; the meadow holds and supports me with their softness as I sneak in an afternoon nap. The insects and fungi and wriggling life of rock pools entrance and fascinate me endlessly. Nature makes me smile, laugh and cry with joy. It's certainly a form of deep companionship, if not nature's answer to a best mate.

'Yes! Totally!' Leif agreed, his attention now focused on a tiny bee who was busy burying their head in the colossal yellow Dandelion they'd landed upon. He told me how shy he was as a kid, at one point being barely able to speak to anyone. During this time, he found he could hang out in nature without any need to chat or socialise. The natural world wouldn't judge him or expect anything of him in return. He plucked two more sunshine-yellow flowers from the ground, saying thank you to the Dandelions before giving me one to try.

FACE DOWN, BUM UP

The sixth course of our botanical feast tasted like a mouthful of sunshine – a mix of planty savouriness and sweet pollen burst on my tongue so that I could taste it in the back of my nose. We followed it up with a chaser of White Clover, subtly sweet to the taste. As I chewed away, I mulled over Leif's words. I liked the way he had explained his gratitude to nature, his thankfulness for the presence it had in his life growing up. He expressed it in the same way you'd be grateful to a mentor or a supportive friend, and I thought it was a beautiful way to look at it. I feel gratefulness towards nature too; it's something I try and consciously cultivate in the everyday.

It's quite a fun thing to do – nurture gratitude in small, unlikely places. To make a deliberate effort to notice and appreciate the mundane, the subtle and the ordinary. Take spiders' webs. These used to be things that generated a bit of an 'ick' response, a slight shudder as I'd accidentally walk through one when taking the bins out on autumnal mornings. But now I know – and love – spiders, this experience has flipped on its head. To feel the strands of silk whispering across my skin – an almost imperceptible tickle – actually feels quite nice. Now, when I walk through a cobweb, I appreciate the sensation as though it's a tiny massage – as well as apologising profusely to its creator.

And then there's the even more simple. Have you ever *really* appreciated a bush wee? Yes – I mean having a wee outside, in a bush, a field, a little patch of scrub. Whether you're a squatter or stander, I've found discovering the free joy of weeing outside is something that's hard to beat and I find myself keeping a mental note of the best pee views I've experienced. I've weed on clifftops, watching the fizzing waves crashing below whilst tasting the salt on the air. I've weed in the woods, bathed in the dappled light of towering Oaks. I've weed in the undergrowth, coming eye to beady eye with a Woodcock, as mottled as the leaf litter they crouched in. I've even weed at the top of mountains, watching a Golden Eagle soar on the thermals in front of me. It's a grounding, animalistic experience that I find myself regularly being grateful for.

When you're consciously thankful for something, it means you recognise its value and you don't take it for granted. To feel gratitude to the natural world is to respect what it gives us and teaches us, and it's to pay reverence to nature for those gifts. After all, nature is something we all take value from. It brings us joy and fascination and wonder. It feeds us, heals us, clothes us and nurtures us. When we're showered with all of these gifts, it only seems right to respond with thankfulness and recognition. This type of gratitude can even serve as a sort of meditation, a zooming out of your personal scenario into the wider ebbing and flowing of life.

We can be grateful to nature in a personal sense too. In the same way every one of us has our own relationship with the natural world, we also have our own reasons to be thankful to it. When I was ill and undergoing chemo, nature rocked up like your best mate rocks up after a break-up, armed with tissues and ice cream and a bottle of wine. During a scary and frankly weird time, the natural world provided escape, fascination and distraction by the bucketful. It was there to show me beauty in the everyday – hoverflies on thistles and House Sparrows building nests in gutters. It was there to help me physically, tempting me outside with sunshine when I hadn't left the house for three days. And it was there to soothe me, the cool caress of a stream when my veins ached from my medicine. Sure, I know none of this was a conscious effort by nature, but does it really have to be for me to feel thankful for it?

This isn't to paint everything in nature as being hunky-dory; along with beauty, wonder, food and fascination, nature has another side too. Where there is life, there is death. Where there is life, there is also suffering, disease, parasitism and decay. Nature, after all, is wonderfully indifferent and apathetic, as I've said before. But in these things, doesn't nature also gift us lessons? The lessons of safety – of being careful with that insect because it stings, of those Brambles because they prickle. Nature teaches us about pain and discomfort, and in doing so teaches us resilience and strength. I wonder, if we were to reframe our thinking around nature and consider her to be actively generous, would it change things?

The path led us across the wide field of Dandelions and clover towards a thick stand of trees in the distance. In the foreground stood a medley of bright, lime greens – the colour of a fresh spring canopy of deciduous trees.

Ducking under a few drooping branches, Leif plucked a couple of young Beech leaves from their spindly twigs. He handed me one and I held it up against the light at the edge of the wood. It folded in satisfying crinkles away from the midrib, a bit like those really good crisps, and was still soft and bright in the way early spring Beech leaves tend to be. This was another unexpected edible treat; they were light, slightly citrusy and tasted nowt like salt 'n' vinegar.

LOVE IS A TOAD

It was moist and muddy in the woods, and our boots squelched satisfyingly in the mulchy black soil underfoot. Beech seemed to dominate the canopy and the cumulation of thousands of fresh, new leaves cast a bright, limey light upon us. By now it was late afternoon and the light had an early evening quality to it, peeking through the thick, smoky storm clouds that threatened a downpour.

As we walked, I pondered, asking aloud questions about our feelings of gratitude towards the natural world. Why don't we feel it? Why isn't it common practice to give thanks to nature in our culture? Leif smiled sadly.

'We've become so removed from it, as a society, that we've forgotten how to be grateful for what the land gives us, for what nature gives us.'

The answer was one I had heard on many of my walks over the course of the last year: that the systems lots of us live within are inherently exploitative, extractive and ultimately unsustainable.

Leif went on to describe how being forced to live in these systems means that most of us aren't taught, and therefore don't understand, what it takes from nature to give us the things that it does. In turn, this removes any opportunity for gratitude.

When we think about gift giving in a human sense, we understand where gratitude fits into the equation. It's something we're taught from a young age – when you are given something, you always say thank you. We practise it as we grow up, making the conscious effort to remember friends' birthdays in return or to let them know you're grateful for the advice they gave you at a difficult time. But outside of the structure of birthday and other physical gifts, it's different. We don't feel gratitude towards the natural world as a result of the mindset of othering and the forces of detachment I'd discussed with Mel and Nick. When the resources we consume seemingly appear in abundance, without limits or repercussion, it's understandable that we then don't recognise them as gifts. We've fallen out of the practice of giving thanks; gratitude is like a muscle we must exercise, something we can put conscious effort into getting better at.

We wandered into the murky stand of plantation we'd seen from afar, the path taking us between two orderly rows of conifers. Here, the woodland floor was quite dark and dingy, peppered with brown pine needles, pine cones and snapped branches. Dotted here and there were vibrant green clumps of haircap mosses and, in one spot, a small carpet of Wood Sorrel. Their bright green leaves, arranged in an adorable trio of hearts, zap like the peel of a Granny Smith apple or the tang of lemon juice when you bite into them. This was another edible plant with a colloquial common name; Leif told me Wood Sorrel is also known as 'bread and cheese and cider' – I imagined the cider part was where the tang came in. We crouched and nibbled on the little leaves, some of which had folded backwards on themselves. Wood Sorrel tucks itself away each night, folding its leaves into little tents and closing its small, white flowers to protect itself from cold spring nights. Plants aren't inanimate, they shift and move around – they just have a different way of looking at time than we do.

'I think lots of people have a little voice in the back of their mind telling them something's not quite right.' Leif picked up where we'd left off. 'I think if you already know nature, you might yearn for the landscapes that have been lost, or for what they could look like again in the future. You long for the wildlife that you know is missing.' The plantation around us seemed to emphasise Leif's words at this point – quiet and devoid of birdsong in the middle of spring. 'But I suspect everyone has this subconscious understanding that there's something missing, whether we recognise it or not.'

Again, I thought Leif made a good point here. Whilst people who study nature and ecology might be acutely aware of its plight, I think lots of people know on a subconscious level that there's something missing. How many of us seek further meaning in our lives? How many of us struggle to operate and function in the way society expects us to? Perhaps on some level, we recognise that we're not built to live this way.

I came across a German word a little while ago – *sehnsucht*. We don't really have an equivalent in English, but it roughly describes a sort of deep, aching yearning for something we don't know or can't explain. It's a longing for something that's missing. When I read about it, I wondered if lots of us are experiencing *sehnsucht* when it comes to our relationship with the natural world.

After a short, straight stretch, the plantation gave way to deciduous trees again, the path now following a wide-open ride lined with grassy embankments. Leif agreed with my theory of a widespread *sehnsucht*.

'This love for nature – there's like a hunger for it,' he said enthusiastically. 'There's a hunger for knowledge; people just *love* learning about it. Even the simplest things, you can feel the interest and curiosity oozing. Like, if you open up the world of a Daisy . . .' He bent down at the side of the path, plucking the familiar, sunny-centred flower from the ground.

'No one really thinks about Daisies, until you tell them what's behind the name, the fact that the word "Daisy" comes from the "day's eye" – they close at night and open in the morning. Or that they can eat them.' He placed the Daisy on to his tongue and bent down to pick me one too. 'Or you tell them that they've got those two different flower types, the yellow and the white.'

Leif explained to me that a Daisy is not simply a Daisy. What we take to be a single Daisy flower is actually a flower head, made up of loads of individual flowers. If you look closely at the yellow centre of a Daisy, you can easily make these out: each little dot or bump is a tiny flower in and of itself. But it gets better. The classic white petals around the edge of the Daisy aren't just petals, they each belong to their own individual flower – a flower with a single petal. In this way, Daisy heads have two different types of flowers. The white, single-petalled ones are infertile; their job is to simply act as kind of signposts for pollinating insects. In the same way an air traffic marshal signals to a pilot of a plane, the Daisy's white petals direct pollinators to the centre of the flower. This is where the yellow flowers come in – these dinky flowers are the fertile parts of the Daisy that want to be visited by invertebrates. There are loads of them and, again, if you look closely, you can see they're arranged in a really satisfying pattern, like something drawn with a Spirograph. These patterns aren't random either; they're mathematically perfected to squeeze the maximum number of yellow flowers into the Daisy. Change the angle of them by even a tiny bit, and you can't fit nearly as many in.

I looked closely at the beautiful Daisy I held – perhaps more closely than I ever had before – before gently placing it in my mouth. It had a distinct flavour, planty but also quite peppery, with a hint of pollen too.

It's easy to make assumptions. When someone doesn't know a lot about wildlife or nature, we can take this to mean that they're therefore not interested in it, that they don't care. I think Leif was on to something here; generally people love learning about these things – there's something that every person can be interested in. Give people a chance to learn, a chance to see, to touch and connect, and they'll generally take it. Foraging is a great example of this; people love to scoff stuff. Isn't taste one of the most exciting, tantalising senses we've got, after all? To twin taste with the exploration of our environment, and to uncover hidden, edible secrets, is undeniably exciting. There's nothing like seeing someone's eyes light up when they smell Pineapple Weed for the first time or understand they can eat the flowers they made chains out of as kids.

A short distance further along the wide track, Leif peeled off to one side, heading deeper into the woods. As we ducked beneath the sweeping lower boughs of a particularly colossal Beech, he turned around and smiled cheekily. 'Brace yourself!'

I was not ready. In front of us sprawled the thickest, richest carpet of Bluebells I'd ever encountered. It almost hurt my eyes to look at. The dim, verging on stormy evening light seemed to only amplify their colour, so that they almost glowed beneath the heavy Beech canopy. And the smell! A sweet, rich, syrupy fragrance hung in the air. The sea of drooping bells stood stock-still without so much as a whisper of wind to tickle at them, so that their beauty lay in their inanimation.

'This has got to be one of the best colour combinations of the woods.' Leif was pointing at some splodges of bright yellow poking up from between the nearest clump of Bluebells. The crayon-yellow flowers were arranged on spikes and had funny little hoods. They looked a lot like the flowers of the White Dead Nettle we'd nibbled on earlier and had similar leaves, resembling those of Stinging Nettles. 'Yellow Archangel!' he exclaimed. 'Don't they look amazing next to the Bluebells?'

He was right – the yellow and the blue complemented each other brilliantly. I liked their vibe. Leif explained that, along with other flowers we could see nearby, the Yellow Archangel was a sign that the woodland we were standing in was really old. He pointed out all of these plants with 'wood' in their names – Wood Melick (a pretty, drooping grass), Wood Speedwell (small, lilac-blue flowers) and Wood Anemone (those familiar, white star-like flowers) – and told me how the presence of these plants is used as an indicator of ancient woodland. They were telling us that where we were standing had probably been wooded for hundreds of years, if not longer.

I liked this idea of plants telling us stories. I wondered what else they could tell us, and I wondered what these woods used to look like. Leif seemed to read my mind and told me he wished he could see what his patch looked like in the past, well before the planting of the conifer plantation we'd walked through. He explained the wood we were walking in would probably have been a mix of mature woodland, full of gnarled and towering Oaks, with patches of messy scrub and some soggy, wetter areas too.

'It's weird,' Leif continued. 'I feel like I miss the past, even though I've never known it. You know, we get so much joy and happiness from what little we have left. If we feel these things now, imagine what it could feel like if things were different.' We spotted a winding, skinny track through the Bluebells, probably made by deer, and followed it in single file so as not to trample the flowers around us. I asked Leif to expand on what he was saying, to delve into that feeling of 'missing' a little bit more.

'It's a feeling that's split into two for me,' he said. 'One part of it is the shadow of what once was, ways from the past that I really long for. A time when we humans lived alongside plants and functioned and thrived. What did that feel like? What did nature look like then?' He paused, stooping to take a no doubt Instagram-worthy snap of the Bluebells from shin height. 'But it's also a deep longing to return to something like that in the future. It's a yearning for something different going forwards.'

I agreed. It's not that I want to hop into a time machine and travel back to some sort of wildlife utopia, perhaps 10,000 years ago. I don't pine for a sort of idealist vision of rewilding, nor do I believe in the concept of 'wilderness' as a sort of pure, wild expanse generally perceived as being people-free. Instead, I find myself longing for a time and place where people lived and worked alongside a wonderfully ordinary abundance of wildlife. As Leif described, this deep longing doesn't just stretch backwards in time, but forwards too. Whilst grieving the losses of the past, I also yearn for a wilder future – one where we have a more intimate, equal and respectful relationship with the natural world. It's in this that I see that yearning can bring about positive emotions too. Perhaps by daring to want something different so badly, it can help fuel hope and, in turn, drive the changes we need to see.

Wandering through the Bluebells, the vibe of the woods subtly shifted. The Beech trees – until this point the main characters on our walk – were now replaced by thick, gnarly Oaks and wizened Hazel trees. Here the Bluebells gave way to an understory of Wild Garlic, dense mats of wide, dark-green leaves punctuated by their bright white pom-pom flowers. This plant needed no introduction and we each plucked one of the flower spikes, relishing the oniony pungency they released on to our tongues. This bit of woodland felt like the *proper stuff*. The canopy was flickering with birdlife. A Robin with a pinch of insects zoomed past, taking food to a nest of young tucked somewhere in the undergrowth. A pair of Marsh Tits fed three fresh fledglings, their adorable *pitchoo* sneezing calls interspersed with the sound of their young's whinge-like begging. And somewhere high up above us was that high-pitched tinkling again. What *was* that?

This part of the woods was wonderfully moist, the floor spongey and giving to walk on. As a result, it felt like every surface had been plastered with mosses and lichens, and I paused to take a closer look at a particularly encrusted-looking Hazel close to the path. Every branch, limb and twig had a suite of other lives occupying it. I zoomed in on a couple of square inches, admiring a particularly lovely patch of script lichen, pale, smooth splodges growing on the bark, adorned with black scribbles that looked a bit like unintelligible handwriting, hence the name 'script'. These squiggles are the lichen's spore-bearing structures and they're utterly beautiful.

As I admired the lichen's calligraphy, I noticed something a bit weird – a twig, snapped at either end, appeared to be defying gravity by resting on the lichen-encrusted branch at a funny angle. A closer look revealed something that looked like spooky black goop. It was an organism I'd only ever read about before: Glue Crust Fungus (mmm!). A fungus that lives its life in the tree canopy to avoid its forest floor competitors, Glue Crust Fungus feeds on decaying wood, so it's evolved a clever way of preventing dead twigs from falling to the ground where plenty of other decomposing fungi are waiting. It forms gluey pads, sticking its chosen twigs to other living branches on the tree, suspending them there whilst it feeds on them. Its sticky tendencies also help it move around the forest, transferring between trees when their twigs touch one another. I love it when nature's a weirdo.

At this point, I realised I'd lost Leif. I turned around in an almost 360-degree spin, looking for him amongst the trees. I would've totally missed him if his bum hadn't been sticking quite so dramatically into the air. Leif was on his knees a good 50 metres away, assuming the classic face-down-bum-up position of a botanist (bottomist?) who'd found something interesting. I was tempted to go over and see what he was ogling, but *there it was again* – that tinkling pulling at my subconscious. I've learnt that, when it comes to nature, it's as important to think with your body as it is with your mind.

FACE DOWN, BUM UP

My ears were telling me something. The high-pitched noise was raining down from the darkest part of a towering Holly tree – it sounded a little bit like a Goldcrest but wasn't quite right, as if the same voice was saying some different words. Then I spied it, a tiny dot flitting in the highest branches. The dot dropped lower and for a gorgeous couple of seconds perched out in the open, belting its little heart out from a lower branch. From here, I could see the white eyeshadow with the black eyeliner. A splodge of olive green, complete with a punk rocker's hairdo in vivid orange, looking like a Goldcrest in drag. It was a Firecrest! It was the first time I'd found one of these stunning little birds by sound alone. I hissed and waved at Leif, beckoning him to join me. For a few moments, we watched the Firecrest together. It made its way down the hanging branches of the Holly with attitude, tumbling and singing, until it disappeared once more.

By now, it was really threatening to rain; there was pressure in the air, that sort of heaviness you feel inside your skull. The gently winding path drew us towards the edge of the woods, the light of the clouds poking between trees making me feel weirdly uneasy.

Where the tree cover opened up on to the path, more woodland plants awaited to greet us. We nibbled at the purple petals of Early Dog Violet (like parma violet sweets), the pretty, notched heads of Greater Stitchwort (quite lettuce-y) and the pastel-yellow flowers of Primrose (wonderfully floral), adding several more samples to our foraging efforts for the day. I looked at each flower or leaf closely before scoffing, taking in their forms, their colours, and giving them a good sniff too.

LOVE IS A TOAD

Ahead of us lay a huge field, raked into neat rows over its smooth curves. The path hugged the edge of it and our walk took us alongside a thick and bushy hedgerow. The hedge was made up of some of the usual characters but there were other less familiar plants in there too. Dotted amongst the regular Hawthorn, Blackthorn and Hazel, Leif pointed out Spindle and Wayfaring trees too.

Our chat earlier had got me excited (maybe some of that was down to the Firecrest too) and I found myself daydreaming about some of the things we'd imagined. These are changes we both want to see – and I suspected lots of other folks do to – but how can they happen?

'I think it comes back to that gratitude again,' Leif answered, walking ahead of me along the hedgeline. 'Without gratitude, there can't be reciprocity. If we don't know we're being given a gift then we can't return that gift.'

Leif explained he'd first come across the concept of reciprocity when reading books by Robin Wall Kimmerer, a Potawatomi botanist and next-level plant gusher. I too adored Robin's work, and had felt the neurons in my brain fizzle and rearrange as I read her thoughts on healing relationships between people and the land. *'Know the ways of the ones who take care of you, so that you may take care of them,'* Leif recited from memory. 'I think this is so important, especially when it comes to plants.'

This was right – thankfulness can't mean simply smiling at an Oak tree and saying 'Cheers, mate!' (though I do love the thought of folks doing that) – it's got to be something more. To help nature, our gratitude needs to be made up of actions. To reciprocate means to give back, to match a gesture or offering with something of comparable worth. Reframing our relationship with the natural world as a reciprocal one has the potential to help us shift the way we do things – be that grow food, harvest materials or help restore ecosystems. In this sort of relationship, nature still nurtures us, but the process of nurturing becomes a two-way street.

Leif explained what he meant about a reciprocal relationship, outlining a long-nurtured relationship between humans and plants. He gestured back along the bushy wall behind us, telling me how hedges are a perfect example of this. For thousands of years, humans have created and then maintained hedges, rejuvenating and refreshing their growth before they grow into tall trees. This ancient tradition involves bending and partially snapping the stems of young hedgerow trees before weaving them together, he explained. This helps form a connected, dense and interwoven barrier – a useful structure that humans have used for centuries. Well-laid thorny and bushy hedgerows provide a solid boundary for the control of livestock, creating an impenetrable natural fence. They also act as a natural windbreak, something we learnt to use for the protection of our crops. On top of all this, hedgerows would provide us with nourishment and healing – each one made up of plants that give us fruit, berries, nuts and medicinal herbs. Plus, the act of laying and relaying the hedgerow keeps it in a perpetual state of growth, effectively replicating the natural scrub habitat that lots of wildlife thrives in.

'So, ultimately, we're helping these plants thrive – the Hawthorns and the Blackthorns, the Elms and Dog Roses and Hazels,' Leif concluded. 'All of these scrubby hedgerow

LOVE IS A TOAD

plants are important – not just for us, but for all sorts of different wildlife. We benefit, the Hawthorns and the Blackthorns benefit, the insects and the birds benefit – and that relationship is both long-term and sustainable. It's a case of you scratch my back, I'll scratch yours.'

To be fair, you probably would end up with a quite literally scratched back if you spent too long rolling around in a Hawthorn hedge. But Leif was right: hedgerows are a perfect example of this concept of reciprocity in action. We're quite good at recognising bad hedgerow management in one sense; when we see them standing battered and flailed to oblivion, slowly fading away before being replaced by barbed wire facing, we know this is bad. But it can go the other way too: hedgerows can just as easily be undermanaged. This is a classic Goldilocks conundrum; you want to find the 'just right' bit in the middle. The sweet spot exists when we come to know the hedge, when we understand what it needs to keep it healthy, thick, bushy, bearing fruit and continuing to grow. This is where nature benefits from the tender, nurturing hand of *us*. And when we know how to help the hedgerow, it can give us all of those things that help us in return.

Without warning, Leif disappeared into the hedge ahead of me. I followed him, squeezing through a gap into a bushy and lush Hawthorn tunnel before reaching a slippery, slightly wonky stile. Clambering over it, we stumbled into a sloping expanse of grassland. One that was absolutely *buttered* in Cowslips.

'Welcome to Bentleigh Bank!' he said with a smile.

It was getting late, the sun slouching in the sky, dipping below the thick grey cloud above us. After a mooch around the meadow, we wandered to the brow of a slope and nestled between two dense clumps of Hawthorn. From our vantage point, we could nosey out across the whole landscape, overlooking a few farms, some houses and more rolling hills in the distance.

Leif bent forwards, plucking some small leaves from close to the ground. 'It's Salad Burnet, our twentieth species of the day!' he said, handing me some of the tiny, delicate leaves. 'It tastes just like cucumber!' He was right; it was refreshing and cool on the tongue, like water that had had cucumber in it.

'Whenever I'm foraging plants to take home, I have a little ritual,' Leif said, smiling shyly at the ground. 'I like to quietly tell the plant my name, say who I am and say thank you.' He petted the little patch of Salad Burnet nearest to us. 'I try to take them in a way that isn't going to negatively impact their life long-term. If I forage Nettles, I only take the top few leaves from each plant and make sure I don't uproot it. When I'm picking blackberries, for every few that I take, I pick another and I throw it down the hedge – helping spread their seeds. And I also make sure not to take every berry on the bush because other species like to eat them too.' I liked the image of new Brambles sprouting where he'd cast the odd berry aside. 'It's an inevitable part of being an animal; you have to consume life in some form or another. So I think it's about *how* you do that, not *that* you do that. Having that sense of gratitude for non-human beings reminds us that we're part of this complex, tangled ecosystem of life, rather than separate from it.' We looked out over the landscape below us. In a field at the foot of the hill, a Fox slowly prowled

LOVE IS A TOAD

along the shadow of a hedgerow, only metres away from an oblivious group of bunnies on the other side.

Leif had made a good point here – something I think we in Western societies tend to forget. We – all humans – are as vulnerable to the rules of the nature that we live in as any other species. To have an impact on our environment – including causing death of other life – is an inevitable part of being an animal in an ecosystem. So it's not about the fact that we *do* have an impact, it's about *how* we decide what that impact looks like.

There's a joy to be had in slowing down, in softening ourselves and in cultivating gratitude. We might begin in the mind, mentally giving thanks for the food, medicine, water, company, beauty and sunshine nature brings us. We might do this by way of our own little rituals or ceremonies, whatever those might be. We might also begin to show thanks in our actions – litter picking, helping with a community garden, caring for neighbours, spreading knowledge and telling stories. You might simply spit out the seeds of blackberries or push an acorn into the soil in autumn. Gratitude can come out in lots of ways; I think it's just important that we practise it.

By now, the evensong was in full swing. The bushes either side of us chattered and rattled with the voices of the Blackbird, Blackcap, Chiffchaff and Dunnock. Perched on a loop of Bramble close to us, a male Linnet puffed his blush-stained chest outwards as he started his own chorus of gorgeous tinkles and whistles. The sky had melted into a burning, molten sunset, the grey-bellied clouds now doused in hot pinks and flaming oranges.

'Just imagine what this could be,' Leif began, gesturing at

the landscape in front of us. 'Imagine this scene with thick bushy hedgerows full of Hawthorn, Wild Cherry, Blackthorn, Wayfaring tree and Spindles, with thrushes, Yellowhammers and Whitethroats singing from them. Imagine lots of smaller fields buttered yellow with Cowslips or speckled red with Poppies or blue with Cornflowers. Instead of those tiny blocks of trees, we could have big, bushy pathways of woodland, connecting everything up across the landscape. And in all of this, we could have people working outside and close to nature – where there are lots of jobs for people of all abilities. Where gratitude is being enacted in everything we do. People reconnected and working in an environment that we're grateful for. Because if we're not grateful for it, it disappears again.' He looked back at me, his face full of hopeful excitement.

'*Can you imagine?*'

CHAPTER 13

Two for Joy

We shake with joy,
We shake with grief,
What a time they have, these two
housed as they are in the same body –
'We Shake with Joy', Mary Oliver

1 May – Dawn Chorus Drizzle

There's a Blackbird in my bedroom. I sit up, my eyelids involuntarily tugging themselves closed as I try to peer at the wardrobe and the darkest corners. Where are you? You're so loud.

I realise, as the stupor of sleep slowly evaporates, that there is not, in fact, a Blackbird in my bedroom. But it sure sounds like it. Instead, he's sitting outside, skinny-knuckled claws clinging to the gutter above my window (I sleep with it open every chance I get). He's belting, whistling, positively throbbing his little heart out. It's 4.47am.

Might as well get up. I pull on the soft hug of a dressing gown and tiptoe out of the flat. The air is stock-still, not a splutter or whisper of wind. The mizzly drizzle, thin *and spray-like, falls straight downwards in a silent, gentle shower.*

4.59am. Here's Song Thrush, each repeated phrase sounding like his own echo in the stillness.

5.12am. Hello, sweet Robin.

5.24am. Dunnock.

5.36am. Wren . . .

When I first put pen to paper (or finger to keyboard) to write about nature, I was angry. I was fuming. I opened my laptop, wanting to rant and rage and type out all of the hurt I felt into a fresh document. But when I took pause and thought for a little while about why I wanted to write about nature, I found an altogether different driving force hidden underneath. Like rooting through the crispy-then-moist layers of leaf litter on the forest floor, I worked to uncover what this force was. Peeling back one leaf after another, digging through the mulch, it revealed itself. Ah-ha. I wanted to write about nature because it makes me feel things. I wanted to write about nature because I love it. Because I witness, value and treasure the mind-boggling variety and complexity of other life on this planet. When I realised this, I understood that the grief was inevitable. You can't love nature, know nature and value nature without seeing her plight. To witness this loss and harm is to grieve.

I was still angry but I could see that I wasn't only that – I was lots of other things too. And so, I set out to write a book full of much more joy than anger, because there's much more joy than anger in me.

TWO FOR JOY

3 May – Two Magpies

The Magpie flutters in a floppy sort of way across the road. I like the way their tails trail in flight, a bit like they can't quite be arsed. They land in front of me, all monochrome and strut, tail now cocked with corvidian confidence. One for sorrow.

I feel sorrow today, the heaviness of the headlines, all war and genocide, loss and destruction. The Magpie pecks at an invisible morsel, then raises their head and clacks into the sky. More monochrome, more strut. Arriving in a splay of black and white and aurora feathers; another.

Two for joy. I smile.

We most often think of grief through the lens of personal loss. The death of a loved one, the loss of kith or kin, the ending of a relationship – this is where grief is both expected and acceptable. Grief happens when we lose something and we are changed by that loss. It's an ongoing process and not something we can stop – there's no pause button with grief. It's not predictable, or orderly, or linear; it's turbulent and unique to each person's experience of it. Grief is not always obvious or acute either; it can be difficult to grapple with, slippery like a Frog in a bucket of water. It's also not easily labelled, especially when we're still in the eye of the storm, the midst of the loss.

The eye of the storm is where we find ourselves now. Collectively, we witness ongoing harm and loss on a widespread scale in the natural world, and we also feel the nature-shaped hole in our daily lives. So of course we feel ecological grief! Our capacity for empathy makes sure that we do. Humans are emotional, feeling beings, and so it's inevitable that we will feel grief for the loss of other, non-human life. When we see the mighty Oak in the park toppled, when we see the Knapweed and Herb Robert tinged yellow with herbicide, when we have another bad butterfly summer – grief is the outcome, and it's the right one.

9 May – Hare

Your crumpled, bumper-bruised body lies close to the spot where I saw you running a year ago. The sinew has been laid bare amongst darkened, dried blood and twisted legs and ruffled fur. Your caramel eye, dimmed and empty, stares straight up at nothing. I pause on the road and wonder if you are who I think you are. The tears sting my cheeks on the cycle ride home.

We in the West aren't particularly good at dealing with grief; it's something we shush, ignore or avoid, something too uncomfortable and raw to let it reach the surface where it might embarrass us. Heaven forbid we sob or wail when we're hurting. Grief is often held and processed privately, and this is where it can consume us, feasting on our minds and souls like worms in the gut. This to me feels apparent in the world of conservation: toxic positivity, anger, resentment and misanthropy appear rife in a sector that hasn't started to face and process its grief yet. It seems to be all around; most people I know are experiencing it. There's a widespread and pervasive sorrow amongst us.

But here's the thing. Ultimately, I think our ecological grief

TWO FOR JOY

comes from a wonderful place. This might sound strange – it is, after all, a painful, uncomfortable and sometimes suffocatingly heavy experience. But I believe it's true, for two reasons.

One. If we're not feeling grief, it means we're not paying attention. To feel sorrow at the state of things is to say, 'I see this is happening and I don't like it.' To grieve the natural world is to pay attention, to witness ongoing harm, and to know that it is wrong.

Two. We can only grieve because we love. We can only miss something, or feel pain at its loss and decline, because we recognise that that something has value. We grieve nature because we recognise that it is worthy of our care and protection. Our grief for nature is born from our capacity to love it. And I think that's something to hold on to.

13 May – Parcel of Blue

Turquoise and garnished with freckles, splodges and spots. I hold the tiny egg between my finger and thumb. A capsule full of potential, a bundle that under the right circumstances could flourish into a new feathered life. A chocolate-shouldered and speckle-breasted life that clings to the treetops and belts his little heart out at dawn.

A Song Thrush egg. Laid by a female in a nest crafted meticulously from twigs and grass, wool and moss. A nest lined with a coating of mud, forming a neat cup to cradle her precious clutch – four or five of these exquisite turquoise things, nestled where she could brood them with her warm, feathered belly.

LOVE IS A TOAD

I find the egg in the grass, cast there for reasons only a Song Thrush needs to know. It was slightly crumpled on one side, no longer a parcel of potential life. But it still fed me. It nurtured a moment of awe and admiration, of belly-deep wonder. I twizzled it in my fingers, contemplating the dual simplicity and complexity of its existence. A speckled parcel of blue, made inside a Song Thrush. Wowee.

Grief can be a very lonely place. But this is something else I've learnt – and something that has been crystallised even further over the last year – it doesn't have to be. Enter, people. Brilliant, hilarious, weird, kind, wonderful people. I see now that it's people whom I owe my love of nature to. Those who have gifted me their time and knowledge, who've taught me how to recognise the voice of the Lesser Whitethroat, or how to tell a Meadow from a Creeping Buttercup. The folks who handed me those little parcels of wonder: my first Adder, my first Bee Orchid, my only Nightingale. Those who have laughed and cried with me, who jumped for joy with the first Cuckoo of spring alongside me and squealed with glee as we opened the moth trap to find a Scarlet Tiger (I still can't believe they exist). Those who walked alongside me in this book – who shared moments of joy, love, vulnerability, sadness and wonderful nerdiness.

The 12 wonderful souls who joined me in the last year have helped me more than I can put into words. Their insights, perceptions and musings have shifted my perspective, helping me knit together thoughts and ideas, and gifting me knew ones.

I can now see that this whole concept of 'nature joy'

is rooted in people who help you see the world in new and different ways, who reveal something to you that was previously hidden. Be they friends or storytellers, teachers or the nerds who wrote about mosses 300 years ago – I owe my love of wild things to my fellow human kin. And that makes me feel much less alone.

Nature joy is a thing; it's as tangible and as real as dragonflies, worms or newts. It's a wonderful concoction of the things that draw us in, that captivate and fascinate us, change our thinking and embed in our memories. In the last year, I've shared moments of nature joy with each of the 12 people who gifted me their time and conversations, who've sparkled with excitement at slugs and Peregrines, Bluebells and beetles. It's the driving force, the thing pulling us forward, tugging at our heartstrings and attention. It's what tells us that nature's a thing worth loving, protecting and fighting for.

17 May – Otter Gratitude

My eyes still prickle with sleepiness by the time I reach the rocky beach. I'm so glad I packed a brew. I hop off my bike and wobble down to the water's edge, clambering on to a big boulder to sit with my tea. The water's still, only intermittently rippled by the tickle of a breeze. It's as clear as glass, and I fall into a trance watching the bob and swill of the seaweed in the almost imperceptible flow.

The Barrel Jellyfish takes me by surprise. They're huge, bigger than a dustbin lid, with big, rubbery tentacles trailing behind them. They've a violet hue to them; they're gorgeous. What a gift.

LOVE IS A TOAD

Speaking of which. 'I'm sorry!' I say to the sun and the air and the trees and to nobody. 'I haven't said thank you for the day!'

I pour a dribble of tea on to the rock, an offering of gratitude, watching it trickle into the blue beneath and disappear.

Otter. Staring, eyes locked with mine. They slipped up from below the surface right in front of me, thick, wiry whiskers splayed and nose flaring as they take me in. A long stare, where I daren't breathe, then the duck of wet, furry shoulders and the slip of a sleek tail. Gone.

Did I just hear nature say, 'You're welcome'?

The joy and grief I feel – we feel – for nature are inextricable. Mary Oliver words it perfectly in her poem 'We Shake with Joy':

What a time they have, these two
housed as they are in the same body.

Nature joy. Nature grief. I feel like my heart hosts a dance between the two. With lots of complicated moves and steps, they foxtrot in a storm of twirling and swaying, the two states inseparable. It's a two-sided coin, a double-edged sword. It's the spiky outer shell of a conker, housing the shiny, marbled treasure within.

Have you ever gotten a Burdock burr stuck in your clothes or hair? Their seeds' hooked fingers seem to grab eagerly at every thread or fibre that they can, matting and snarling themselves into you. Have you ever then tried to pull it off? To disentangle the barbs and unpick each hook? It feels futile; the seed head disintegrates and seems impossibly attached to everything else. Like a burr knotted into your sleeve, I see now that these feelings are linked in a way that we cannot unpick.

To experience wonder-inducing, heart-fizzing, I-can't-believe-Swifts-exist joy, we must also open ourselves up to grief. We must let ourselves mourn the moth clouds, to feel sorrow when the Swifts don't return. There is no way around it. By loving this thing so much, I also have to hold the pain of witnessing its decline and loss. And what a privilege it is to feel such love in the first place.

20 May – Sea Gooseberries

My wetsuit is old and riddled with holes. Do Clothes Moths eat wetsuits? I'm not sure. The cloud's been thick and low today but, if I've predicted right, the sun should drop below its belly at dusk, just as I go for a swim.

I'm a bit nervous. The shore is quiet, there's nobody around. It's deliciously still, no waves or ripples, just right for snorkelling. I strap on my mask and sink into the wet and cold, icy fingers tickling down my neck and chest, through various rips around my gubbins. The first jelly appears suddenly and makes me jump, kicking my legs in an ungainly way and stifling a scream. I'm glad nobody saw it. It's only a Moon Jelly – a non-stinger. Phew. I bob and ogle it; it's gorgeous. Four rings of deep pink set in a gelatinous blob of lilacy purple. A marine lava lamp if ever I saw one. I turn around to spy another, then more still. Like in that scene from Finding Nemo, *I realise I'm surrounded by a (thankfully harmless) swarm of jellies, all drifting in an entrancing, peaceful mass only a few metres offshore.*

LOVE IS A TOAD

There's that sun. It has dropped below the cloud line, firing beams of warm orange light through the surface of the water. Now I'm really inside a lava lamp.

Between the jellies are dots of light, forms that resemble little translucent grapes. There are hundreds of them, each with two dangling tails and what appear to be flashing lights, arranged in rows like the seams of a rugby ball. I've entered a storm of Sea Gooseberries and I can't quite comprehend it.

A frond of seaweed entwines around my ankle and I twist around to remove it. But it's not seaweed; it's a shred of plastic – red and silver and ugly – that has tangled around me in a way seaweed never would. I carry the plastic and the knot in my tummy back to shore.

When I first started to write about nature, I didn't intend to provide any answers. I'm not a practical conservationist. I hold little real power, and I possess neither swathes of land nor mountains of money. I'm falling increasingly out of love with a conservation sector that's losing its soul. But that isn't to say that I – and you – don't have other types of power. Amidst this loss, it's not OK to bury our heads in the sand, nor is it enough to simply give into the sorrow and let the despair overcome us. With the tools and fuel of both joy and grief, there are things we can and must do.

I often think of those who do hold power. The people standing in the halls of Parliament, or who preside over large corporations, businesses and even charities. I wonder, do they know the song of the Skylark? Have they ever smelt Honeysuckle in the dark? Have they sipped the sweet nectar from White Dead Nettle? Felt the wake from a bat zooming over their heads or the tickle of a weevil as they scurry over their skin? Have they felt the hoot of the Tawny Owl rattle in their ribcage in the dead of night? I wonder if they could come to know this magic, they might act differently.

The changes we need to see don't just come down to policy, nor does the solution simply lie in science and technology. We can't grow or buy our way out of a growth and consumption crisis. I believe now that in order to change the way we treat nature, including beginning to see ourselves as a part of it, we must seek a change in mindset – a collective change of heart.

This is tricky. A change of this sort feels intangible, as difficult to grab as the smoky spores erupting from a puffball. It certainly feels less concrete and solid than practical conservation actions. When people tend to a wildflower meadow or create a wetland, the results are laid bare in front of them. But these obscure things – changes of attitude and beliefs – can have physical consequences too, no matter how elusive they seem. When we begin to think differently about something, we also begin to behave differently. And a shift in human behaviour – away from those things that result in endless growth, extraction, dominion, exploitation – will alter how we treat nature and people alike.

And so I've been thinking – what do we do with our nature grief?

24 May – New Life

The House Sparrows have been nesting above the gutter again. I've seen them, squeezing in and out of a flat crack in the peeling painted wood. The gap is so small and tight

LOVE IS A TOAD

that little feathered bodies must momentarily plug the hole as they come and go. A grey cap lands with a clatter of tiny claws and goes in. Hysterical, hungry tweeting ensues. The grey cap leaves. Hello, little male. Silence. A brown back flutters in. More hysterical tweeting. The brown back leaves. Hello, little female.

As I leave to get the bus, I spy your little form on the stone flags beneath the window. Scrawny and pink with eyes bulging beneath stretched, closed lids, your beak still slightly agape. The beginnings of feathers dot your body, little pins with tufts of soft brown protruding from them. I heard your voice only a handful of days earlier. I crouch and watch the fly scuttle apathetically across your face and tiny throat. Soon your skin is adorned with rows of tiny white eggs. New life forming from death.

Above me, a grey cap lands with a clatter of tiny claws and goes in. Hysterical, hungry tweeting.

First, we must name our grief. We must look the beast in the eyes – the one stalking us from the shadows in the woods – and give it a name. Call it grief, acknowledge that it is in fact what we're going through and accept it is now an inevitable part of being a human at this time. Saying it out loud, naming it with friends, like the wonderful people I met in this book, means we can begin to understand it.

Next we must *feel* it. Grief is not something we can skip or avoid; it's something that must be felt and processed. We must give ourselves permission to mourn the loss of nature and to not be ashamed of talking about that openly and honestly with each other. So let yourself mourn the wild things. Grieve the felled tree, the silencing birdsong and mothless nights. Grieve for nature and grieve for people too. Let your grief expand; feel it flow through you in the face of injustice, of suffering, genocide and war. When we've both named grief and accepted its place in our lives, we can then begin to tend to it, helping each other deal with the ongoing loss (because, let's be honest, it's not stopping anytime soon) before jumping into urgent and panicky solution mode.

The third thing we can do with our grief, once we've named it and felt it, is to channel it. When we don't acknowledge and process grief, it can turn into a debilitating sort of hopelessness, a force that can leave us stuck in the mud. But when we do allow ourselves to work through it, grief can become a fuel, just as Charlie, Tom and Nic showed me. It has a certain power to it that we can convert into action. Once we've felt the overwhelming sadness that comes when something is lost, don't we often feel a surge of motivation? We must harness these surges, channel them, and get to work.

27 May – Wolf's Milk

Prod. Mmm, how satisfying. The rotting log in front of me is a sight to behold. Adorned with pinkish-orange bobbles blobbed like witches' warts all over the surface of the wood. Not a fungus but a slime mould, a community of single-celled organisms acting together. It's gross and weird and sublimely, slime-ily wonderful. I thrust at one with my finger and from it seeps some goop of the orange-est orange. Poke. Positively oozalicous.

*

LOVE IS A TOAD

So, how do we get to work? This is where we need the other side of the coin, the gorgeous shiny conker inside the spiky shell. Joy! One of the greatest tools we've got in the face of loss is joy, a big treasure box of love, beauty, awe, fascination and all of the good stuff nature gives us.

I see there are also three things we must do with joy. We have to start by finding it. Nature joy is out there, everywhere, waiting for us. Go seek it out; go and be curious. If we give the natural world our time, if we pay it slow and deliberate attention, we begin to notice things – both the good and the bad. By being nosey we form bonds and attachment, we learn and absorb, we connect. This is the key to developing those deep, intimate relationships, the ones we want everyone to have with the natural world.

Next (and as with grief) we must feel joy. This may seem obvious, but to do it properly requires a lot of letting go. So, let joy in. Absorb it, guzzle it up like a bumblebee guzzles Foxgloves or a slug slurps up algal slime. Make that joy a part of you, a force that buoys you and fuels a love that can't be extinguished. To choose to seek joy in the face of loss and destruction is a wonderful act of rebellion. So . . . rebel.

Finally – and I want to screech this from the treetops like a cackling Kestrel – *share it*. Take the love for nature that you've cultivated and nurtured, and share it with others – like the 12 nerds I've walked with this year. Share it with your family, friends, peers – that random bloke down the pub – *just share it*. When we do this, when we turn ourselves outwards to share our passions, our stories, our little jewels of awe, we give the biggest and best gift there is. Let yourself gush about woodlice, fawn over ferns and bubble about Buttercups.

TWO FOR JOY

Tell the stories of the Oaks, spread the songs of the thrushes, the crickets, the Aspen. Whisper these things like they're the best-kept secrets, spill them like the hottest rumour you know. Keep returning to them, tending to your joy like a much-loved garden that will provide bountiful and juicy harvests again and again. *Then share those harvests.*

29 May – Turned Tables

Can plants be sexy? I ponder this as I stare at your red-tipped tentacles, bejewelled with drops of glistening dew. You're one of a little mat of Sundews I have stumbled across, tiny and protruding from the soggiest bit of ground at my welly-clad feet. Your leaves are an arrangement of splayed and betentacled arms, reaching outwards like sticky spoons.

I crouch for a nosey and see you're mid-meal. Still wriggling yet thoroughly stuck, a midge sits upon a leaf, entrapped by your gluey dew. The leaf has started to curl over, enveloping your snack ahead of digestion. Plant eats animal. Bloody ace.

Come and sit with me for a moment, down here on the woodland floor. Lie back in the crunch and look up at the treetops. See the Oak and the Ash, the Ivy intertwined between them. See the woodpecker, the Nuthatch, the bickering Blue Tits. Smell the rot of the fungi, hear the hum of hoverflies. Isn't it beautiful?

Do you know that you are nothing but simply an expression of nature, squeezed into a blip of consciousness in one moment in time? Before this life, you have been rocks and moss and lizards and ants. And after this life, *oh*. After you'll be lichen and fish and ticks and soil and thistles. Maybe one day you'll be an Oak – like the one towering above us – or one of the hundreds of beings living on them. Today, you are simply nature contemplating itself. And you are only one part of it. Nature thinks and perceives and presents differently in everyone. Isn't that wonderful?

Right now you – yes *you*, nature – are witness to loss. A loss that we understand to be bad, one that risks all of this beautiful everything. And one that hurts us too. The coincidental bundle of neurons and nerves you've inhabited allow you to understand this, and to feel it – in sorrow and sadness and grief. But your nerves and neurons also bring you a joy; a light brighter than every Glow Worm's bum in the world. That's pretty wonderful too.

With our blips of consciousness in one moment in time, we have a chance to push back against this loss, to turn things around. Between all of us blips (and there are lots of us, I promise), we have a chance to raise a ruckus.

So, will you raise a ruckus with me? I don't mean the sort with loud bangs and flashing lights, no. But the sort nature shows us. A ruckus like the dawn chorus, like the buzz of a thousand insects in a meadow in June. A ruckus like the frenzied plunging of Gannets into shoals of fish, like the shriek of a sexed-up vixen at midnight. Let's raise a ruckus like a screaming party of Swifts, weaving and zooming between chimneys and satellite dishes, drawing eyes upwards, drawing attention.

We've got it in us. All of us. A ruckus of nerds, each with something to share in the push for a better future. So get sharing. Share stories. Share knowledge. Share questions and then answers. Share the locations of the best Blackberry bushes. Share adventures and share laughter, share relentless giggles whilst swimming naked in the sea in January. Share tears, share sorrow and grief. Share cuddles when the Oak topples or the wildflowers wilt.

Share love – buckets of it, please. And always, always share joy.

31 May – Toad

Love is a Toad. I know this to be true. I can feel it; it sparkles somewhere in my chest as I stare into your squashed and inky pupils. Pinpricks swimming in a cauldron of molten gold, cuddled by a thick drooping eyelid. This truth, as you squat gruffly upon my palm, squirms in my belly and sits in my throat in a heavy lump.

Toads are lumps, sort of. Yes, you. A lump of grumpiness, a small bulge of defiance. Slow, ugly, lumbering and not even remotely apologetic for any of it.

You, little Toad, are impossibly tiny. How? My mind fizzles. How can something so small be made of the same things as me? Inside this warty, furious-looking parcel of every brown on earth, how can there be ribs? Be guts and nerves and a beating heart tinier than the big mole on my left knee? You have toes and I do too. We're not so different, you and I, little Toad.

I think about you for the rest of the day. Long after I lifted you from the path and plopped you in the undergrowth out of the way of busy feet. The joy flickers and bubbles as I picture your toes again. And your nostrils, and your gurning

LOVE IS A TOAD

pout, and your little Toad bum. I love you – and I mean that. For your ugliness and lumps and warts and all. I love you for being a Toad.

References

Chapter 1: A Nod and a Wink
Page 36: *This is the biophilia hypothesis – literally the 'nature loving' hypothesis.*
    The Biophilia Hypothesis, Stephen R. Kellert, Edward O. Wilson, Paul Shepard

Chapter 2: A Telltale Peep
Page 66: *As Greenpeace have said: 'The problem isn't that people aren't recycling enough. The problem is that there is still far too much throwaway plastic being produced.'*
    https://www.greenpeace.org.uk/news/plastic-recycling-export-incineration/

Page 69: *The truth is, there's only a certain amount of countryside we're actually allowed to access, especially in England. Public rights of way – footpaths and open-access land – make up a tiny proportion of the total.*

https://www.ramblers.org.uk/go-walking-hub/understanding-public-rights-way

Chapter 4: Hoardyceps

Page 110: *Flow state is linked closely with skill; it happens when we're engaging our brains on some sort of task, be it physical or mental, that challenges us, that requires effort and motivation, but something that's not too difficult.*

https://www.sciencedirect.com/science/article/pii/S0028393224000393?via%3Dihub

Chapter 5: Pincushion of Opportunity

Page 136: *Nev mentioned shifting baselines – full name 'shifting baseline syndrome' – which is an interesting concept. It's defined as 'a gradual change in the accepted norms for the condition of the natural environment due to a lack of experience, memory and/or knowledge of its past condition'.*

https://esajournals.onlinelibrary.wiley.com/doi/abs/10.1002/fee.1794

Acknowledgements

To the nerds who made this book – Nadia, AJB, Indy, Chan, Nev, Charlie, Chris, Tom, Mel, Nick, Nicola and Leif – your brilliant minds and words gave me more than I could've hoped for, and I'll treasure our wanders forever. I'm grateful for your time, knowledge and unique takes on joy, grief, Dandelions and earwigs – thank you.

A big thank you to my agent Claire, who kicked me up the bum multiple times in order to get the ball rolling on this book – it wouldn't have happened without your encouragement, tenacity and nudging. Thank you also to Ellie, my editor at Bonnier, who picked up my ramblings with confidence, immediately grasped what I wanted to say, and helped me shape it into a whole book, all the while encouraging me with kind words.

To my parents, for giving me a childhood that let me get to know Oak and Robin and Toad, I'm forever grateful. To

LOVE IS A TOAD

my friends who've always bigged me up and listened to me whinge, those named above, and also Jane, Sam, Samuel, Ryan, Nathan, Hannah and Megs – it means the world. Thank you to Matt, who encouraged me in the early days and always cheered me on.

My love, my partner, L, I literally couldn't have written this book without you; your content planners, spreadsheets, brews, cuddles, softness and patience guided me through. Thank you.

And of course, thank you to the big mother; to nature for being a crux during the stress, worry and self-doubt. Your honeysuckles, slugs and seaweeds soothed me more than I can put into words.